St. Olaf College Libraries

REVEALING ANTIQUITY

· 14 ·

G. W. Bowersock, General Editor

The Invention of Jane Harrison

MARY BEARD

HARVARD UNIVERSITY PRESS
Cambridge, Massachusetts
London, England
2000

Copyright © 2000 by the President and Fellows of Harvard College
All rights reserved
Printed in the United States of America

Library of Congress Cataloging-in-Publication Data

Beard, Mary.
The invention of Jane Harrison / Mary Beard.
p. cm. — (Revealing antiquity ; 14)
Includes bibliographical references and index.
ISBN 0-674-00212-1
1. Harrison, Jane Ellen, 1850–1928.
2. Classical philology—Study and teaching—England—Cambridge—History.
3. Literature and anthropology—England—Cambridge—History.
4. Classicists—Great Britian—Biography.
5. Archaeologists—Great Britain—Biography.
6. Mythology, Classical—Historiography.
7. Newnham College—Biography.
I. Title.   II. Series.
PA85.H33 B43 2000
938'007'202—dc21   99-086699

Designed by Gwen Nefsky Frankfeldt

Contents

Foreword
by G.W. Bowersock

The series Revealing Antiquity was designed to illuminate new approaches to the culture of the ancient Greeks and Romans in a form that would be both exciting to general readers and rewarding to professional scholars. It is often wrongly supposed that these two constituencies have nothing in common, even though the most influential works in the field prove exactly the opposite. Ronald Syme's *The Roman Revolution* and E. R. Dodds's *The Greeks and the Irrational* are two superb examples of revolutionary works of scholarship that have won a broad and appreciative general audience. The books in the present series are obviously on a more modest scale but have a comparable objective. Each is designed to be traversed in one or two sittings and to leave behind a clear image of a significant part of the classical past and its timeliness for the present. From the first volume on Dionysus to the latest on the end of the Roman Empire, we have endeavored to place new research and fresh perspectives in an engaging format.

The thirteen volumes that have been published so far all directly illuminate the ancient world. But since any choice of topic is a reflection of the time in which it is chosen, works that reveal antiquity also inevitably reveal their authors and their age. The name for our series is deliberately ambivalent. The word *revealing* can function as a verbal noun with *antiquity* as its object (in that we hope to reveal antiquity), but it can also function as an adjective (in that antiquity can itself be revealing). Antiquity can reveal *us* just as much as it is revealed by us. This is the first book in the series to exploit that other sense of Revealing Antiquity—what the study of antiquity tells us about ourselves. A modern pioneer in the interpretation of Greek archaeology and religion, who was equally a pioneer in opening up classical studies to women after generations of male domination, seems a worthy subject.

Mary Beard's vivid and infectious prose has been able to invest a mass of documents, to which she has had access in Cambridge (England), with all the fervor with which they were originally written. The emerging celebrity of the young Jane Harrison in the last two decades of the nineteenth century reflects the growing prestige of archaeology at the time as well as the dominant role of German professors, upon whom Schliemann's discoveries at Troy had conferred unanticipated authority. Dr. Beard evokes Harrison's popular lectures in London. Harrison used lantern slides and plaster casts in a dramatic and innovative attempt to escape from the tyranny of ancient texts through the interrogation of works of art.

Thus we see the process whereby Jane Harrison revealed antiquity to an astonished and admiring world. But we also see the turbulence of her own career in Victorian England and the forces that drove her to interpret the Greeks as she did. Dr. Beard calls up from her documents, through riveting detective work, a virtually unknown connection between Jane Harrison and another pioneering woman in the field of ancient art, Eugénie Sellers (Mrs. Arthur Strong), whose scholarly reputation is wholly tied to her study of Roman antiquities. She participated in Morelli's revolution in the analysis of ancient objects by means of affinities in tiny details, a revolution better known today from Berenson and from Beazley's work on Greek vase painting. In the London of the 1880s, amid Victorian theatricals and lectures for the general public, we find Harrison and Sellers working together, and even living together. In later years neither, it appears, wanted to remember their shared beginnings.

Proceeding from her discoveries about Mrs. Strong, Dr. Beard goes on to attack the foundations of the supposed school of Cambridge Ritualists, to which the recent history of classical scholarship has conspicuously attached her. In a recent article in the journal *Arion* (vol. 7, no. 1 [1999]: 184) Karl Galinsky has labeled the anecdotal character of much of this so-called history of scholarship "*Wissenschaftsgeschichte*-lite." What Dr. Beard has provided is an altogether refreshing and heady brew. The concoctions of J. G. Frazer and F. M. Cornford, which were fed into the mainstream of modern literature through T. S. Eliot's *The Waste Land,* are reexamined here. We can watch the construction of reputations and the imperfect recollections of participants, notably the aged Gilbert Murray. This is a case study in the tendentiousness of archival sources and the efforts of an older generation to secure the future through the careful selection of the documents it leaves behind.

Greece itself is part of this story. No work on antiquity can (or should) avoid the country where the classical past was played out. Jane Harrison and her friend take their place in a long and distinguished line of intrepid English women abroad. Unlike Lady Mary Wortley Montagu in Turkey in the previous century, she had ample companionship from compatriots and European scholars traveling abroad with classical antiquity on their mind. But a Mediterranean country was still a strange and liberating force for a Victorian gentlewoman.

Dr. Beard's book works on many levels at the same time. It is a record of a doomed friendship between two gifted women with a passion for ancient art. It is a memorable account of the dawn of archaeology in Britain and the post-Schliemann era in Greece. It is a reminder of Victorian manners and tastes. And, when all is said and done, it uncovers the process by which the art of classical Greece became a key to unlocking those myths and rituals that lay at the core of the civilization of Pericles and Plato.

Preface

Jane Ellen Harrison changed the way we think about the ancient Greeks; she infuriated the academic establishment at the turn of the nineteenth and twentieth centuries with her uncompromising refusal to play the submissive part; she fell repeatedly and hopelessly in love—usually with entirely unsuitable men, who were also her academic colleagues; she gave some of the most remarkably theatrical lectures that the University of Cambridge has ever seen; in the very male intellectual world of a century ago, she put women academics and women's colleges (dangerously) on the map.

These are some of the myths of Jane Harrison that I shall be exploring in this book, wondering how and why we cast her as we do. It is an exploration that extends very widely: from the dusty world of museum basements to the glamour of late-Victorian amateur dramatics; from the culture of sapphism in early twentieth-century Paris (and Cambridge and London) to the theory and practice of contemporary biography. *The Invention of Jane Harrison* is, in one sense, an experiment in rejecting that tone of assured certainty in which most biographies strive to be written, and in exposing the processes through which we construct a narrative out of a life. It is a biography that aims to "show its working." But it is also, and principally, a book about

Classics written by a classicist. It is an attempt to understand how Classics invests in its history, and how that history is embedded in our understanding of the ancient world itself.

Many people have helped me in the attempt. Kate Perry (of Girton College, Cambridge) and Anne Thomson (of Newnham College) have welcomed me to, and guided me through, their archives; likewise Pauline Adams (Somerville College, Oxford), Peter Asplin (University of Glasgow), Michael Bott (University of Reading), Nancy Reinhardt (Colby College, Maine), and Valerie Scott (British School at Rome). Glen Bowersock, Peg Fulton, and the readers for Harvard University Press have tightened the style as well as the argument of the book. Friends, family, and colleagues in Cambridge and elsewhere have given a hand (and put me right) on points that range from old Persian to modernist poetry: Robin, Zoe, and Raphael Cormack; Tony Boyle; Nigel Cassidy; Alistair Crawford; Lindsay Duguid; Stephen Dyson; Pat Easterling; Jean Gooder; Richard Gordon; Edith Hall; William Harris; Keith Hopkins; Fiona Macintosh; Basim Musallam; Ian Patterson; Michael Reeve; Annabel Robinson; Anthony Snodgrass; John Sturrock; and Gill Sutherland. But I owe an enormous debt to two friends in particular: Chris Stray, who read every chapter and came up with a host of suggestions, new ideas, and documents; and John Henderson, with whom for years I have taught and talked the history of Classics, who read and improved the manuscript more times than I care to think, and finally insisted that it be finished.

The Invention of Jane Harrison raises big questions about why we write the history of Classics as we do, and about the biographer's personal investment in their chosen subject. For twenty-five years, on and off, I have lived, studied, or taught in Newnham College, Cambridge, the very institution in which Jane Harrison wrote her most famous books. I was first "introduced" to her in 1973 by my Newnham teachers, Joyce Reynolds and Pat Easterling, each of whom conveyed an affectionately wry view of their predecessor; and now a charcoal portrait of her (in which she looks anything but dangerous, more like a benign grandmother) hangs in my college study. In matters like this the author herself may well be the worst judge. But I suppose that *The Invention of Jane Harrison* must somehow be a product of that familiar combination of irritation and gratitude, devoted loyalty and rebellion, that almost anyone feels for their own institution and its icons. As a piece of rebellious loyalty, it grew out of my Jane Ellen Harrison Memorial Lecture, given at Newnham in 1996.

Illustrations

Illustrations 1, 4, 8, and 9 reproduced by permission of the Principal and Fellows, Newnham College, Cambridge; illustrations 2, 5, 6, and 7 by permission of the Mistress and Fellows, Girton College, Cambridge; illustration 3 by permission of the Syndics of Cambridge University Library.

Illustrations 1, 2, and 4 through 9 photographed by Nigel Cassidy; illustration 3 by the Department of Photography, Cambridge University Library.

The Invention of Jane Harrison

CHAPTER ONE

Prolegomena

If I try to think what was most characteristic of Jane Harrison's work, as compared with that of contemporary scholars, I think perhaps it is that, though she was capable of much steady grind and long research among potsherds and heavy volumes of German, she was always in pursuit of one or two other things: either of some discovery which was not a mere fact, but which radiated truth all about it, or of some creation or fresh revelation of beauty . . . If a fact had a living message she embraced it and loved it; if it had not it was entirely unimportant to her . . . Her lectures had a combination of grace and daring, of playfulness and dignity, which made them unlike any others. Her private letters were, not by study but as it were by instinct, works of art.

An embarrassing eulogy to our ears, maybe. But on October 27, 1928, Gilbert Murray's words struck just the right note. Jane Ellen Harrison had died in April of that year, and without delay her friends in Cambridge and elsewhere had clubbed together to endow an annual lecture in her memory at Newnham College. Some of the most famous figures in the academy and the arts (including Sir James Frazer and Sir Arthur Evans, the excavator of Knossos) had put their names to the original "appeal brochure"; two hundred or so others (among them such more or less remarkable figures as Leonard and Virginia Woolf, Franz Cumont, Roger Fry, Paul Valéry, G. M. Trevelyan, and André Gide) had

responded with cash and were recorded on the list of subscrib-
ers.[1] To deliver the first of what they hoped would be a distinguished series of lectures, they chose the greatest classical name
around, the Regius Professor of Greek at the University of Oxford and a long-time friend of Harrison, Gilbert Murray.

It must have been a tense occasion. Not least because the fu-
neral itself, in the middle of April, had been an ill-organized and
badly attended affair: "Many [people] I know were away on their
holiday. But one somehow felt as if she was deserted," wrote
Murray, regretfully, shortly afterward. Virginia Woolf, too, had
found the ceremony, not to mention the scattering of other
mourners, "very drab"; "it was only barely full of the dingiest
people." She and Leonard, in fact, had mistimed their arrival and
only "marched in" just as the service was ending—blaming, it
seems, the unfashionably suburban location ("somewhere out of
the world where buses pass only one every 15 minutes").[2]

At Newnham things were run more efficiently. The Principal,
Miss Pernel Strachey (sister of the biographer Lytton Strachey),
started the proceedings off with the required words of welcome
and the appropriate pieties, lauding Harrison as "a shining example to her College of the scholar's simplicity and integrity of
life."[3] A. B. Cook ("ABC," as he was commonly nicknamed, the
leading archaeologist in town) was allotted five minutes to speak
on behalf of the University, and Hope Mirrlees (Harrison's impossibly close friend in the last years of her life) followed—with
a quick reading from Proverbs (this first lecture was, after all,
doubling as a memorial service). Then, at 5:15 sharp, it was
Murray's turn. He came up with just what her pupils and admirers, colleagues and companions wanted to hear: an address
on Harrison herself.[4] Mirrlees, at least, was delighted: "It was
pitched," she later wrote, "in a key that gave the audience comfort and reassurance of her fundamental greatness." And she
wrote to Murray in terms of studiously deferential congratulation: "I hope you won't think it a liberty if I tell you how deeply

moved I was by your lecture . . . Some of your phrases evoked her almost unbearably."[5]

Murray's lecture is one of the founding texts of the story—perhaps, better, the *myth*—of Jane Harrison. His well-judged performance was not simply pious eulogy; the first Jane Harrison Memorial Lecture also launched one of the orthodox narratives of Harrison's scholarly career. He chose to say nothing about her family and childhood. (She was born in 1850, and her mother died when she was only a month old; but, whatever her emotional deprivations, she had, albeit haphazardly, been taught Greek and Latin at home and ended up at Cheltenham Ladies' College, one of the best schools in Victorian England).[6] He skipped lightly, too, over her undergraduate career at Newnham, where from 1874 to 1879 she had been one of the earliest students at the (still tiny) new women's college, founded in 1871.[7] This was a wise move, no doubt, in front of the home audience who must have known, or thought they knew, this side of Harrison rather better than he did. Besides, although her brilliance had been the talk of Cambridge while she was an undergraduate (and although, even before she arrived at Newnham, she had apparently been dubbed "the cleverest woman in England"[8]), when she sat the Classical Tripos examinations in 1879 she was judged to be only "second class." She was the "top second," admittedly, but still only a "second"; and in an academic and social world where such classifications mattered (and marked you for life), it was a result that rankled.[9] Nor did Murray linger long over her time in London through the 1880s and 1890s: an independent "New Woman," surviving comfortably enough on the combined support of a private income she had inherited from her mother and the fees she earned from lecturing on Greek art and archaeology at the British Museum and elsewhere; with most vacations spent as "Englishwoman abroad," traveling in Europe (from Greece to Russia), seeing the sights, taking the waters—and doing a good deal of hard archae-

ological research in museum basements. (Illustration 1 was almost certainly taken during this London period.)

Murray concentrated instead on the story of the intellectual
revolution that she inspired after her return to Newnham as a
fellow in 1898 (she was then almost fifty). It was essentially a
matter of two exceptionally influential books. *Prolegomena to the
Study of Greek Religion* ("what I can only call a work of genius,"
puffed Murray) appeared in 1903, making its now classic claim
that (in Murray's words again) "we must escape from the tyranny
of the fully articulate and finished literary accounts, and wring a
deeper and truer evidence from the inarticulate and half-under-
stood rituals which the Greeks really practised. We must study
the things done at festivals . . . and discover the stuff of religion
that was there before the Olympians, before anthropomorphism,
before theology." These *Prolegomena* were followed in 1912 by
Themis: A Study in the Social Origins of Greek Religion—less favor-
ably received in general and (as the subtitle suggests and Murray
himself delicately hints) driven by a Durkheimian fervor that
makes it hard going for anyone not similarly inclined to the *école
sociologique;* here Greek religion, its ritual and myth, was more
uncompromisingly presented as a *social process* than it has ever
been, before or since. But for Murray the occasionally shaky arguments that supported some of the major planks in her theories—"the tribal initiations; the year-festivals with their projection, the Eniautos Daimon; God as the projected desire; and
Themis as the tribal custom"—did little to undermine either
their truth or their importance. In fact *Themis* stole a march on
Prolegomena precisely because of its anthropological universality,
precisely because it threw "light on Greek religion not so much
for its own sake, as for the sake of the religious adventures and
aspirations of the human mind everywhere." It was, in other
words, a book that spoke about the Greeks *and us.*[10]

Murray's Harrison is, inevitably, a trimmed-down version of
the "real" Jane Ellen Harrison. She lectured and wrote on a

Fig. 1. Jane Harrison strikes a pose; a photograph probably dating to the 1880s.

much wider range of topics than he had space in his well-timed hour to suggest: from contemporary French poetry to women's suffrage. Unsurprisingly she favored votes for women—albeit with some characteristically idiosyncratic arguments: "Personally I have no more interest in or aptitude for politics than I have for plumbing. But, embarrassing though I should find the possession of a vote, I strongly feel that it is a gift which ought to be given, a gift which I must nerve myself to receive." In fact, she used the issue of suffrage as a prompt for a wide-ranging discussion of what we would call gender: "The virtues supposed to be womanly are in the main the virtues generated by subordinate social position. Such are gentleness and the inevitable 'tact.' They are the weapons of the weaker, physically or socially, of the man or the woman who dare not either strike out or speak out . . . they are virtues not specially characteristic of the average duchess."[11]

Besides, she devoted many more years to the study of Greek art and archaeology than Murray's few passing lines would ever indicate: her *Introductory Studies in Greek Art* ran to four editions between 1885 and 1897; her commentary on Pausanias' account of the monuments of Attica became the standard handbook for an archaeological visit to Athens (the "Blue Jane");[12] and there were five other major archaeological books or translations, as well as articles that spanned subjects from Greek vases in Florence to new discoveries on the Athenian Acropolis.[13] Not to mention the quite different intellectual interests that (re)surfaced in the last years of her life: in 1922 she turned her back on Newnham, on Cambridge and on Greek studies, moving on to Paris and the full-time study of Russian language, literature, and folklore (her contribution to Russian studies being the subject of the second Jane Harrison Lecture, by Prince Mirsky in 1930).[14] As she left Cambridge, she burned most of her private letters and papers (in a bonfire to which I shall return); ironically, when Murray in his lecture quoted lovingly from the "works of art" that were her letters to him ("spontaneous and informal . . . bubbling with wit"), he did not yet know that she had torched all his replies.[15]

For obvious reasons Murray glossed quickly over the uncomfortable fact (for Newnham) that its most famous fledgling had flown the nest—offering instead an intellectual biography of Harrison, the student of ancient religion, that still defines her place in the history of classical scholarship and the interpretation of Greek culture. Her view that ritual must always come first, that the *things done* have precedence over the *things said,* has had a complicated afterlife: regularly conscripted, on the one hand, as the legitimating ancestor of a whole variety of contemporary approaches to Greek myth, ritual, and religion (from the "new ritualism" of Walter Burkert to the "proto-structuralism" of Louis Gernet, and through him to J.-P. Vernant and the so-called Paris School[16]); derided, on the other, as an embarrassing relic of early classical anthropology barely worth talking about (something "it will be wise to reject from the outset"[17]). But the basic message of her work—that somewhere underneath the calm, shining, rational exterior of the classical world is a mass of weird, seething irrationality—is a tenet that almost everyone working in the history of Greek culture would now take for granted; so much for granted, in fact, that we have become more interested in how and why the pure "rationalist" vision ever came to be invented in the first place, and in how our predecessors ever imagined that "rationality" could be so easily distinguished from "irrationality." Harrison's "irrationalist" message may have been more sharply, economically, and accurately expressed since (by E. R. Dodds, for example, Murray's successor in the Oxford chair of Greek); but she still sits pretty securely in Murray's terms among our pantheon of intellectual ancestors.[18]

Gilbert Murray was not, of course, the only promoter of the Harrison story; nor was that story entirely a scholarly one. It was also about cleverness, wit, and style—and about a new vision of the Greek past that found a ready audience among modernist writers and critics in the first half of the twentieth century.[19]

T. S. Eliot had read *Themis* as soon as it appeared and discussed it in a Harvard graduate paper—and his later construction of the "primitive" was explicitly influenced by Harrison and her "fascinating" books.[20] Hilda Doolittle (H. D.) figured a version of the ancient world that drew directly on Harrison (not surprisingly: her lecture notes taken on a Greek cruise in 1932 show that the lecturer was feeding his audience pure *Prolegomena*).[21] Virginia Woolf, in *A Room of One's Own*, pointed to Harrison's work on Greek archaeology (together with Vernon Lee on aesthetics and Gertrude Bell on Persia) as a prime example of distinguished (nonfiction) writing by a woman. And she gave her ghost a famous walk-on part, haunting the gardens of Fernham College (a thinly disguised Newnham): "Somebody was in a hammock, somebody, but in this light they were phantoms only, half guessed, half seen, raced across the grass—would no one stop her? . . . could it be J—— H—— herself?" *A Room of One's Own*, don't forget, was based on lectures given in Cambridge at both the women's colleges, Girton and Newnham, only a few days before Gilbert Murray's Memorial Lecture.[22] J—— H—— really was in the air.

I shall turn later to other writers who had a yet more personal investment in Harrison's heroization. But for the moment, we must recognize that probably the most vigorous promoter of the Harrison legend was Harrison herself. Almost all the classic anecdotes of Harrison's career come from her own autobiographical sketch, archly entitled *Reminiscences of a Student's Life*,[23] and from its series of wryly triumphalist (and brilliantly told) accounts of its author's encounters with the world. A checklist of the most famous of these stories, those lodged most firmly in the Harrison mythology, would run something like this:

- Harrison, as an undergraduate at Newnham, faces down the grand old man of British politics, William Gladstone himself, on a visit to the college (where his daughter was also a student): "He sat down and asked me who was my favourite Greek author. Tact counselled Homer, but I was perverse and not quite truthful, so I said 'Euripides' . . . the sceptic Euripides! It was too much, and with a few words of warning he withdrew."[24]

- Harrison swoons at the compliments of George Eliot on her wallpaper (or was it on her looks?): "She came for a few minutes to my room, and I was almost senseless with excitement. I had just repapered my room with the newest thing in dolorous Morris papers . . . I remember that she said in her shy impressive way 'Your paper makes a beautiful background for your face.' The ecstasy was too much, and I knew no more."[25]

- Harrison, during her London lecturing days, makes her well-known impact on the boys at Winchester College: "One of the masters asked a very small Winchester 'man' if he had liked the lecture. 'Not the lecture,' he said candidly, 'but I liked the lady; she was like a beautiful green beetle.'"[26]

- Harrison, back at Newnham as a fellow, entertains the Crown Prince of Japan—interested, but not *too* interested, of course, in the whole royal razzmatazz: "If you must curtsey to a man young enough to be your grandson, it is at least some consolation to know that he believes himself to be God. It was that which interested me . . . The Prince was good enough to say his own royal name to me two or three times, but alas! I forgot it."[27]

And so it goes on, with many, many more. *Reminiscences* is a brilliant piece of writing from the heart of an elite culture in which ironic self-depreciation was highly prized. It is a wonderful example of how to write yourself *up,* as if you were writing yourself *down;* of how confession can be the most effective form of boasting; of how sophisticated you have to be to pretend to be naive. And it is aimed at an audience who well understood the relationship (and the difference) between the conventionally misleading tropes of autobiography and the "truth."[28] "It is said by Southerners," she writes in one of her most playfully ironizing passages, "that we Yorkshire people are exclusive, gruff in manner, harsh and unsympathetic in soul. Gruff in manner I grant it, but our bark is worse than our bite . . . I think that we Yorkshire people have another trait in common with the Russians. The vice we hate above all others is pretentiousness . . . You may break every commandment of the Decalogue . . . but try to show off, to impress [the Yorkshireman] in any way, and you are done."[29] The self-parody of the successful non-Londoner was, and remains, one of the most complex conventions of British humor,[30] and here it cleverly sets the trap of literalism for any biographer eager to cast Harrison as a social inferior in the classy society of London and Cambridge, handicapped throughout her life by her provincial upbringing. As if it did not take the self-confidence of success, money, and fame to parade (so artfully) the apparently artless qualities of the provincial backwoodsman. Read *Reminiscences* as a simple text of self-revelation (as most modern students of Harrison seem happy to do) at your peril.[31]

This book is an exploration of the myth(s) of Jane Harrison. It asks not only how those myths are constructed and reconstructed—from Harrison herself, through Murray and beyond—but also what they encourage us to see in Harrison's career, and what they work hard to occlude; in short, what those myths are for. Inevitably the Harrison story (*our* Harrison story) is a loaded story, a carefully selected, edited, and narrativized version of a life, told and retold by those (Harrison and myself included) with a stake in its telling. Just how loaded it is, we shall discover by thinking about how differently it might have been told. Chapters 4, 5, and 6 present some entirely new material (from the archives of Newnham and Girton Colleges in Cambridge) on the early period of Harrison's academic career in the

1880s, and so bring a new cast of characters, friends, and intellectual allies into the Harrison legend. This is not the Jane Harrison we thought we knew.

My aim here is not to replace one mythic version with another, an old story with my own brand-new, and necessarily better, one. But I do want to show that if we choose a different route into Harrison's life, if we concentrate on a different period, a different group of friends, we must end up with a very different kind of tale (and so also a different place for her in the history of Classics). In other words, by adding to the story of Harrison, I am trying to expose it all the more clearly *as a story;* not as a "real life" (recoverable by careful historical effort), but as a series of competing narratives, a battleground of biography. Traditionally, "biography contracts to deliver a self . . . if the life does not take shape, if we do not in reading it encounter a distinct person whose voices, gestures and moods grow familiar to us, then we judge the biography a failure."[32] By contrast, the aim of this book, as its title indicates, is to question the procedure by which the biographical person is "invented."[33]

I have chosen quite intentionally to concentrate on a short and an early period of Harrison's life. Short, because by looking hard at a decade or so we can explore the fainter traces and the more fragile connections that tend to get lost in a grand lifetime's narrative; we can enjoy the detail (and see the significance) of the day-to-day; we can think more closely about how exactly elements of a life are reconstructed—friendships, quarrels, decisions, passions, influences; we can expose the process of biographical writing more clearly to view. And early, because people's lives look different at the start of their career. Of course, we can never tell a life "forwards," as if we did not know what happened next.[34] Biography is about hindsight (it is, after all, only because of "what happened next" that we are now concerned with the story of Jane Ellen Harrison). At the same time, by concentrating on a period before she had made her name, by sensing how unfamiliar her career appears from that standpoint, how differently it might have turned out, we can read (productively, I hope) against the grain of the teleology that normally marks the written life story of Harrison—or anyone.[35]

Meanwhile, I shall be wondering how biographical narratives can contribute to an "intellectual history" in its broadest sense (not, that is, the narrow set of "grand theories" that have come to stand for the history of ideas). I am interested in why people—classicists in particular, now or "then"—think and write as they do; and I am even more interested in the kinds of explanation that satisfy us when we write about other scholars' writing. What are we looking for when we look to explain ideas? What counts as a good answer to: "Why did she write that?"

Inevitably, in exploring how the orthodox versions of the Harrison myth have become orthodox, I shall be tracing them back beyond the published sources to the apparently (but deceptively) raw documentation gathered in the Newnham College Archive. Archival research of this sort is a strange and slightly uncomfortable pastime. These are, after all, *other people's letters.* How could you not feel rather awkward (as well as blissfully transgressive) prying through them?[36] But part of the point of my book is a tactical reminder that, for all our belief in its artless neutrality, an archival collection is itself a rhetorical construction, no less than (or not much less than) a carefully crafted biography; that personal mythologies already determine (and are determined by) the peculiar selection, preservation, and classification of letters, diaries, minutes, notes, and reminiscences that make up an archive.[37] Chapter 9 will focus on the two women who between them constructed the Harrison archive at Newnham and, along with that archive, some other orthodoxies in the Harrison mythology.

My argument depends crucially on another female scholar, Eugénie Strong (before her marriage, Eugénie Sellers)—Harrison's contemporary, more or less; historian of Roman art; Assistant Director of the British School at Rome; and one-time glittering star (and influential patron) in the academic society of cosmopolitan, expatriate Italy. More precisely it depends on attempting to re-establish a connection between Strong and Harrison, on finding a different version of Harrison through Strong. But to juxtapose these two raises further questions of academic myth making. Both Harrison and Strong have a good claim on our intellectual time—for the books they wrote and the impact they made within the (men's) classical profession. Yet, while Harrison continues to get her due share of attention, and more, Strong is passed by largely unnoticed. There is no place for *her,* unlike Harrison, in Briggs and Calder's heavyweight encyclopedia of the pantheon of classical scholarship—from Porson to Momigliano.[38] *She* doesn't provide the theme for conferences nor (yet) for intellectual biographies. *Her* ghost, haunting the library, is the laughingstock of the British School at Rome, not an elegant phantom making its mark on a great work of literature. *She* must make do with a brief hagiographic memoir, rather inelegantly composed shortly after her death at the request of her surviving sister (and stolidly titled *Mrs. Arthur Strong: A Memoir*).[39] This book must wonder why this is so; we cannot help but reflect on what determines winners and losers in the race for (posthumous) academic fame.[40]

CHAPTER TWO

Mrs. Arthur Strong:
Apotheosis and After Life

When Mrs. Arthur Strong, who had been Eugénie Sellers, published in 1907 her book on Roman Sculpture, she put at the head of the Preface a quotation from D'Annunzio:

> . . . *ha in sè la luce d'un astro:*
> *Non i suoi cieli irraggia soli ma il mondo Roma*[1]

The lines fittingly express not only the leading motive of her scholarship, but, more than that, the motive which as she grew to maturity, informed her whole life. It is a motive which can be summed up in the word Romanità.

It was eighteen years after the publication of that book, on 14th July, 1925, that a dinner was held in the Hotel Cecil in London. The dinner was given in honour of Mrs. Strong, who had recently retired from the post of Assistant Director of the British School at Rome. The names of the guests are a reflection of that cross-section of English men and women who, in those uneasy years of peace between the wars, retained the tradition of doing honour to scholarship.

So Gladys Scott Thomson starts her memoir, *Mrs. Arthur Strong*[2]—with the party that marked her "retirement" from her post at the British School at Rome in 1925. It was a glittering way to go: almost two hundred (important) guests.[3] At the top table, a handful of Mrs. Strong's closest friends and relations (her sister, Charlotte, and Miss Jex-Blake, from college days) ate their way through the feast, elbow to elbow with the most distinguished of her patrons and acquaintances: a minor royal, Princess Helena Victoria, granddaughter of Queen Victoria; the Italian ambassador and "Her Excellency the Marchesa della Torretta"; Sir James and Lady ("Tiger Lil"[4]) Rennell Rodd (he was a superstar diplomat and one-time British ambassador to Italy); Sir James Frazer O.M. (Lady Frazer came too, but didn't make it to the top table); Lady (Arthur) Evans; the Earl of Oxford and Asquith (as he was then called; Asquith the Prime Minister, as he is better known). The rest of the room was a stylish combination of aristocracies (intellectual, artistic, and political), plus their wives and more friends: G. M. Trevelyan; Mrs. (Bernard) Berenson; a whole party of Macmillans (the publishers, politicians, and Hellenists); Mrs. Holman-Hunt (widow of the artist, for whom, a long time before, Mrs. Strong had modeled[5]); Sydney Cockerell (Director of the Fitzwilliam Museum in Cambridge); Gisela Richter (at the very beginning of her long reign over classical antiquities in the Metropolitan Museum in New York). These were the men and women who (in Thomson's words) "retained the tradition of doing honour to scholarship." No surprise, then, to find a number of the very same people, only three years later, digging deep into their pockets to fund the Jane Harrison Memorial Lecture.[6]

Over the coffee, various members of the party rose to their feet to say a few words of tribute to Mrs. Strong. Lord Oxford and Asquith had no qualms (he said) in asserting "that there is no more distinguished woman scholar to be found anywhere today." He "pointed out how wide was Mrs. Strong's range, how varied her interests, how she had taken all Western archaeology for her province. He need not, he said, in one of the peculiarly happy phrases of which he was the master, enumerate all the beads on her rosary of honour."[7] Sir James Rennell Rodd, who followed, chose a more personal idiom. He started from their first meeting sometime in 1889 or 1890, during his posting in Athens: "He saw her standing between the columns of the Parthenon. And, he said, having first so seen her at the sunset hour, he naturally always associated the friend of after years with Attic forms and Attic harmonies." (In fact, as we shall see in Chapter 4, Rennell Rodd was quite wrong about this first meeting; he had actually come across her years before, in 1883, in much more unlikely circumstances.[8]) He then moved on to their more recent encounters during her long years in Rome. "Identifying herself more and more with the presiding spirit of Imperial Rome, she would reconstitute for us the Altar of Peace or illuminate the Dacian campaigns on the column of Trajan . . . Years passed . . . There was something added which suggested evolution from the sterner outlook of earlier years . . . and once more we sat at the feet of Mrs Strong exploring the mysteries of forbidden cults or rehabilitating the reputation of Bernini."

Of course, these gentlemen had a rather trickier job than Gilbert Murray. *Their* honorand, after all, was not merely alive, she was present at the party and was given the last word before they all went home. True, she put up a proper show of reluctance: "I am terrified," she wrote to one of the organizers, "for I hear there is no getting out of giving a speech . . . I can lecture before anyone without being in the slightest nervous, but you cannot imagine what a bad speaker I am at meetings or after dinner."[9] But, terrified or not, she did not let slip the perfect opportunity—among generous thanks to her hosts, no doubt—for summarizing her views on the importance of Rome in human culture: "From Rome we derived more than a legacy. A legacy implied relations to the dead rather than to the living. Was not, she asked, Rome's gift rather a continuous infiltration of ideas vitally transformed in each successive generation and proceeding from an organism that never died?"

Besides, there were a few skeletons in the cupboard that must have made the eulogies all the more awkward. As we shall see, the circumstances of Mrs. Strong's departure from the British School at Rome were closer to summary dismissal than to voluntary resignation or "retirement," and any eulogist would have had good reason to feel slightly edgy about it. There were some political question marks too. Maybe in 1925 enthusiasm for *Romanità* or for "the presiding spirit of Imperial Rome" was not yet tainted by Mussolini's imperialist projects, with their identical slogans. Maybe many of this particular assembled company would, in any case, have remained pretty unmoved by Mrs. Strong's later—and, to some, embarrassing—fondness for Il Duce. All the same, "fascist sympathizer" was a regular slur after her death, and it certainly made its impact on Strong's admiring biographer, who betrays some nervousness when she insists: "It is characteristic of the trend of her thought that each of the two visits she paid Il Duce was connected with his interest in archaeology."[10] In a sense, the accusation is both fair (how could Strong fail to be tainted by the views of those she counted as her friends, and whose letters—occasionally strident in their anti-Semitism, notably Ezra Pound's—she chose to cherish?) and, at the same time, wildly misleading (a drastic oversimplification of the complex social and academic world of Roman archaeology under Mussolini that cannot straightforwardly be classified in terms of pro- or antifascist). But who knows how it might have affected the frankness of those who chose to celebrate her?

There were extenuating circumstances then. Nonetheless, it is hard not to suspect that the eclipse of Strong's fame was due in part to the sheer inadequacy of these, and her other, eulogists; hard not to think that they could have done a better job.

The rest of this chapter offers a brief account of Mrs. Strong's career. It is no eulogy but an attempt to write her back into the history of Classics. If, in the process, *her* biography seems to escape some of the skepticism that I paraded in the last chapter (if Strong appears to have "got off lightly" compared with Harrison), that is a consequence of the particular task at hand. Complicated games of representation and self-representation have their place in Strong's life too—as we shall see clearly in later chapters.

Eugénie Sellers was, like Harrison, one of the first generation of women students at the University of Cambridge: an undergraduate at the rival women's college, Girton; one of the "Girton Pioneers." She came up to read Classics in 1879, at the age of nineteen—just a few months after Jane Harrison had finished her undergraduate career at Newnham. The college was still very small, with only three tutors and just a handful of students, reading Mathematics and Natural Sciences as well as Classics, and it had only recently moved to the outskirts of Cambridge, after ten years in the little town of Hitchin (an inconvenient twenty miles away, but safe—so its founders thought—from the prying eyes of the Cambridge male establishment). Like Newnham, then, which had just left its makeshift city-center lodgings and was busy creating its own elegant "campus" only a couple of miles away from Girton, it must have been as much a building site as a college.[11]

How Sellers coped with the demands of the course we can only guess. Apart from a few years spent at a French convent, she had had little formal schooling, and she herself talked of "her complete lack of preparation" for the degree. Had she gone to Newnham, she would doubtless have been allowed to take an extra year or so to catch up (for there the college authorities considered it entirely fair to allow women more time than the male students to prepare for university examinations, to compensate for what they were likely to have missed in school). But Girton's Principal, Emily Davies, insisted that her students take the university exams on exactly the same schedule as the men (for only thus would they be counted equal to the men). No great surprise, then, that Sellers failed her preliminary mathematics requirement at least once and finally left Cambridge with the equivalent of a "third" in Classics in 1882; not just a third, but in the third division of the third class, one of the worst results that you could possibly get.[12]

Some of her teachers were quite happy to write testimonials, assuring the world that she was brighter than her degree result implied (and her later career suggests that they were right). After all, the examination she took was almost entirely a test of Latin and Greek language, designed for men who had been drilled in almost nothing else for most of their secondary school career; although a few women excelled over these linguistic hurdles (as Harrison very nearly had), most came to do better in the new optional, and much less narrowly philological, Part II of the Tripos—which Sellers did not choose to take.[13] "I can confidently say," wrote Alfred Cooke MA of King's College, "that her place in her final Examination is by no means a true measure of her real capabilities." And J. P. Postgate (of Trinity College and, simultaneously, from 1880–1909, Professor of Comparative Philology at University College, London) thought highly enough of her abilities, third-class degree notwithstanding, to engage her in 1888 to help him on a proposed revision of his *New Latin Primer,* and to attempt strenuously to dissuade her from the switch away from Latin ("I own the glamour of Archaeology . . . I believe myself that your gifts are specially literary").[14] She herself (as many before and since) came to believe that her heart had not been in it, and that the poor result was not entirely her fault, as the course had simply not engaged her own particular talents and interests: "I am quite a beginner w[ith] Plato," she wrote to her friend Vernon Lee some years later, when they were arguing about theories of art in Plato's *Phaedrus,* "for what I did at Girton was chiefly to examine how his use of the past participle differed from somebody else's."[15]

Teaching school was a safe enough destination after Girton, even with a third-division third. But after just one year of teaching Latin and Greek at St. Leonard's, a leading girls' school in Scotland, Sellers opted for a more exciting life in London. For the first few months, at least, she shared a flat with her sister and a college friend, Hertha Marks (a political radical and later to become a famous electrical engineer—and the model for Mira in George Eliot's *Daniel Deronda*),[16] while studying classical archaeology and earning money from private tuition and lecturing at the British Museum and elsewhere. It probably wasn't as "reckless" a career move as she herself would have us believe.[17] At any rate she was certainly rich enough (whether from private investments or teaching income) to travel widely in Europe through the 1880s and 1890s and to study with the state-of-the-art German archaeologists of the day, both in Germany and at the German Institute in Rome. (See illustration 2.)

She also had the money to have the leisure to write—no sign yet of the *Romanità* that was to "inform her whole life," but in-

Fig. 2.   Eugénie Sellers. A copy of the photograph that Sellers sent to her new friend "Miss Paget" (Vernon Lee) in 1887.

stead a series of publications on Greek archaeology. Some of these were serviceable translations, bringing the cutting edge of German archaeological discovery to a home readership. She started, in 1891, with an English version of Schuchhardt's handbook to the excavations at Troy (*Schliemann's Excavations*)—an extremely handsome production from Macmillan, with a no-expenses-spared gold embossed cover. It came complete with corrections ("I have ventured to alter one or two matters of detail . . ."), new footnotes, an introduction by Walter Leaf,[18] and an appendix ("by Dr. Schliemann and Dr. Dörpfeld") on the most recent discoveries; letters preserved in the publishers' archive hint at the complex series of negotiations that finally extracted this new material from Mrs. Schliemann (Schliemann himself having died) and from the willing but overcommitted Dörpfeld.[19] In 1895 she followed this up with a translation of *Meisterwerke* (*Masterpieces of Ancient Sculpture*) by her friend and teacher Adolf Furtwängler ("a splendid barbarian," as she called him in a letter to one of her publishers: "Sir Charles [Newton] has christened him 'The Dying Gaul'"); again the book—another lavish production (this time from Heinemann)—was politely corrected and edited.[20]

But there were some notable original contributions too. In 1896, with her old friend from Girton days, Katharine Jex-Blake (now college tutor in Classics, and a future Girton Principal), she produced an edition of *The Elder Pliny's Chapters on the History of Art.* Jex-Blake provided the translation of the relevant sections of Pliny's *Natural History;* Sellers wrote the introduction and commentary, which discussed the whole tradition of art historical writing in Latin and Greek and attempted to match up the works of art mentioned by Pliny with surviving remains.[21] (On this occasion, sharing the honors with her German colleagues proved more troublesome: H. L. Uhrlichs complained that the acknowledgment in the Preface of his help on the project was far from adequate, and the dispute ended in pamphlet

warfare.[22]) Some of her other work of this period has so much entered our currency that we no longer remember it specifically as
hers. Buried in small type and between square brackets in *Masterpieces* is a detailed two-page discussion (signed only with the
initials "E. S.") of the so-called Aberdeen Head in the British
Museum—a fragmentary, battered, and unattractively stained
piece of sculpture, which she argues is an original work by the
fourth-century artist Praxiteles. The precise attribution of this
head, inevitably, continues to be debated (Praxiteles? Skopas? an
unknown sculptor working somewhere between their styles?).
But no one now doubts that it is a late fourth-century (or possibly early third-century) "original," and no one much remembers
that it was Eugénie Sellers who was largely responsible for rescu-
ing it from obscurity. Her arguments were, in the 1890s, strikingly up to the minute. She writes of making a lantern slide to
compare the Aberdeen Head with that of the well-known Her-
mes of Praxiteles: "When the two heads, much enlarged, were
projected on to the screen, the agreement between them of form
and technique was exact beyond all expectation."[23]

Strikingly up to the minute, too, was the theory lying behind
this demonstration (as well as behind the identifications of various sculptures proposed in the edition of Pliny). On July 13,
1893, Vernon Lee wrote home to her mother, telling about her
friend's archaeological researches: "Miss Sellers is doing such interesting work . . . She is applying to antique sculpture the
method lately invented by Morelli for painting—namely accurate and minute study of the single forms and methods of representation of each master. A man gets dominated by certain
forms, or manners of vision, quite as much as by a technique,
and it becomes an infallible means of identification. Thus Poly-
clite and Myron see[k] to represent hair in quite a different
way."[24] Hence the identification of the Aberdeen Head by the
modeling of the cheekbones, the shape of the nose, the form of
the eyeball, and so on.

It is perhaps not surprising that Sellers should have caught on to the "Morellian revolution" in art history, and that she should have seen uses of her own for Morelli's (then) radical claim that the *imprint* of an individual artist lay in the apparently insignificant details of the treatment of minor features (earlobes, hands, eyebrows), which could identify a painter as reliably as his handwriting. Nor is it particularly surprising that she should have taken a copy of Morelli's *Italian Painters* on her travels ("Morelli you probably have with you," wrote her future husband while she was away in 1895), or that she should have wandered around Italian art galleries in an "aesthetic trio" with her friends Bernard Berenson and Mary Costelloe—later to become Mrs. Berenson—enthusiastically "re-writing the picture galleries" in Morellian fashion ("The young man is far from stupid," conceded one observer, "but it is an unfortunate postion to be in: the teacher and prophet of two admiring spinsters, one of whom [i.e., Costelloe] is a widow."[25]) What *is* surprising is the way that we have so comprehensively forgotten this aspect of her work. According to most histories of classical art history, it is Sir John Beazley (ultimately through the influence of Berenson, and with Gisela Richter's father, the medieval and Renaissance art historian Jean Paul Richter, as another intermediary) who brought the Morellian revolution to Classics, in a whole stream of articles (and later, books) on Greek vase painters, published from 1910 onward—even though, as is reluctantly admitted, Beazley never so much as mentions the name of either Morelli or Berenson in any of his published works. In fact, a good fifteen years earlier Eugénie Sellers had been deploying the Morellian method in classical art history, and in much closer contact with Berenson than Beazley had ever been.[26]

In 1897, just one year after her collaboration with Miss Jex-Blake, Sellers entered a new partnership, marrying Sandford Arthur Strong—who was (simultaneously) Professor of Arabic at University College London, Librarian for the Duke of Devonshire at Chatsworth, and Librarian of the House of Lords. Strong's letters written in the course of their (very) long courtship are preserved in the Girton Archive, still tied up in the ribbons in which Mrs. Strong had bound them. Still with them are the notes she added, chronicling her version of the ups and downs in this relationship: "Letters written between Aug 12 93 (after our engagement was definitely broken off by me) and Dec 93 when I attempted a further break . . . In Aug [95] SAS came to see me in Schwabing when I for the second time since the breaking off of our engagement attempted to put a stop to our 'friendship.' The correspondence was returned . . .").[27] In the end she married him; but it did not last long. By 1904 he was dead (*we* would suspect overwork; *they* diagnosed pernicious anemia). He left his wife a job (she inherited his post of Chatsworth librarian), the kind of connections that distinguished bereavement can bring, and the name and status that she enjoyed for the rest of her life: Mrs. Arthur Strong, widow.

It was in this guise that she migrated to Rome in 1909, at the age of forty-eight, to take up the position of Assistant Director and Librarian of the British School of Art and Archaeology, which had been established (on paper at least) in 1899 and, from 1907, was offering scholarships to artists and architects, as well as archaeologists and historians.[28] At first, she made a brilliant team with the Director, Thomas Ashby: playing the glamorous hostess to all comers, "from cardinals to art students in corduroys," and holding the fort while Ashby was locked up in his study, tramping around the Roman Campagna (he was to all intents and purposes the inventor of modern archaeological "field survey"), or absent fighting for king and country.[29] But trouble lay ahead. Local gossip traced the rot back to Ashby's marriage in 1921. By all accounts May Ashby was very keen on animals and none too keen at all on her new husband's closest colleague. Whether she was, as some have thought, an "unpretentious"

woman, overwhelmed by (and increasingly resentful of) the unbearably queenly style of Mrs. Strong, or, alternatively, a schem-
ing manipulator who had plotted the Assistant Director's over-
throw from the very moment she hooked Ashby, is impossible
now (as it ever was) to decide. It is equally impossible to know
(though hard not to wonder) whether the new wife was in fact
largely a scapegoat for trouble long brewing between Ashby and
Strong. But however the blame is to be apportioned, by the early
1920s the almost continual quarreling between the Assistant
Director and the Director (with his wife just behind him) had
turned even the most trivial domestic decision into a major diplomatic incident, bordering on warfare, and the School was left
virtually ungoverned.

A flavor of the sheer madness of these disputes (as well as
of the paranoia that thrives in small expatriate institutions) is
found in the collection of letters and denunciations preserved in
the Girton Archive on the subject of Strong's alleged support of
bullfighting.[30] Had she, or had she not, encouraged the British
School students to attend a bullfight? (*Not,* she claimed—un-
convincingly to some.) In the light of these suspicions, was the
Duchess of San Teodoro to welcome Strong's presence at a celebrity lecture in aid of the Italian Society for the Prevention of
Cruelty to Animals—or not? (*Not,* of course . . .) Whose side
was Ashby on? (Hardly difficult to guess, since Mrs. Ashby, with
her enthusiasm for animal welfare, was busy organizing a con-
cert at the British School in aid of the very same society, without
even consulting the Assistant Director.) And was he, as Strong
inevitably suspected, bad-mouthing her around the School and
among the Roman glitterati?

The School's managing committee in London took the only
option and got rid of them both in 1925.[31] The cover was (as
usual) "resignation" or "retirement"; Strong was, after all, in her
midsixties. But she (and the rest of the world) recognized it,
rightly, as the sack: "These gentlemen had as much right to dis-

miss Dr. Ashby or me," she wrote to Lord Crawford, "as you have to dismiss your cook. I only wanted . . . that their dismissal of me should not be represented in the crude, not to say cruel, terms that were actually printed in the *Times*."[32]

Mrs. Strong could at that point have returned to England. She had been elected the first Research Fellow of Girton, for life, in 1910, and would have been welcome to take up residence there. But she chose instead to stay on in Rome until her death in 1943 (just a few days after the Germans entered the city, when most people in the world had bigger things on their minds). For more than thirty years she wrote, lectured, and held court there: "Social life in the British School," wrote one student, "[had] revolved entirely around her."[33] Hospitality, one senses, now became even more of an obsession. Her papers include literally thousands of visiting cards from this period, trophies of "the great and the good" who came to call—from Ezra Pound to Franz Cumont—all carefully collected and filed away, as well as their letters, in even greater numbers. Lodged now in Girton College, Cambridge, and at the British School at Rome, they are a startling, and sometimes unsettling, collection: a still almost unknown archive, parading—and this was surely the intention—a galaxy of Mrs. Strong's tame stars, and not just from classical archaeology; there were also high-flying Vatican apparatchiks, European aristocrats, up-market artists, novelists, critics, and poets (Henry James, Andrew Lang, Mary Kingsley, Vita Sackville-West, Flinders Petrie, Evelyn Waugh, Giacomo Boni, and more cardinals than one could hope to imagine).[34] Though it was clearly sorted and, in some places, annotated by Strong's sister, Charlotte Leigh Smith, and by her biographer, Gladys Scott Thomson, much of this archive appears still to be arranged as it was by Strong herself; or so the handwriting on some of the labels, the ribbons binding the letters from her fiancé, and the parodically self-glorifying system of classification ("Letters from distinguished foreigners") must suggest.[35] We shall see later how strikingly this contrasts with Newnham's Harrison Papers.

In the period after her husband's death, Strong published prolifically, from a major monograph on the church of Santa Maria in Vallicella (la Chiesa Nuova) to some briskly journalistic articles for the *Times Literary Supplement* on recent archaeological discoveries in Rome.[36] But two extremely important books stand out. The first is *Roman Sculpture from Augustus to Constantine* (1907), unsurprising enough as a title, but in fact the first ever systematic *history* of Roman sculpture to be written in English. The second was *Apotheosis and After Life* (1915), which explored the relationship between the visual arts and Roman ideologies of the afterlife and the deification of the emperor. Its three main chapters were based on the Charles Eliot Norton lectures she had given in the United States (under the sponsorship of the Archaeological Institute of America) in 1913—together with an "Introductory Address to Students" and a chapter on "Rome and the Present State of Roman Studies."

If you brush the dust from *Apotheosis and After Life,* if you refuse to be put off by its early twentieth-century jargon, you find a book that is still disconcertingly interesting. It is quite different from her early work on Greek art and culture, not least for its striking and sustained polemic—spirited or silly, depending on your point of view—against those who valued Greece above Rome. Whatever the reasons for this change of perspective (she herself was later to claim that an interest in Rome had been lurking since childhood: "The seed had been planted . . . under guidance of my Jesuit teacher in Spain"[37]), her introductory tirade in *Apotheosis and After Life* makes it all too plain why her college obituary felt bound to allude to the "irritation" she caused to "the more Hellenically inclined."[38] Greece may have had, she admits with treacherous generosity, "an infinitely clearer vision of beauty"; the truth was, however, "that this vision was attained by the sacrifice of certain things pertaining to the spiritual world, which the Romans . . . came to realise and to express . . . In spite of all efforts to combat it, the determination to praise the Greek at the expense of the Roman persists."[39]

But amid all this polemic, there is also a sustained attempt to come to grips with the particular qualities of Roman culture and artistic production in a way that strikes a distinctively modern chord. Two of her claims stand out. The first is her stress on what she (like many more recent writers) saw as one of the most important paradoxes of Roman culture: its combination of conservatism and innovation; the Romans, for her, were simultaneously highly conservative *and* radically innovative—their innovation thriving on (and legitimated by) an ideology that ostensibly rejected change in almost all its forms.[40] The second is her insistence on the inextricable connection between visuality and religion: visual representations, she argued, must be central not only to our own understanding of Roman religion but also to Roman religion itself; art, in other words, does not merely *illustrate* religious claims, it *is* religion. "English scholars especially have a tendency to underrate the role played in the formation of religious ideas by the visible form given to deities and abstractions." Think, she urges her audience, of the triumphant Roman general: he did not merely dress up as Jupiter; by adopting the god's costume, he *became* the god. Or think of the Roman emperor: deified more emphatically by the statues that displayed him as a god than by the formal title *divus*.[41] In a sense, for all their differences of approach, Strong was doing for Rome what Harrison had done for Greece: linking the visual arts and archaeology to a cultural anthropology of the ancient world.

A whole series of honors followed (rather more for Strong than for Harrison, in fact). By the time of her death, at age eighty-three, she had been loaded with honorary degrees; she had become one of the first four women to be made Fellows of the Society of Antiquaries; she had been decorated with the British Academy's Serena Gold Medal for Italian Studies, with the gold medal of the city of Rome, and with letters after her name (C.B.E., Commander of the British Empire). This can hardly have been far short of her wildest dreams.

CHAPTER THREE

Unanimism

You do not have to look very far to spot some insistent similarities between the careers of Jane Harrison and Eugénie Strong. Both were among the first handful of female undergraduates at Cambridge, both read for the Classical Tripos. True, they were at different colleges and their undergraduate years at Cambridge did not directly overlap (Harrison "went down" a few months before Sellers "came up"). But, unless all the stories of her prominence on the Cambridge scene are flagrantly untrue, Harrison must still have been fresh in the collective memory (even at Girton) when Sellers arrived; Sellers can hardly have failed to know that she was following in the footsteps of the glamorous (and self-glamorizing) Miss Harrison, with her circle of admirers, her stunning wallpaper, and her so very nearly first-class degree.

Both of them also picked up from somewhere a determination to learn more about classical archaeology. Neither gives much credit here to the Classics course at Cambridge. Jane Harrison's own story, in her *Reminiscences,* was that "all my archaeology was taught me by Germans. The great Ernst Curtius . . . Heinrich Brunn . . . Dörpfeld was my most honoured master." There was room for only the slightest influence from teachers in Cambridge: during her final year, so another story went, she hap-

pened to go along to hear some lectures by Sidney Colvin, the
Slade Professor of Fine Art, on recent discoveries at Olympia; it
was these which, in the words of her friend Hope Mirrlees, "gave
a focus to her studies & interests & decided her on specialising in
Greek art." But that meant going abroad.[1]

Eugénie Sellers was even more strident, ferociously denying
that Cambridge had had any archaeological influence on her
whatsoever. Her story, too, was that all her archaeological exper-
tise had been the result of German training, whether in Munich
or at the German Institute in Rome: "As previously in Germany," she wrote of her stay at the Institute in 1892, "I received
fullest encouragement and help contrasting painfully with the
blank my effort had drawn in England, more especially from my
own university of Cambridge. Archaeology indeed was a study
at that time barely recognised there, whether by classicists or
historians." We may detect here an oblique—and unkind, given
all his help—reference to her friend and patron J. P. Postgate,
who had indeed once attempted to dissuade her from moving
into archaeology: "Archaeology has always seemed to me a vast
sea," he wrote to her in 1889, "at present almost without a
shore; and archaeological studies to be in a position which does
not make them easy or profitable to teach."[2] For Arthur Strong
(whom she had certainly managed to convince of her point of
view), those attitudes were typical of Cambridge in general. Just
after the publication of her edition of Pliny, he wrote to her
commenting on an otherwise favorable and well-meaning review: "One thing in it annoyed me, and that was the airy assertion that the book expressed the results of *Cambridge* training."
"But," he continued, "nothing I suppose will ever impair (much
less destroy) our insular self sufficience."[3]

None of this can be quite accurate. As we shall see in Chapter
5, this pair certainly did not learn *all* their archaeology abroad.
Both of them spent a good deal of time at the British Museum,
working and studying with Charles Newton, the Keeper of

Antiquities, as Mrs. Strong grudgingly concedes ("In London I did find sympathy and some encouragement when good fortune brought me in contact with Sir Charles Newton . . . Intercourse with him confirmed my zest for the study of ancient sculpture— Greek at that time—but brought me no nearer turning it to practical purpose."[4]). Besides, there was considerably more interest in archaeology among scholars in Cambridge than either Harrison or Strong chose to admit. The late 1870s to early 1880s was exactly the period when archaeology first gained a real foothold in Cambridge Classics: Colvin (whose lectures inspired Harrison) was busy for most of that time assembling a huge collection of six hundred or so plaster casts of Greek and Roman sculpture to be displayed in a brand-new university museum (officially opened in 1884); the Classics course was reformed to include, in its optional new Part II, a major element on classical archaeology; and the first lecturer in classical archaeology, Charles Waldstein (himself German trained), was already in post during the academic year 1880–81—had she wished, Eugénie Sellers could have attended his lectures, and had she stayed on to take Part II, she could even have specialized in archaeology.[5] For all their denials (probably as much to do with a desire to parade a connection with German traditions in the face of what they saw as British ethnocentricity and insularity as with a rejection of what they had learned in Cambridge and London), it is hard not to imagine that something of this new local excitement for the material culture of the ancient world had rubbed off on both of them.

The parallels between the two women are even more striking after they leave Cambridge. Both of them tried out the same career (teaching school—if only for a short while); both of them gave it up to live, independently, in the same city (London), studying and writing on the same subject (classical—mostly Greek—archaeology), working and lecturing at the same museum (the British Museum); and they were writing articles in the same periodicals (the new *Journal of Hellenic Studies,* the *Classical Review*), publishing books with the same publisher (Macmillan),[6] traveling abroad to the same cities and sites (Florence, Athens, Olympia) and to meet the same scholars (notably Dörpfeld); and they both proclaimed, at least with hindsight, the same influence (Germany) on their archaeological career. How could their biographies not be intertwined? How could these women not have had some part to play in each other's life? How could they not have known each other well? It seems inevitable that they did; unbelievable that they didn't.

Or so you would think. But it is, in fact, a more complicated story than that. For all the similarity we have detected in the underlying principles of their major work, for all the common preoccupations of religion and visual culture that bind *Prolegomena* and *Themis* to *Apotheosis and After Life,* there is no sign whatsoever of any direct contact linking those books, no parade of acquaintance between their authors. It is more than a question simply of physical separation: Harrison returning to Cambridge in 1898 and increasingly concentrating on (primitive) Hellenism; Sellers marrying in 1897 and turning (both metaphorically and literally) to Rome. We find no expression of intellectual debt from one to the other; no grateful thanks in a preface; hardly a reference, let alone a warm one, in the footnotes. On my reckoning, Strong admits just two bare citations of Harrison's work in *Apotheosis and After Life,* and in 1928 she is recorded as donating a (not particularly generous) "guinea" (£1.05p, or $1.70) to the Harrison Memorial Fund.[7] Harrison herself—amid all her expressions of gratitude to Gilbert Murray, Francis Cornford, ABC, and A. W. Verrall; her acknowledgment of the influence of Henri Bergson and Emile Durkheim; her dedicated sparring with William Ridgeway—had not a single word for Mrs. Strong in the preface to either *Prolegomena* or *Themis.*[8]

So too in the biographical tradition. Miss Sellers (and/or Mrs. Strong) usually merits, at most, a passing mention in published accounts of the career of Miss Harrison. She does not appear at all in Jessie Stewart's *Portrait* of Harrison; Sandra Peacock admits a connection of sorts in just one casual reference: "Eugenie Sellers, an acquaintance who later became an expert on Roman art, angered Jane by the 'unscrupulous way she used people just to get on.'"[9]

There is a slightly clearer hint of their connection (and of its possible significance) in Thomson's *Mrs. Arthur Strong,* though it is still only a hint. She refers darkly to a "friendship, with intense admiration on one side, and then disaster," and she continues (with a biographer's defensive loyalty to her own subject): "The two temperaments were incompatible with one another. And, as was to occur again later, the very generosity and warmth and enthusiasm with which Eugénie Sellers could fling herself into a new friendship often intensified the catastrophe in the end." Thomson also knew enough to pinpoint two particular locations in which (during their London years) Harrison and Sellers were to be found *together.* First, she refers to the British Museum: "Jane Harrison was, like Eugénie Sellers, a disciple of Sir Charles Newton . . . both were students working at the British Museum." Second, she observes in passing that in 1883 they had both taken part in a notable theatrical show entitled *The Tale of Troy,* an ambitious adaptation for the stage of the *Iliad* and *Odyssey.*[10]

The next two chapters will follow up these hints. They are the story of my own exploration in archives (in Cambridge and much further afield), on the trail of a lost friendship and a forgotten collaboration. The hunch that lay behind my exploration was simple: that there was a lot more to the links between Harrison and Sellers than most biographers have recognized (or chosen to tell). It was a very lucky hunch; the connection between Harrison and Sellers turns out to have been very close indeed.

For the time being, I shall be focusing on the 1880s and 1890s—after Cambridge, but before Harrison returned to

Newnham in 1898 and before Miss Sellers became Mrs. Strong in 1897. This period has usually been treated as a rather murky, ill-documented prequel to Harrison's triumphant and hugely productive career in the early years of the twentieth century, a period that can be illuminated, if at all, by reflection backward from later events—seen, in other words, through the lens of the future. Hence the isolation of one or two key events (such as Harrison's disagreement with D. S. MacColl) as explanatory of what was to come.[11] In fact, it is not half so ill-documented a period as people have imagined, and there is a good deal of (new or unexploited) contemporary evidence for Harrison's activities during her seventeen years based in London (particularly if we look beyond the Harrison Papers lodged at Newnham College). Chapters 4 and 5 will try to capture something of the fin-de-siècle world in which Harrison and Sellers lived, worked, acted, studied, taught, and traveled; they offer a new perspective on Classics and the classical world in the late nineteenth century. At the same time, I hope to show that a new look at her "London period" must make a difference to our understanding of Harrison's career as a whole, that it enables a significantly different story to be told of her work, its roots, and her intellectual influences.

Inevitably too (and this problem will guide the book to its end) I shall be reflecting on why Harrison and Sellers have been so comprehensively written *out* of each other's narratives. There is more than one answer. Thomson's memoir clearly suggests a catastrophic falling out, a bitter break, a "disaster." I shall be looking for traces of this quarrel (which, in turn, will prompt questions about the *kind* of friendship we are to imagine between these two women). But there are wider issues of classical and intellectual history at stake too. Part of the answer almost certainly lies in the subject boundaries within Classics that we ourselves have inherited (and which we, as well as they, partly constructed): wherever they started, Harrison and Sellers ended up on opposite sides of the great divide between Greece and

Rome. Who would now think of bringing Mrs. Strong (with all her uncompromising *Romanità*) into Miss Harrison's story of ur-Hellenism? But, as we shall see, the answer is also connected with the (apparently) raw materials out of which we resurrect past lives. As I have stressed already, archival collections are loaded constructions; biography, even before it reaches the printed page, always has an ax to grind. One of the reasons that Sellers has been effaced from Harrison's (written) life is that a number of people (Harrison herself included) did not want her there.

But now, we shall watch them together in *The Tale of Troy* and explore the background to their partnership in a characteristically late-Victorian theatrical (and, as we shall shortly see, archaeological) enterprise.

CHAPTER FOUR

Myths of the Odyssey
in Art and Literature

The London season of 1883 was enlivened by some high-society theatricals, performed to raise money for a good liberal cause—the new Lectures for Women at King's College London. One performance is memorably described by a young American visitor, Maud du Puy, in one of her letters home; she had been taken specially from Cambridge for a day's shopping, followed in the evening by some elegant culture:

> Gladstone, Sir Isaac Newton, Sir Frederic Leighton and some other great codger sat immediately in front of us . . . Gladstone looks exactly like the caricatures of him, only his collar is a little larger and his eyes are so keen and bright and twinkle so when he laughs. Sir F. Leighton had charge of the scenic effects and succeeded very well, only all the rouge and powder and Greek dresses could not make perfect beauties of the English girls. The play was called *The Tale of Troy*, and this night was spoken entirely in Greek. Mr. Stephen was Hector and acted remarkably well. Lionel Tennyson as Ulysses would have been better had he known his part. I enjoyed the play very much and equally so the people. Such dresses!!! Words fail me for description.[1]

Part of the evening must, in fact, have been hard going for du Puy. Her only connection with the Greek language came through her aunt (and host), who was married to Richard Jebb (later to become Regius Professor of Greek at Cambridge); and we know from various reviews that the performance lasted a good two and a half hours—and no doubt felt considerably longer if you knew no Greek. It is pretty clear, too, that she had misunderstood quite a lot of the careful explanations that her host had surely given her—about who was, and who wasn't, there. "Sir Isaac Newton" had, after all, been dead for more than a hundred and fifty years; though it must have given the young visitor a buzz to imagine that she had sat so close to the discoverer of gravity, the Newton sitting in the row in front was presumably Mr. *Charles* Newton, the Keeper of Greek and Roman Antiquities at the British Museum and one of the leading lights behind the production.[2] All the same, details apart, du Puy has it absolutely right; it was a glittering social occasion, and the dresses must have been (unspeakably) beyond description.[3]

If anything, Miss du Puy rather underestimates quite how glittering it was, on both sides of the curtain. The play was the brainchild of Professor George C. W. Warr (Professor of Classical Literature at King's College London), who had selected key moments from the Homeric epics and adapted them for the stage, with the addition of a few songs, "in some cases derived from Homer or Theocritus, in other cases original."[4] To heighten the atmosphere, he had commissioned a series of tableaux—set displays of memorable scenes from the *Iliad* and *Odyssey*—designed by the contemporary stars of the art world: Sir Frederic Leighton, already by 1883 President of the Royal Academy and on his way to brief enjoyment of that yet grander title by which we now generally know him, *Lord* Leighton[5] (his ennoblement a direct consequence of his shrewd investment in precisely this kind of neo-Hellenic dream; he was "a mixture," as one contemporary commentator called him, "of the Olympian Jove & a head waiter"[6]); the up-and-coming Edward Poynter (another President of the Royal Academy in the making); G. F. Watts; and L. Alma-Tadema; along with a Pre-Raphaelite duo, Edward Burne-Jones and John Everett Millais, keeping company among the

Hellenophiles.[7] Right up to the last minute, this strange assortment of talent busied itself with the finishing touches to the painted backdrops and with capturing just the right "hang" on the garments of the players who filled the stage—motionless mannequins in a series of frozen mimes of the poems' greatest moments. One member of the cast later recalled the steamy atmosphere, her "willing slavery" to "all the great artists of the day," and the faintly ludicrous interchanges between actors and academicians: "'What about my *chiton?*' and 'Please drape the folds of my *himation.*'"[8]

The performance took place in the private theater in Cromwell House, the London home of the now completely obscure, but then extremely rich, Sir Charles and Lady Freake. There were, in fact, two different versions of the show, in Greek and in English, staged on alternate nights—four performances altogether. (Miss du Puy was perhaps unlucky to have hit a Greek night, but then again it probably made for a more self-consciously cultured audience). Inevitably, two epics and two languages demanded an enormous cast of something like eighty different actors drawn mostly from the inner ranks of the chattering classes (with a couple of up-market professional thesps thrown in—Mr. and Mrs. Herbert Beerbohm Tree). It may have been, as one of the actresses was to claim long after, "rather an absurd affair . . . laughed at for giving Society ladies an opportunity for dressing up and displaying their beauty,"[9] but nonetheless, "everybody of note—except Bernard Shaw—[was] in it."[10] J. K. Stephen, as du Puy mentioned, played Hector on the Greek night (the painter Whistler had apparently turned the honor down, but Stephen, well-connected young don about town, later to be in the front rank of celebrity suspects for Jack the Ripper, filled in well enough[11]); Mrs. Bram Stoker, bride of *Dracula* Stoker, took Calypso on the English night; there was a Sitwell or two among the cast; plus Lionel Tennyson, the poet laureate's son, as Ulysses (pater turned up with the other celebrities one evening to watch junior stumble through his lines); Mrs. Andrew Lang, wife of *Myth, Ritual and Religion* Lang; Rennell Rodd, whom *we* last met more than forty years later, in his real-life role as ex-ambassador to Rome and chief eulogizer of the (not-so) retiring Mrs. Strong;[12] right down to Jane Harrison (Penelope in Greek) and young Eugénie Sellers (Helen in English and Cassandra in Greek) adding youthful female talent to the show—not to mention that it was female talent that knew some Greek. Unlike their generous hostess, Lady Freake, whom Jane Harrison's friends rather tritely mocked for her "great wealth but little culture" (Sir Charles had made his millions out of real estate and property development in South Kensington) and for pronouncing *H*omer as 'Omer.[13]

Behind the scenes it was the usual amateur dramatic mixture: fanatical, obsessive directors, demanding total loyalty to the show (in a style that veered from flattery and bribery to fits of temper and violence); a group of thespians who had other things on their mind (and found the self-importance of the organizers faintly amusing); vain would-be stars, rubbing shoulders with the walk-ons, who weren't quite sure why they were there or what they had let themselves in for (and who certainly weren't going to polish their lines).

Strong's papers still contain the initial notes of invitation-plus-persuasion from Warr himself, carefully balancing politeness, self-interest, and prudent economy: "I hope very much you will be able to play Helen—do *please* if it can be managed" (March 1883); "When you wrote before, I of course gave up any hope of your playing and asked Mrs. Beerbohm Tree to play Helen on the Greek night, as she happens to know Greek" (April 9, 1883); "Most fortunately your telegram came just in time, and I have kept the part of Helen for you on the English night. On the Greek night you must appear too (I think, as Cassandra). The same dress will do for both" (April 15, 1883). And the stream of letters continues through the rehearsal schedule, the dinner invitations (that were meant to sugar the pill), the last-minute cancellations, and the arbitrary decisions from the various directors and designers. "I have asked Mr. and Mrs. Beerbohm Tree, Mrs. Lang, Miss Harrison and Mr. Cecil Smith to come to my house tomorrow week for a sub rehearsal. Mrs. Sitwell is also coming and Mr. Warr. There will be dinner at 6:30 and rehearsal afterwards" (Charles Newton on May 11, with still a fortnight to go); "if *4:30 tomorrow* suits you *all* I shall be at your orders to arrange the tableau" (Leighton, "Thursday"); "Just after I had fixed the 21st for our Helen Hermione tableau, Mr. Warr informed me that . . . he had found it necessary to suppress that tableau altogether. That leaves you free for the 21st" (Newton, May 15, and rather less than a fortnight to go).[14]

From Harrison's side, the story is told with hindsight; it is (predictably) sharper, the anecdotes nastier. Lady Freake wasn't the only target of their "jokes." Professor Warr, Harrison's friends decided, was a look-alike Mr. Pickwick—and with about as little talent as Pickwick for dealing with the "bevy of high-spirited beautiful young ladies who rustled & 'bussled' on every side." Baiting the director was obviously part of the sport: "The suave ironical gravity of Jane's manner to him was one of the subsidiary amusements of the rehearsals." And so was watching the rows between the men: "There was the scene when George Alexander (who was stage managing), exasperated by the woodenness of J. K. Stephen finally shook him, to which JKS responded by knocking him down! Poor Mr. Pickwick must many times have wished himself back with the docile audience of his lecture room."[15]

Perhaps it serves them right that the contemporary reviews did not rate *The Tale of Troy* an unqualified success. The tableaux were widely agreed to be great, especially as enhanced by the "bevy of high-spirited, beautiful young ladies." "No doubt," wrote the commentator in the *Saturday Review,* "the chief attractions of *The Tale of Troy* lay in the beauty of the numerous nymphs and goddesses who revealed themselves to mortals; in the arrangement of the tableaux; in the variety and agreeable colour of the dresses, and in the music and processions of singing women." Likewise the reviewer from *Vanity Fair* singled out the "dresses of a wondrously irrational kind, and lovely women rolling out hexameters after a fashion that would rejoice Girton and startle their grandmothers." Other critics were full of admiration for the overall Hellenic (not to say Homeric) impression conveyed: "It is impossible to conceive," gushed *The Times* on May 31, "how this could be done with a more scrupulous regard to the spirit of the poem or with a more sympathetic or more refined appreciation of the beauty of Greek art. Costume, scenery, grouping, music, the product of many minds were blended into a whole and impressed the spectator no less with their admirable harmony than with their severely classical correctness."[16] (Something of the style of this "severely classical correctness" is captured in the commemorative publication, *Echoes of Hellas,* that followed the performance;[17] see illustration 3.)

It was the acting that was the problem. Individually, every review agreed, there were very some creditable performances; after all, Warr had engaged a couple of professionals to compensate for the likes of young Tennyson: the Beerbohm Trees were (at least) "effective," and Mrs. Tree performed valiantly as Helen (in Greek), "commanding sympathy, and even respect, in spite of her sin and its fatal consequences."[18] Some of the amateurs, too, pulled out the stops when it counted: however "wooden" he might have been in rehearsal, "Mr. J. K. Stephen, who supported the character of Hector yesterday, acted with admirable force"; Rennell Rodd made Eumaeus "a figure of picturesque homeliness"[19]; and Sellers herself (as Cassandra) touched the critic from *Vanity Fair* with "decidedly the sweetest-spoken Greek in the play."

Contemporary debates (both inside and outside the academy) about the pronunciation of ancient Greek underlie some of these views on the acting. The man from *Vanity Fair* particularly liked

Fig. 3. Tableau design ("The Pledge of Aphrodite Redeemed") from Warr and Crane's *Echoes of Hellas.* Aphrodite (on the right) brings Paris to Helen, while (on the left) Peitho, or Persuasion, whispers in Helen's ear. Originally designed by Frederic Leighton.

Sellers's "modern Romaic" version of Greek—unlike the flat
tones of many of the others. "It is apparently vain to protest
against the flat pronunciation of Greek. Cambridge is obdurate
so far, but there is a warning in the delivery of Cassandra's three
lines, and surely some of these days our English boys will be
taught to speak Greek that would be intelligible to scholars outside our own island."

But overall the performances left something to be desired. No
doubt, as our man at the *Pall Mall Gazette* realized, the audience
expected too much: "more [in fact] than any company of professional actors, not to say amateurs, could have done. Homer on
stage may be a simple thing enough to imagine . . . but in practice it is seen at once to be as arduous a task as any performers
could impose upon themselves." But on the Greek nights, the
language itself was a barrier, even for these classically drilled late
Victorians. So, at least, it was for the reviewer in *The Athenaeum:*

> I am bound to admit that some of the actors spoke their Greek as
> if they had only a dim idea of what they were saying, and this gave
> a distinct sense of unreality to the action . . . Miss Harrison's
> Penelope was very good on the whole, and she spoke the Greek
> with the intelligence of perfect knowledge; only I would suggest
> that excessive declamation and too great emphasis on unimpor-
> tant words tend rather to destroy than create natural effect. Too
> often the impression was not of a Greek lady speaking her own
> language in a natural way, but of an accomplished scholar de-
> claiming Homer and anxious to give due weight to every word.

There were critics, too, of the enterprise as a whole (not just
its particular faults). "An awfully clever piece of writing" in the
Fortnightly Review ended up with a spirited attack on the very
idea of what it called "South Kensington Hellenism." Written
by the fashionable satirist H. D. Traill, this took the form of
a spoof dialogue between Plato and the poet, critic, and essay-
ist Walter Savage Landor—a parody of both (second-century)
Lucian's *Dialogues of the Dead* and Landor himself, who was best

known for his *Imaginary Conversations*. The *Conversations* were a version of *Dialogues with the Dead,* and part of the joke in 1883 was that Landor himself was now dead, conjured back to talk to the even longer dead Plato, in a parody of his own style.[20] The self-consciously witty readers of the *Fortnightly* must have loved it; Warr and company were irritated.[21]

Traill gives us a Plato who combines well-meaning innocence with total cultural misunderstanding. He finds it rather flattering at first (notwithstanding his well-known opposition to Art) that Greek drama is so much the rage in 1880s Britain. He has already heard of the Oxford production of the *Agamemnon* (1880) and the Cambridge *Ajax* (1882),[22] but when Landor tells him all about the latest "scenic representation of Homer" (assuming that he will disapprove of this corruption), he is even more delighted. He is particularly taken, in fact, with the idea that the Freakes' show featured the work of "the first of your philosophers"—until Landor explains that Leighton's Royal *Academy* is a school of painting, not of philosophy.[23] But gradually (and Socratically) his interlocutor argues him round to seeing this Hellenic modishnesss for what it is: modishness, no more, no less. "Suffice it to you to know," concludes Landor, triumphantly, "that the nation in whom you take such an interest have no more become votaries of Homer than they have become worshippers of the elephant. The drama and poetry of Greece take their turn in our world of fashion with the latest traveller, the latest murderer; and they will be thrown aside in their turn for some newer novelty of vacuous minds." A cynical prediction which, of course, came absolutely true.

Whatever the papers said, it's clear enough that in private the friends of both Sellers and Harrison managed reassuringly to turn each of their performances into the triumph of the season. Warr himself had lavished praise on Sellers during rehearsals: "I hope very much you will not try to *alter* your rendering of Helen—it is quite beautiful and altogether *right,*" he wrote on

May 27, just a couple of days before the opening night. This flattery may have been meant to sweeten the instructions that followed: "The only thing necessary is to emphasise judiciously—some *few* words and *only* those should be dwelt on, all the rest should be flowing—and to keep in the same way to a *few* grand attitudes and gestures." It is hard to resist the conclusion that Miss Sellers had, in fact, been shouting her way through the part, staccato, and throwing her arms around with operatic bombast.[24] But if any criticism was intended here, there was certainly no sign of it after the show, when Warr issued his pressing request for a picture of her in her Greek costume: "I shall be so glad to have it as a memento, and I shall always be thankful to you and to the gods who 'put it into your heart' to play Helen so beautifully."[25] In fact, the photographs that she did eventually distribute were a disappointment; one of the recipients responded frankly: "[It] recalls to me the costume but does but scant justice to the wearer. It gives you a Clytemnestra expression which is not in character."[26] Harrison, too, was offered plenty of admiration by her friends: "One of the triumphs of the Greek night was Jane," wrote her friend Hope Mirrlees half a century later. "Everything about her performance—her appearance, movements, voice, diction—was EXQUISITE."[27]

Predictable enough (and that's what friends are for); but in fact these various eulogies of their youthful excursions into amateur drama give us a first hint of the later incompatibility of the Harrison and Strong legends; a forewarning that, in the end, there would be space for only one of them to triumph, that they were competing for a prize that could not be shared. In this case, the prize was the admiration of the most important man in the audience, the Prime Minister William Gladstone. "How beautiful you looked," wrote another of Sellers's correspondents, in (presumably) carefully rehearsed enthusiasm. "Now I suppose hundreds have said so including old Gladstone who I hear would not listen to Mrs. Tree but said you were his first and only love."[28] In the same vein, Hope Mirrlees reassures herself, and us, that it was the exquisite performance of *Harrison* that was "singled out for special admiration by two of the most distinguished members of the audience, Gladstone & Tennyson."[29] Of course, we may now suspect that Gladstone spread his prime-ministerial praises widely (and without much discrimination, for *that* a prime minister should praise is more important than *what*). But, in the end, legendary fame can admit only one of these young actresses as Gladstone's favorite; if Harrison wins, it must be at the expense of Sellers, and vice versa.

For the time being, though, both of them felt confident enough about their acting to take on more, and more ambitious, roles. The 1880s was, after all, the crucial moment—both in Britain and the United States—for the revival of Greek drama (in Greek as well as English), with universities on both sides of the Atlantic almost in a race to reestablish a tradition of stage performances.[30] Ironically, it was a race that the students at Newnham would easily have won (beating Balliol College, Oxford's famous 1880 *Agamemnon* by three years)—if only their planned performance of Sophocles' *Electra* in 1877 had not been called off at the last minute, through the intervention of the college Principal; she objected to the bare flesh that was to be on view, not to mention the dubious morality of young ladies playing male parts. ("She would not hear of our acting with 'bare arms and legs' before the Miss Kennedy's and Miss Adams etc. . . . She went on to say that she disapproved of theatricals & could not hear of our acting as men."[31]) But—official disapproval or not—only a few years later, outside Newnham at any rate, there were plenty of Greek plays to choose from and plenty of parts on offer, particularly for those ladies who knew Greek.

Sellers clearly found Helen of Troy an agreeable form of type-casting. She played her again in the spring of 1884, in a new set of tableaux, *The Dream of Fair Women*,[32] and she was strenuously courted in the same year by John Todhunter to appear in his creative version of a Greek drama, *Helena in Troas* (which was eventually shown in London in 1886): "I still hope that you may consent to be my Helena. I think you will be fascinated by the part when you see it, & I want you to intoxicate the world with her divinity!"[33] At first she was tempted by the idea: "I am glad you seem to think that there is a possibility of your being able to act," he wrote in May, while consulting her about some of the other parts. "A Hecuba I may perhaps get from Girton . . . I think the man who took the part of Achilles in The Tale of Troy would do very well for Paris if I could get hold of him. Who is he?"[34] But in the end, for whatever reason, Sellers did not appear (though she went to watch, courtesy of Charles Newton).[35] The play itself had a mixed reception in the reviews—particularly for its far from professional acting ("A Greek chorus . . . loses a considerable amount of its charm when it sings habitually false . . . We grant that the acoustic principles of the new Greek theatre are difficult to master . . . but the protagonists do not better matters by shouting," complained the man from the *Daily Telegraph*[36]). Nonetheless it, too, was a glittering social occasion (with the Prince of Wales as sponsor and guest of honor), and it became a milestone in the history of the performance of Greek tragedy in Britain, notably for its ambitious attempt to reconstruct the exact physical conditions of the fifth-century Athenian theater.[37] Jane Harrison went to see it and was so impressed that she wrote effusively to Mrs. Todhunter, not without some clearly implied criticism of *The Tale of Troy*. "After a long and somewhat bitter experience of amateur performances," she writes, "I had come to what was almost a conviction that a Greek play in modern times could never be anything but painful . . . your husband has achieved a triumph for which I for one am profoundly grateful to him."[38]

In the very next year, 1887, Harrison herself was back on the boards—in Oxford, playing Alcestis in Euripides' play staged by the Oxford University Dramatic Society (OUDS). Vice Chancellor (Benjamin D.) Jowett had laid down some tough regulations for OUDS: first, it could perform only Shakespeare or Greek tragedy; "2nd . . . the ladies' parts should be played by ladies & . . . no undergraduate should disguise himself in women's attire."[39] To perform their *Alcestis,* the students needed a woman (preferably with experience of acting Greek, in Greek), and Jane Harrison was conveniently on hand giving lectures on Greek art.[40] The reviews tell the same old story. The set and costumes were great, and so they ought to have been, for OUDS had bought up what was left from Todhunter's *Helena in Troas.*[41] Not so the acting—even if the friends of the performers, as usual, came up with the required praise. "Her rendering and appearance were enormously admired," writes Hope Mirrlees of Harrison's performance, thinking perhaps of a colorful account given by the Arthur Sidgwicks (he was an Oxford classicist, the brother of Henry Sidgwick, Newnham's founder—and Harrison was the guest of the family while the play was on): "A truly piteous Alcestis! Such a sight as goes to the heart of even the policeman in the Gallery (who is waiting for the end of the performance very patiently & is a little uncertain as to whether he ought or ought not to run in Herakles for being drunk and disorderly) & altogether unnerves the spirit of any mother present. JEH takes the motherhood on her naturally." Even the Sidgwick children learned to echo this chorus of praise, remembering her years later as "a figure of beauty . . . a fairy princess" ("[she] came up to our nursery in her Greek dress, all white, with arms bare to the shoulder, and bracelets on her *upper* arms. This struck us greatly!").[42] It is a vision that was captured in a (now) famous photograph of Harrison, carefully preserved in a Newnham College album. (See jacket illustration.)

The press, on the other hand, took a particular dislike to Harrison's whining, high-pitched voice: "Miss Harrison's Alcestis was a little disappointing," complained the *Cambridge Review,* "for though her acting was decidedly good, she thought it necessary to keep her voice at such an artificially high pitch that it became monotonous and almost expressionless." This view was shared by the reviewer in *The Athenaeum*: "In gesture and in general demeanour Miss Harrison succeeded in conveying much of the mingled sweetness and dignity of the character; and her speaking of the beautiful lines which fall to her part was as that of a woman using her own familiar tongue. But unfortunately, whether from an unwise attempt after realism or from a desire to make herself heard all over the house, she pitched her voice throughout in too high a key."[43] None of this seems to have dampened the enthusiasm of Eugénie Sellers and *her* friends for the occasion. It is far from clear whether or not Sellers was actually involved in the production. The cast list does not give her any of the smaller female parts or mention her work behind the scenes. However, her own skeletal "time chart," recording where she lived and major events in her life (presumably an aide-mémoire for the autobiography she had started to prepare shortly before her death), marks out 1887 with "Alcestis at Oxford" among such events as her sister's wedding and a trip to Italy, which suggests that the play meant more to her than just one visit to the theater among others.[44] Besides, we know that she used the occasion to host one of her oldest Girton chums. Katharine Jex-Blake wrote instantly to thank her: "I had the most rapturous time yesterday; never in my whole life did I enjoy anything more than going there and seeing you and that lovely place, and everything, and everybody, and above all Alcestis. Dearest I do enjoy myself so with you."[45] How much you enjoy a play, obviously, depends a lot on who you see it *with*.

These theatricals show us Sellers and Harrison operating together (and in incipient rivalry) among the chattering classes of 1880s Britain—along with a cast of characters with whom they would intersect for the rest of their lives. Several of the major players in this book were already acting on the very same stage in *The Tale of Troy*. But the perfomances also had a specifically archaeological dimension. For one of the most important impulses behind the fashion for Greek plays in the late nineteenth century—from Oxford to Cambridge, London to Harvard—was a zeal for accurate archaeological and antiquarian restoration. The plays were, in other words, not simply literary and dramatic endeavors; they offered a chance to re-create ancient theatrical settings, Greek costumes, jewelry, hairstyles, and architecture. This was demonstrated brilliantly in Todhunter's *Helena in Troas,* with its circular auditorium and reconstruction of the Athenian stage. But the link between archaeological and literary fashion can be seen just as clearly in the performances of *The Tale of Troy* at the Freakes' Cromwell House.

The awkward task of coaching the vast team of actors (self-regarding and self-willed to a man and woman, one suspects) was given to Charles Waldstein. Waldstein had some experience of what was required, albeit on a more manageable scale. Only twelve months earlier he had been one of the leading lights behind the production of the first Cambridge Greek play (Sophocles' *Ajax,* in which the young J. K. Stephen, our Hector, had taken the title role—a fearsomely suitable part for a Ripper suspect).[46] Despite first appearances, Waldstein managed to impress Harrison, among others, with his thespian skills. "Jane never forgot the dramatic gift he disclosed . . . She used to tell me how at one rehearsal, dissatisfied with the acting of 'Helen of Troy' he showed her how it ought to be done. 'And that ugly little man,' she used to say, 'BECAME Helen of Troy.'"[47] But, as we have already seen, Waldstein was better known as an archaeologist: the first Lecturer (then Reader) in classical archaeology at Cambridge; one of the founders of the Museum of Classical Archaeology there (with its collection of hundreds of plaster casts of Greek and Roman sculpture[48]); later Director of the Fitzwilliam Museum, and of the American School of Classical Studies in Athens (from where he masterminded the excavations of the Argive Heraeum).

An even grander archaeological figure than the still junior

Waldstein had a big hand in getting the show on the road. Warr's partner in the whole enterprise (and "the tempter" who had invited Sellers, and probably Harrison too, into the company) was the Charles Newton behind whom Miss du Puy, so we guess, had sat. Keeper of Greek and Roman Antiquities at the British Museum from 1861 to 1885 (and from 1880 to 1888 Yates Professor of Classical Archaeology at University College London), Newton was best known for his earlier sensational discoveries in Asia Minor. He was still hard at work in the 1880s restoring the sculptures of one of the wonders of the ancient world, the Mausoleum of Halicarnassus (Newton's most glamorous trophy and his finest (re)construction), which had arrived in London in 1859 to be housed in the British Museum.[49] Though most modern accounts portray him as a rather austere character ("a hard and demanding taskmaster"[50]), a quite different image—of a generous, gregarious, and rather jolly old widower—emerges from the Harrison and Strong archives. For *The Tale of Troy,* he was assigned (or, more likely, chose) some particular scenes to direct; he gathered his actors for rehearsals at his own home and had them decked them out in the appropriate, archaeologically bona fide, ornaments. It was a generous enthusiasm that occasionally threatened to backfire: one letter to Sellers shows him anxious to retrieve from her all the nice bits of gold jewelry a friend of his had lent her specially for the "Helen of Troy" photograph.[51]

But archaeology of the nontheatrical kind was always near the top of Newton's agenda, even in the stream of mutual congratulation that accompanied *The Tale of Troy.* Writing, for example, to Sellers just a few weeks after the performance, he tells her of plans for a revival of *The Tale,* as well as "our idea of bringing out the scenes of the Shield of Achilles in a series of tableaux"; then, in the very next sentence, he is back to the nuts and bolts of museum work: "I am . . . trying to restore the head of Mausolos with long hair falling on each side of his neck. He is beginning to look like a medieval Christ!"[52] And it was as a museum man, not as an amateur theatrical impresario, that he made the most impact on the lives of Harrison and Sellers (as I have already hinted), and it is through the British Museum and Greek art that we can begin to trace a whole tangle of connections between the two women that runs much deeper than their share of the limelight in the South Kensington theatricals on a few summer's evenings in 1883.

CHAPTER FIVE

Introductory Studies in Greek Art

When Jane Harrison left Newnham College in 1879, she tried her hand at teaching—at Oxford High School, where (or so *her* story was) she was so popular that the girls would book appointments to "take her arm" on the playground during the morning break.[1] She seemed glamorous to the girls maybe, but she wasn't a great success at the job, or she soon tired of it. The next year she moved to London, where she was to be based (give or take some lengthy foreign trips) until her return to Newnham in 1898.

Despite her later claims that she had learned *all* her archaeology from the Germans,[2] she did in fact spend a good deal of time in the British Museum learning from Charles Newton, to whom she had been introduced (most likely) by the family of a friend from Newnham, Mabel Malleson.[3] It was under Newton's aegis that she found the ideal way of supplementing her (not quite sufficient) private income: lecturing on Greek art and archaeology, first at the British Museum itself, then in packed series held throughout London and notable one-off occasions all over the country.[4] It was a crucial and deliberate step in her public career—even if in retrospect she chose to present it as just one of life's chances, simply a matter of being in the right place at the right time. It all started "quite accidentally," she explained to a reporter from the *Pall Mall Gazette* in 1891 (who had come to interview "the lady to whose lectures during the last ten years the revival of popular interest in Greece is almost solely due"). "I was studying at the British Museum when Sir Charles Newton, the then Keeper of Antiquities, asked me one day if I would not take some parties of ladies round. He could not ask me officially but he thought I might explain some things to the ladies. And so I began."[5]

Harrison's admirers always particularly admired her lectures: "a combination of grace and daring, of playfulness and dignity," as Gilbert Murray put it in his memorial address. They were inventive, atmospheric, theatrical. "I have a vision of her figure," chimed in Francis Cornford (also after Harrison's death), "on the darkened stage of the Archaeological Museum, which she made deserve to the full its name of theatre . . . The hushed audience would catch the nervous tension of her bearing . . . Every lecture was a drama." They were also lavishly illustrated with up-to-the-minute lantern slides, laboriously handmade by Harrison's friends and pupils. These slides are the closest we can now get to the atmosphere of her lectures. Four large wooden boxes in the Newnham College Archive still contain more than a hundred of the fragile squares of glass, just as she left them when she finally abandoned Cambridge in 1922, last lecture done: careful black and red brush strokes delicately copy the designs on Greek figured pots and even now project dramatic images (illustration 4); in the 1880s they must have been mind-blowing. On other slides key words are engraved on opaque blue glass, for projection through the magic lantern onto the screen and into the memory—the equivalent, perhaps, of the modern photocopied "hand-out" ("Athenian virtues: $\alpha\dot{\upsilon}\tau\acute{\alpha}\rho\kappa\epsilon\iota\alpha$ / self-sufficiency, $\mu\epsilon\gamma\alpha\lambda o\psi\upsilon\chi\acute{\iota}\alpha$ / greatness of spirit, $\sigma\omega\phi\rho o\sigma\acute{\upsilon}\nu\eta$ / discretion, $A\dot{\iota}\delta\grave{\omega}\varsigma$ $\kappa\alpha\grave{\iota}$ $\chi\acute{\alpha}\rho\iota\varsigma$ / Reverence & grace").[6] Harrison herself showed little (false) modesty about her lectures' success, however "accidental" she made their origin. "Fatally fluent," she

Fig. 4. One of Jane Harrison's lantern slides: a scene from a black-figure Attic *hydria,* showing Athena seated, a priestess in front of a blazing altar, and an ox(?) inside a shrine. Harrison used this same image in *Mythology and Monuments* (p. 428) in discussing the Athenian ritual of the Bouphonia ("Ox-slaying"), and in *Themis* (p. 145) to demonstrate "the supremacy of the ox and the nullity of the goddess . . . [it is] a holy ox, holy on his own account, with a sanctuary of his own." For the vase (by the Nikoxenos painter), see Beazley *ABV* 393, 20 (with *Addenda*); it is now in Uppsala.

calls herself in *Reminiscences;*[7] to the reporter from the *Pall Mall Gazette,* she boasted of addressing an audience of 1,600 people in Glasgow on the unlikely (or perhaps very Victorian) subject of Attic grave reliefs.

But it is not hard to imagine that these performances might also have been intensely irritating, especially if you were not one of Miss Harrison's fans. A letter written to Eugénie Sellers a few months after the article in the *Pall Mall Gazette* gives a plausible alternative version of Harrison's lecturing style. Sellers had asked a friend, Violet Buxton, for some frank comments on her own recent series of lectures. After some gentle criticism ("You do sometimes repeat yourself, but lecturers generally seem to . . . I don't think you speak too loud—and last time I did not think you spoke too fast either"), Buxton ends up by comparing Sellers and Harrison: "I like the lectures very much and prefer them to Miss Harrison's, for she is always so desperately patronizing to her audience. 'Sufficient is it for *you* to know' is one of her favourite phrases—though she does put her lectures together wonderfully."[8]

Some among Harrison's audiences found the whole display, if not patronizing, embarrassingly flamboyant. Even her most loyal admirers occasionally expressed a few doubts: "Her enthusiasm, though one might think it a trifle overdone at times, was very catching," wrote one of her Newnham friends, defensively, in a college obituary notice;[9] not to mention her impatience (directed, no doubt, at the long-suffering projectionist) when the slides went wrong.[10] Others—most notoriously D. S. MacColl, who wrote a blunt letter of criticism to Harrison in 1887—seem to have found her performances unbearable.

MacColl was an outspoken and influential art critic, an uncompromisingly avant-garde champion of "modern" French art, and later (between 1906 and 1911) Keeper of the Tate Gallery in London.[11] As friend and colleague, holiday companion and coauthor, he played (as we shall see) a significant part in the early careers of both Harrison and Sellers. Frank criticisms of his colleagues' lectures seem to have been part of his stock-in-trade: thirty years later we find him writing to Mrs. Strong, giving her, presumably, much the same treatment ("You are a first rate lecturer . . . But I was, I confess, surprised and even dismayed to find at what point you have 'come out' after all these years of study. You are too valuable a force to be expended in the wrong direction").[12] On the occasion of his letter to Harrison, written in the course of their growing friendship, he made a characteristically direct onslaught (as tactless as it was well meaning, we should guess) on her teaching of art history. The letter he wrote has become famous in the Harrison legend, despite, or largely because of, the fact that it does not survive ("I tore it up in the fury of first reading, but unhappily that only made me remember every word of it").[13] But from her responses to MacColl, it is clear enough that one of his principal targets was the vulgar sensationalism of her delivery; what she called (disguising it under the cover of a Greek title) her "$\dot{\epsilon}\pi\iota\delta\epsilon\iota\kappa\tau\iota\kappa\grave{o}\varsigma$ $\lambda\acute{o}\gamma\circ\varsigma$," or "display oratory."

Harrison's reaction to the attack veered from anger to abjection; but in one letter, at least, she promised reform: "I have quite decided . . . to give up entirely next year all lecturing that is purely lecturing, because I see only too clearly that it is the $\dot{\epsilon}\pi\iota\delta\epsilon\iota\kappa\tau\iota\kappa\grave{o}\varsigma$ $\lambda\acute{o}\gamma\circ\varsigma$ that has been my undoing."[14] It would perhaps be naive not to suspect some irony in this protestation, for it came as a response to MacColl's request (he had a nerve . . .) that she should take over some of his lecturing for the following year. But certainly, if she ever did reform, it didn't last long. She was soon back with all the old (audiovisual) tricks: the noisy props (Cornford recalls her getting two friends to swing "bull-roarers" at the back of the lecture room, to capture a particular religious sound), the dark lighting, the power dressing, the specially high-pitched voice. You either loved it or hated it. It certainly made her name.

In the interview in the *Pall Mall Gazette,* Harrison claimed that she herself was now tired of the lecture circuit and promised to hand the torch over to her younger followers. Like all great actresses, she was always (and sincerely, maybe) on the point of retirement from the stage: "As my former pupils come forward to carry on the work I began," she explained to the reporter, "I am gradually withdrawing." One of the former pupils mentioned by name was Eugénie Sellers: "Three, at all events, of my pupils during the last ten years have followed in my steps by becoming professional lecturers: Miss Sellers, Miss Millington Lathbury and Miss Raleigh."[15]

Sellers, as we have already seen, had taken very much the same path as Harrison. It started with teaching school, in Scotland. "Her lessons were delightful . . . how much we enjoyed the *Epistles* of Horace we read with her," applauded one ex-pupil.[16] Sellers herself, however, expressed a different view: "I did not take to it kindly. Nor indeed did St. Andrews, where I had my first post, take kindly to me"; she was (as failed schoolteachers so often like to claim) too "'foreign', critical, innovating in my methods."[17] In less than a year she had moved to London, and it was presumably in 1883 in rehearsals for *The Tale of Troy* (and *chez* Charles Newton) that she first met Harrison and became her "pupil." Before long she had built up a clientele of pupils of her own, including the fashionable (and fashionably reluctant to pay) Humphry Wards. Mrs. Humphry Ward was a novelist, a leading light in the foundation of Somerville College, Oxford— and later a strident antisuffrage campaigner who was to be the bête noire of radical London ("Reading Mrs. Ward, [Virginia Woolf] once said in her smart way, was like catching flu.").[18] At this stage, in the 1880s, she was keen to start Greek, while the children, with varying degrees of enthusiasm, were being put through both Latin and Greek (happily interspersed with some junior versions of the classical tableaux that were all the rage— the death of Cleopatra, and Diogenes in his tub).[19] In the competition for such private teaching and lecturing appointments, Jane Harrison was no doubt a useful patron; she certainly provided a glowing recommendation for Sellers in a letter of February 1890: "I am so glad Lady Enniskillen is going to Miss Sellers [for classes in archaeology]," she wrote to another of her pupils. "I am very anxious Miss Sellers should get on as she is really a first rate teacher."[20]

But letters to and from Sellers throughout the 1880s, preserved in the Girton College Archive, suggest a much more inti-

mate collaboration between the two women than simply the patronage of a clever pupil by a caring teacher. For much of this
time Sellers was effectively Harrison's secretary, business manager, and (eager) publicist. In 1885, for example, she handled all
the arrangements for a series of subscription lectures on art and
myth in the *Iliad,* given by Harrison in aid of the fledgling British School at Athens: she placed the advertisements; she pro-
cessed the requests for tickets; she tried to arrange a decent press
showing at the series (unsuccessfully, as it turned out—news of
Miss Harrison's lectures didn't quite match news of the general
election, pleaded the editors). She also issued a whole series of
timely personal reminders to the Great and Good, exploiting
old Cambridge and *Tale of Troy* connections: Sidney Colvin
hoped to make "some" of the series; J. W. Mackail, Latinist and
reforming administrator in the Board of Education, promised to
turn out to support the School ("though I have an innate and in-
curable horror of lectures of every sort and kind, I shall enjoy the
magic lantern"); Sir Frederic Leighton (in)conveniently found
that he had a regular engagement clashing with every single
one![21]

In the end there was a smaller turnout than they had hoped;
in truth it was disappointing. A letter from George Macmillan
to Sellers hints at what must have been part of the reason: "I am
only sorry," he writes, "that I did not know before that the place
had been changed and that men could therefore attend."[22] Nonetheless, the whole series came to be judged (politely) a success,
and Walter Leaf (the classical scholar, banker, and, appropriately,
treasurer of the British School) conveyed his thanks to Miss
Sellers, paying generous compliments to her administrative ef-
ficiency and commitment to the cause: "I must take the opportunity of expressing my feeling—and I need hardly add, that of
the Committee also—of our debt to yourself also for all that you
have done for the School. I am sure you must feel very pleased at
the way in which all your arrangements worked, and the bril-

liant success of the whole course, which must in very large measure be put down to the credit of the business management."[23]

But it was more than "business management." Sellers was also Harrison's companion and friend; they went *together* about town. Casual references in their letters help to fill out the picture. Sometimes it was to meetings of the Society of Psychical Research, or tea at the Alma-Tademas (Sellers took Harrison to meet the Alma-Tadema daughters and a friendship ensued).[24] On other occasions, it was a joint expedition to the British Museum (for study, to teach, or to fuss over Newton): "I shall see Mr. Newton to-morrow I hope," wrote Sellers to Vernon Lee. "Miss Harrison and I are going to tidy his diagrams for him—he gets them into hopeless disorder." For all his reported austerity, Newton seems to have appreciated this kind of treatment, and, for both ladies, he reciprocated with dinner and trips to the theater; he even commissioned a portrait of Sellers—to make up, perhaps, for the disappointing photograph taken after *The Tale of Troy.*[25]

Behind the scenes Sellers was pulling what strings she could in Harrison's interest. In 1888 Harrison applied for the Yates Chair of Classical Archaeology at University College London, to succeed Newton himself (who since 1880 had held the chair simultaneously with his position at the British Museum). Sellers was busy pumping her old teacher J. P. Postgate (now Professor of Comparative Philology at University College) for useful information—softening him up in Harrison's favor at the same time.[26] Unsuccessfully, as it turned out. Despite an international array of talent signed up as her sponsors, the job went to the older, more established (but strikingly less clever) Reginald Poole, Keeper of Coins in the British Museum. Wilhelm Dörpfeld, from the German Archaeological Institute in Athens, had backed Harrison; so had Ernest Babelon, the great French numismatist, as well as the brothers (Henry and Arthur) Sidgwick and Richard Jebb, now in the Regius Chair of Greek in Cambridge. But Newton himself (who must have been influential), faced with a choice between his long-standing museum colleague and his engaging female pupil and theater companion, backed the colleague.[27] The whole election was widely reported ("I think the press notices will do Miss Harrison's chances harm," wrote Postgate to Sellers) and became a cause célèbre. The list of rejected candidates also included such prominent figures as L. R. Farnell (the crustily reactionary author of *Cults of the Greek States*), E. A. Gardner (Director of the British School at Athens, who was to be successful the next time round, in 1896), and the aggressively self-promoting Charles Waldstein (one-time voice coach for *The Tale of Troy,* now Reader in Classical Archaeology at Cambridge and Director of the Fitzwilliam Museum: "The Committee was not satisfied that the solidity of his attainments was equal to the reputation which he enjoys").[28] But it was only Harrison who split the committee on ideological grounds: two members signed a document stating that it was "undesirable that any teaching in University College should be conducted by a woman."[29] The shock waves of the appointment evidently reached as far as Italy. At the beginning of 1889, a friend (Margaret Smith) wrote to Sellers from Florence about a chance encounter with a lady there. Smith was sure they had met before: "I said 'Have you been at Miss Harrison's lectures?' She said she had & as a parting shot called out 'Did you hear that she was not elected to the Professorship?' I lacked presence of mind to reply 'No more was my brother' [A. H. Smith, then assistant in the British Museum, another failed candidate]."[30]

On the other side, we find Harrison playing her part in launching Miss Sellers. Some time (probably) in 1886, she wrote to arrange an introduction for Sellers to D. S. MacColl:

A very fair lady—so fair that she is used to considering her will as law—demands of me your acquaintance. I stand in too great awe of her to refuse any request she may honour me with, so, in the interests of chivalry, I lied & said I was certain the desire wld be mutual. She (Miss Eugénie Sellers) comes to me next Sunday to 'tell me in Spanish' many things but I am afraid latterly I have taxed your Sundays too heavily for business to ask you even to tithe another for pleasure, So if not next Sunday—when?

I think her the most beautiful woman in all London so proba-bly—out of sheer cussedness—you will refuse to admire her. But I will not quarrel with you before the event.

I send you the Danaë pots that led me (pots have their uses) to Simonides. Please look at No. II. It is the uniform shape of *bed* for children as well as grown ups. Cradles with rockers seem un-known . . . [31]

It is impossible now to reconstruct in any detail the set of rela-tionships inscribed in these few lines, just as it is impossible (in-tentionally so, no doubt) to disentangle the complexities of Har-rison's self-irony. MacColl could presumably have been relied on to spot the oblique reference in "tell me in Spanish" to Brown-ing's steamy verse, "The Flower's Name," where a lover longs to learn Spanish—just to be able to repeat the flower's name that his/her beloved had identified in Spanish. "Is there no method to tell her in Spanish / June's twice June since she breathed it with me?" runs part of the last stanza.[32] But what exactly was he to conclude from that about the relationship between Harrison and Sellers? Were they close confidantes, romantic friends, or what? I shall return to that question at the end of this chapter. But let us note now that part of what Harrison wrote stuck forever in MacColl's mind. More than fifty years later, on the death of Mrs. Strong, he volunteered a supplement to the obituary published in *The Times* in which he recalled this letter (in a conveniently simplified form): "Miss Jane Harrison, inviting me to meet her, wrote 'I think her the most beautiful woman in London' and the claim was not extravagant."[33]

Not just student and teacher, then, Harrison and Sellers were close friends and colleagues—and (as we shall presently see) "flatmates" and traveling companions too. Toward the end of her life Mrs. Strong started to gather together material for an autobiography, now deposited with her letters at Girton. This includes not only some already worked-up passages of memories and memoirs but also a rough sketch of her life: a skeleton story of major events, career steps, and (particularly) the places she lived, waiting to be filled out with more ample reminiscences in due course.[34] Here, in the middle of what she (melodramatically) entitles the "Years of Awful Struggle" (that is, 1882 to 1889), she pinpoints 1885, noting "?short while with Miss H?" What this implies is clear enough: over the period when Sellers was acting as Harrison's business manager they were conveniently sharing the same apartment.

This interpretation certainly matches some remarks by Hope Mirrlees in her notes on Harrison. She writes: "I am not quite clear about the Mrs. Strong affair. Sometime in the 'nineties Jane got to know Eugénie Sellar [*sic*]. And (Get being away) Eugénie came to live with her for a time."[35] As we shall soon discover, there was ample incentive for Mirrlees to parade ignorance, confuse the dates (she must mean the '*eighties*), and insult Sellers with a clumsy misspelling of her name; ample incentive for both her and Strong, with hindsight, to underplay the significance of the friendship. But there can be little doubt that during the period of her "awful struggle" Sellers was very much at home with Harrison, and for some part (or parts) of it, quite literally *at home*. In fact, as late as 1889 a letter notes that a parcel of books is being sent to Sellers from Italy to Miss Harrison's address—no necessary indication, of course, that she was then actually living there, but a clear sign that she was confident enough to treat it as her base and mailing address.[36]

Confident enough too, as I shall shortly argue, to travel abroad with Harrison—to Italy, and perhaps to Greece as well. Both of these women spent a good deal of the 1880s and 1890s out of the country. Foreign travel (subsidized by the teaching income) was high on their agenda, for a variety of reasons. The universities and museums of Germany were an obvious entice-

ment for anyone who aspired to the cutting edge of classical archaeology.[37] Harrison had already visited Germany, en route to
Italy, in 1881, shortly after she had given up teaching school and
just as her first book, *Myths of the Odyssey,* was in press. She took
along with her her Mabel Malleson (who, though she had graduated
in History at Newnham, on this trip was relegated to tracing
vases for Harrison), as well as bundles of letters of introduction
from Newton and Reginald Poole (the one who was later to beat
her to the Yates Chair, and a relation of the Mallesons). The letters and the contacts worked a treat: "At the least mention of
[Newton's] name all eyes lighten," Harrison wrote home to Mrs.
Malleson.[38] She was given free use of archaeological libraries, access to museum basements, and even the loan of an office—not
to mention useful meetings with the local archaeological stars:
including Curtius, Brunn, and the-soon-to-be-important young
Charles Waldstein (presumably on vacation from Cambridge).[39]

At the same time, she was particularly struck by the state of
German museology: "I cannot tell you at all how keenly I have
felt (since I have been here) what a museum *may* be and what
alas! ours in England is not." It was the educational superiority
of the collections of plaster casts that most of all impressed her:
"With the single exception of the Pergamos marbles, these Germans here have not one important original to stimulate them
and yet they have gathered together casts of every single thing
a student can need to set the whole subject in its historical aspect clearly before his eyes and the arrangement is so wonderful
wherever comparison is needed duplicate casts or replicas or
even photographs are placed side by side."[40] It was an aspect of
German archaeology that made its mark on others, too. In fact,
just as Harrison was writing, Charles Waldstein was busy planning (and assembling) a collection of plaster casts, very much on
the German model, for display in the brand-new Museum of
Classical Archaeology in Cambridge.[41]

Sellers, too, made for Germany—though not (for any substantial length of time, at least) until the 1890s. She found a base near Munich, only a few minutes' walk from the house of the archaeologist Adolf Furtwängler (whose *Meisterwerke* she translated in 1895). No further away in the other direction lived the neurotic, agoraphobic (a "consequence of earlier over-indulgence, so it was said, in tobacco"[42]) Ludwig Traube, the philologist and paleographer—these were (as she called them) her "pole stars," and an ideal pair for teaching her about German scholarship and Greek archaeology (nothing Roman here: "Had I spoken of the merits of Roman sculpture to Furtwängler, he would have replied, as he was wont to do when his wife indulged in flights of fancy, 'dummes Zeug, mein Kindchen, dummes Zeug' ['Nonsense, baby, nonsense']."[43]) Not to mention helping her with the edition of Pliny—and (as her nostalgic memoirs, combined with her contemporary appointment diaries, suggest) sharing tea and tennis: "June 2, Pliny with Traube," "June 9, Furtwänglers afternoon," "June 16, to Tr. Furtwänglers for tennis," June 19, "Sent flowers to Tr. for his birthday."[44] From 1892 on, she visited Munich on several occasions, and for several months at a time. But she had certainly encountered (and learned from) German archaeology before the 1890s: in Greece, Italy, and (at one remove) via Miss Harrison.

Both women, in fact, showed off their loyalty to German archaeological friends in one of the most bitterly waged (but now nearly forgotten) academic wars of the nineteenth century: the "Greek theater controversy" of 1890 and 1891 This all started as insignificantly as most such disputes—with the publication in the *Berliner Philologische Wochenschrift* of a review by Wilhelm Dörpfeld of Arthur Haigh's book *Attic Theatre*.[45] It was there that Dörpfeld (the Director of the German Archaeological Institute at Athens, Schliemann's assistant at Troy—and, so it was joked, "his most important find") chose to make public for the first time his own views on the archaeology of the Greek theater. These amounted to two main claims: first, that the surviving remains of the Theater of Dionysus in Athens dated from the fourth century B.C.E., not the fifth; second, that the chorus and actors in the classical Greek theater had performed *on the same level* (that, in other words, the raised stage referred to by the Roman Vitruvius in his treatise *On Architecture* was a postclassical invention). Neither of these claims now seems very startling, and in fact we would probably agree that both are broadly correct. But in 1890 they flew in the face of all (and especially British) orthodoxy, and brought down a torrent of forthright criticism and nasty abuse on Dörpfeld's head. In fact (and in some ways this was to make the bad feeling worse) Dörpfeld had the last laugh—by arguing, convincingly to most observers, that the British were comprehensively wrong about one of their very own excavations.

A key plank in the British argument was the form of the theater at the site of (Polybios' city of) Megalopolis in Arcadia, which was then being uncovered by a team from the British School at Athens, under its Director, E. A. Gardner. So Gardner and his colleagues invited Dörpfeld to come and see, to be confronted, no doubt, with proof of the error of his ways. But when Dörpfeld went over the site on April 15, 1891, he instantly spotted that, far from supporting the British case, the remains much more plausibly backed up his own. He was so convincing about what he saw that even the excavators, with their vested interest in the opposite view, were forced, at the very least, to rethink; some of them surrendered completely. Saving as much British face as possible (not much), they issued a joint communiqué in the *Classical Review:* "Instead of continuing our controversy, we wish to make public at once, in a common statement, certain facts which have, for the most part, come to light during the continuation of the excavations this spring. The English excavators wish to acknowledge that their significance was first pointed out by Dr. Dörpfeld during his visit to Megalopolis." Signed: Wilhelm Dörpfeld, Ernest A. Gardner, W. Loring.[46] It didn't end quite so simply, of course. Under the surface of these careful public utterances, Dörpfeld's victory (won on the "British territory" of Megalopolis) only increased the animosity against him. But German victory it was, and, for all the stiff upper lip so properly displayed in the *Classical Review,* an inglorious and ignominious chapter in the history of British archaeology.[47]

Throughout this controversy both Harrison and Sellers were public allies of Dörpfeld. (As we shall see, this was among the very last occasions on which we find them in alliance, operating in the same cause; so it is worth savoring the moment.) It was Harrison who first broke the story of Dörpfeld's theories in the *Classical Review,* giving a summary of his review of Haigh. She does not explicitly swear her own allegiance to his view, but *we* know that she claimed Dörpfeld as her "most honoured master,"[48] and her final paragraph (quoting her friend Verrall's "literary" argument that Aeschylus could not have been played on a "Vitruvian" stage) is a clear indication—and would have been seen as such—of where her sympathies lay.[49] Meanwhile Sellers (who was herself studying at the British School in Athens in 1891 and working with Dörpfeld on his appendix to her translation of *Schliemann's Excavations*) wrote to the *Classical Review* on March 29 to convey in English Dörpfeld's opinions on the theater of Megalopolis.[50]

As always, Sellers was also active behind the scenes, leaving her traces in the archive. She wrote around to enlist influential support for the Dörpfeld side (a package of photographs with "very clear explanations" that she sent to Professor Richard Jebb in Cambridge elicited a polite, but wisely noncommittal, response[51]), while at the same time "managing" Dörpfeld's press releases back in England. She presented herself, for the most part, as an enthusiastic champion of the German cause. In a letter blazoned *"Private,"* she explained to George Macmillan (her publisher and the leading light in the British School at Athens) not only how "profoundly hurt—& no wonder" Dörpfeld was, but also how awkward the whole business had made her stay at the School—where, predictably, her male colleagues were all paid-up supporters of the Director, Gardner: "I had not been 3 days in Athens before I saw or guessed the silly opposition of the Germans by the English students—& I set my face against it. 'Hinc illae lacrimae.' Later when Dörpfeld honoured me with his confidence on the subject, I was placed in a difficult position towards School and Committee. I saw how wrong Mr. Gardner and some of the students were—and yet I was not at liberty to explain quite why."[52] It doesn't take much imagination to reconstruct the other side of this conflict: the new lady student turns up at the British School and instantly starts to fraternize with the Director's enemy. Hardly surprising that they gave her the cold shoulder.

To some of her friends she seemed to be courting danger with her thoughtless enthusiasm. As the bad feeling rumbled on through the summer of 1891 (the flames fanned, or so it must have seemed, by Sellers herself), Lewis Campbell, Professor of Greek at St. Andrews, recommended caution: "I am sure you will do well to keep your powder dry," he wrote. "The joint letter of Dörpfeld and Gardner has altered the situation for the present, and the most becoming attitude is to 'sit on the fertile ground, with our spears sticking by us' if you will. Even in matters of scholarship it requires watchful circumspection to make a career."[53] In fact, he need not have worried. We know, as Campbell did not, that Sellers was capable of presenting a quite different view of her own involvement in the theater row. Some days before she wrote to Macmillan, and a good week before she would have received the letter from Campbell, she wrote to Charles Waldstein (also "privately") in these terms: "Personally I wish to ask you a favour. This theatre row is most distasteful to me. I got let in for it thro' a piece of ill-luck originally. Now I am feeling utterly bewildered by it. If my humble name strikes your ears in connection with it will you use your influence to make people think my actions of no importance, I feel that at present women are much looked upon as partizans & for this reason alone I now wish to withdraw completely from this business."[54] It's the classic archival problem: quite different explanations and self-constructions offered to different correspondents, and every one of them (in their own way) true.[55]

It was all a storm in a teacup, of course, but a storm all the same—with Sellers and Harrison on the same side, and for the last time. But where *exactly* in the battle line Miss Harrison stood in relation to her pupil and fellow "partizan"—behind, close beside, or (already) at a discreet distance—we can now no longer trace.

Foreign travel (then as much as now) was not only about archaeology and its controversies. Italy and Greece, in particular, offered the excitement of monuments, excavations, and museums, but there was also the excitement of escape, of nights spent under canvas, of donkey rides up remote mountainsides, and of the suspension of (at least some of) the rules of British upper-middle-class behavior. For three months in early 1888, for example, Harrison toured Greece and Turkey with D. S. MacColl and a shifting group of friends who seem to have dropped in or, more often, out of the trip—as money or archaeological enthusiasm waned. After a series of Boy Scoutish adventures (which included getting themselves thrown out of a Greek monastery, encounters with a lecherous abbot, and Harrison forgetting her passport), MacColl and Harrison ended up in the Peloponnese, the only survivors of their original party. There they visited the remote temple of Apollo at Bassae, where they decided to sleep out—miles from anywhere, in the pouring rain, protected only by a couple of tough British macintoshes and umbrellas plus, in Harrison's case, "a shetland shawl and an air cushion." All this was against the protests of their local guide, who was very un-

willing to make for the temple because (as MacColl patronizingly recounted it) he believed it was haunted by "Charones"
(devils)—and besides, he didn't know the way. *We,* on the other
hand, might suspect other reasons for his reluctance: that he had
seen it all before (for what British traveler did not hanker after
the experience of Bassae-by-night?[56]), and that he did not share
their enthusiasm for a soaking night in the open, spent (in his
case) keeping the campfire burning and no doubt watching over
the safety of our "intrepid" tourists.[57]

Both women also found travel a useful refuge whenever the
going in England got rough—or when it was recommended by
their doctors (which must often have amounted to almost the
same thing). For Sellers, throughout the 1890s Germany—and
the company of Furtwängler and Traube—was a convenient escape from the ups and downs of her off-and-on engagement to
Arthur Strong.[58] On her side, Jane Harrison went off to the
Engadine (in Switzerland) in the autumn of 1889 on medical advice, "owing to great breathlessness"[59] (a displacement not entirely unconnected with her failure to win the Yates Chair a few
months earlier), and she left her friends behind, anxiously parading their concerns about her. Some time in the autumn (the letter is undated) MacColl wrote to reassure Sellers: "I have just got
home & found your letter, & must send a line to allay your anxi-
ety. I had a note this morning from Miss Harrison about a business matter: she did not say much about herself, but she was
skating vigorously & enjoying it. Indeed my impression is that
the Engadine has been a great success."[60]

But Sellers was not always left behind—or so various allusions and coincidences in the archive documents hint. At some
point in this incessant traveling, Harrison and Sellers appear to
have spent time together in Tuscany; at least, if that were *not* the
case it is hard to imagine how MacColl's sister Lizzie could have
written to Sellers as she did in 1890. Miss MacColl was staying
in Florence in a *pensione* that was well known to English ladies,

and she passed on to Sellers a message from its proprietor: "Miss Godkin cannot understand why Miss Harrison and you do not come to Florence again and greatly mourns over your non-appearance."[61] An almost inconceivable way of putting things if "Miss Harrison and you" had not on some occasion been there à deux.

Greece, too, may have been on their joint agenda. The evidence for this will lead us on a tantalizing trail, first through the Peloponnese in the 1880s (which turns out to have been much more heavily populated with busy Euro-archaeologists and friends and colleagues of Harrison and Sellers than we would ever have guessed); and then back to the Strong Papers in Girton College, to a puzzling set of photographs and another classic archival problem. The hunch that I am exploring is that Harrison and Sellers may have been, for a short time at least, *together* in Greece in 1888. Whether I am right or not, it is an exploration that reveals both how *much* we can discover about these two women (where they were, who they were with, when they left) and at the same time how *little* we can know them; literally, as you will soon see, how hard it is to recognize them, even when we get face to face. The point of the pages that follow is as much to expose the practicalities of (any) biographical reconstruction, the assumptions, conjectures, and improvizations that make up the story, as it is to pin down the whereabouts of Harrison and Sellers in the spring and early summer of 1888. In the process we shall also discover something of the tensions and conflicts that branded the German archaeological community to which Harrison and Sellers claimed such close attachment.

We have already glimpsed something of Harrison's Grand Tour in 1888: her visit with MacColl to the temple of Apollo at Bassae, and their glamorous (if soaking) camp-out. It was in fact her second visit to the Peloponnese during that year. She had left England at the end of March 1888 and made first for Athens, where the full touring party of Mr. and Mrs. Arthur Sidgwick (her Oxford hosts during the *Alcestis*), the Peveril Turnbulls (he had been a friend since childhood), Harrison, and MacColl all met up. They embarked on an energetic program of archaeological tourism: Athens, Aegina, Eleusis, Delphi, Thebes, and Olympia before the end of April (when all her companions but MacColl returned wearily home). Alone together, these two made east for Constantinople (which was rather a letdown archaeologically, but the trip was enlivened when Harrison forgot her passport and had to be passed off as MacColl's wife), then came speedily back to Athens in time for Greek Easter. By May 13, as MacColl wrote to his sister,[62] they were on a boat bound for Gytheum, the start of their second and longer trip through the Peloponnese, via Bassae to Olympia (again). "I had also a most beautiful and resting time in the Peloponnese," Harrison wrote to Mrs. Malleson on her return, "—who do you think protected me thro' those wilds? I know I may venture to tell *you* what I do not disclose to every British matron that Mr. MacColl and I ventured on that pilgrimage alone—and we have come back firmer friends than ever . . . Arcadia was just one's dream come to life . . . a never to be forgotten experience but inconceivably primitive and savage."[63] After a breathless week of adventures, on May 21 they were on the steamer to Corfu, "our Greek trip at an end"; by the beginning of June, Harrison was back in London, "return[ed] to civilisation with a shock."[64]

In fact, during the the first half of 1888 the "primitive and savage" Peloponnese was rather more heavily populated by intrepid northern European archaeologists than Harrison cares to give away. Dörpfeld himself was very much in evidence. Harrison and MacColl had visited him in Athens during the earlier part of their stay, where MacColl had complained of the "four mortal hours" they spent listening to his peripatetic lecture around the Theater of Dionysus. Harrison, by contrast, had—so she claimed—been enthralled: "[he] used to lecture to one *stand-*

ing out among the excavations for five hours and one scarcely knew he had begun."[65] (I know who *I* believe.) Shortly after this (not without managing to fit in some work at the temple of the Kabeiroi near Thebes) Dörpfeld conducted what was to be the first of his famous series of archaeological "travels" *(Reisen)* around the Peloponnese. He wrote a brief account of the trip in the *Archäologischer Anzeiger* for 1889, detailing his group of travelers (all male—and including Charles Waldstein, still at Cambridge but simultaneously part-time Director of the American Academy in Athens) and their itinerary around southern Greece. According to this, the party made it up to the temple at Bassae *("bei wundervollem Wetter")* on April 21, before moving on to Olympia and (for a smaller group) a six-day tour round Sparta and Messene.[66] It was, of course, only a few weeks later that Harrison and MacColl spent *their* night at Bassae *(not "bei wundervollem Wetter")* and proceeded on to Olympia—following closely in their friends' footsteps.

Sellers, too, as letters and a travel diary show, was on the Peloponnesian scene that spring. We find her preparing to leave London from January through March, in Marseilles by mid-April, and then going on to Florence.[67] Her Florentine diary lasts until May 11; it is packed with expatriate socializing, an introduction to Mommsen, a growing friendship with Vernon Lee—and letters to deliver on behalf of "J. E. H."[68] From Florence (presumably just after May 11) she went to Greece, or so we must conclude from a letter in early August referring to her recent "caravan through the Peloponnese."[69]

It is enormously tempting to reunite all these old friends in the Peloponnese in May 1888. Could it have been that MacColl and Harrison's intimate twosome in southern Greece at the end of May was interrupted for a day or two by the appearance of "the most beautiful woman in all London"? Could it even have been that they joined up with Dörpfeld for a short while, fresh from the first of his *Dörpfeld-Reisen?* These are almost irresistible combinations. Yet almost certainly we *would* resist them—were it not for a group of three photographs, buried (among pictures of assorted cardinals and other Italian dignitaries) in Mrs. Strong's papers.

These three pictures show a woman on a mule, a male companion, and at least one other man in the background; they carry the identification "Olympia c. 1888." In the first (illustration 5) the woman sits elegantly sidesaddle, a hat jauntily (and, for riding, precariously) perched on her head. In the background, almost out of the picture and certainly not intended to be in it, is a figure of a man in a heavy suit, hat, and what looks like a flamboyant mustache. In the second photograph, which appears to have been taken just a couple of moments later than the first, the woman on the mule looks (flirtatiously) down, while the man in the background has almost turned his back on the scene;

Fig. 5.   Woman on a mule: an archival puzzle.

the third photograph (illustration 6) shows the woman again, in the same clothes (albeit with a change of hat and the addition of a shawl, and on a different mule), now accompanied by a young male rider as the central figure; what may be the same building as in the first two photographs, but from a different angle, appears in the background. Same day, same place, same people.

Compare the woman here with the photograph of Jane Harrison in illustration 1 (see Chapter 1). It seems a powerful likeness, so powerful that it is hard not to conclude that these are photographs of Harrison, taken on her Greek adventure of 1888, preserved and forgotten in Miss Sellers's archive. This is a compelling hint that Harrison and Sellers really did meet up in Olympia at the end of Harrison's trip (with Sellers taking the holiday snaps), but it is also a reminder of how easily such archi-

Fig. 6. Taken for a ride: another puzzle.

val material can be overlooked. Who, after all, has ever thought to search for photographs of Jane Harrison in the papers of Eugénie Strong?

Sadly, the solution is not so simple, and I have not come quite clean. The *full* text of what is written on the photographs absolutely contradicts the identification I have proposed. The first photograph is inscribed twice, in two different hands: on the front, "Olympia. E.S."; on the back, "Eugénie in Greece c. 1888." The second has only "Eugénie in Greece c. 1888." The third is again in two hands: on the front, "Olympia. A galop [*sic*] with Herr Heyne"; on the reverse, "Eugénie in Greece c. 1888, probably with Dr. Dörpfeld."

One of these identifications is certainly wrong. The man on the mule in the third picture bears no resemblance whatsoever to Dörpfeld—to judge, at least, from photographs taken at "Troy conferences" at about the same date.[70] Who is he then? Not much more light is shed by the rival identification on the front of the photograph: "A galop with Herr Heyne." *Galop* spelled *auf Deutsch* is obviously part of the joke. But who might Herr Heyne be? Someone we don't know, an unknown bit part in the story of archaeology? We have no more inkling than (presumably) the person who made the desperate conjecture— "probably with Dr. Dörpfeld"—on the back of the photograph.

Except, again, for physical resemblances. If we match up the mule rider with other portraits in Strong's collection, he comes very close to her German star, Adolf Furtwängler, then in his midthirties (illustration 7). But if that is correct, then Miss Harrison is an impossible candidate for the female figure. Let me explain. So far I have treated nineteenth-century German archaeology as a conveniently unitary phenomenon: you either loved it (like Harrison and Sellers) or hated it (like much of the British academic establishment). In fact, of course, it was no more unitary than British archaeology. Young Miss Sellers herself may have managed to keep on good terms with both Dörpfeld and

Fig. 7. Portrait photograph of Adolf Furtwängler,
from Mrs. Strong's collection.

Furtwängler, but they were not on good terms with each other, either personally or intellectually: Dörpfeld, the prehistorian and dirt-archaeologist, the biggest name in Greece, but hardly so preeminent in Germany itself; Furtwängler, the fashionable museum man and Munich professor, connoisseur of *Meisterwerke,* an art-historical systemizer who had left his "prehistoric" past far behind.[71] And in fact Furtwängler so loathed Harrison, with her "fancies" about the origins of Greek religion, that he could barely bring himself to speak to her, let alone gallop round the Greek countryside in her company. (On one occasion in 1901 Dörpfeld had the fun of reintroducing them, with predictable results: "F. as stiff as a pole and looking furious. J. rose in her most gracious manner and forced him to shake hands.")[72] All of which points back to Sellers as the lady on the mule, as the written identification has it—were it not for the fact that it looks so very unlike her. Compare the mystery lady with illustration 2, in Chapter 2 (said, in *its* inscription, to be the photograph Sellers sent "To Miss Paget"—that is, Vernon Lee—and which stood on Lee's mantlepiece in 1887). They seem to have little in common but a prominent nose. And whether that seems sufficient to press an identification all depends on how keen (or desperate) we are to make the match.

We do not know who wrote the names on the photographs, nor do we know what would entitle us to doubt their consistent claims that it is Sellers on the mule—and nothing to do with Harrison at all. If we confidently reject (as I believe we must) the identification of the man as Dörpfeld, does that allow us to reject anything else we choose? The writing on the reverse of the photographs is quite unlike that of Mrs. Strong; it may be her sister's (sorting the archive at her death) or her biographer's (going through the material in preparation for the memoir). But on the front, the coy Germanic joke about the "galop" does have the ring of Strong herself, and the handwriting is not incompatible. Could *her* identifications be wrong? Could she possibly have made such an error as to mistake Miss Harrison for herself?

At this point speculation risks losing touch with reality. Tantalizingly immediate as the images seem, the fact is that we do not *know* who these people are. I have followed the trail to its disappointing end for two particular reasons. First, to show that such trails do end; to make a point of not leaving the exploration while the going is good, and of sharing the kind of impasse that finally blocks further investigation—even when we have the "evidence" so clearly before our eyes. Second, to expose the uncertainty that underlies the apparently simple processes of *recognition.* This is a lesson that no one with a family photograph album of their own should need to have drummed home; we know how often "putting a name to a face," even a single generation back, is contested, how often it calls into question the processes by which likeness is to be judged, and how often it demands an appeal to criteria external to the image ("It can't be Grandad because he died before little Tommy was born." "It can't be little Tommy because Grandad's in the picture"). It is the same problem—only worse—with recognition at the distance of a century or more. Biographers usually turn their back on this issue, seducing their readers with confident identifications of their subjects in murky images from across the decades; as if the famous had their albums better ordered and better labeled than we do ourselves—or as if it was the biographer's job to solve (rather than accept, still less parade) the puzzles. In fact, for the vast majority of the moderately renowned, we rely on little more than our hunches, on their big noses and distinctive hairstyles—and most of all on the identifying labels reliably, or unreliably, fixed by others. We cannot escape the uncomfortable specter of thoroughgoing mistaken identity, of photographs masquerading under (plausible) assumed names—no better nor worse than the mistaken identities in any family album. Here is yet another version of the loaded, and sometimes quite erroneous, assumptions that determine our *picture* of the past and its cast of characters. Never trust a photograph.

If we have followed the trail of Harrison and Sellers to a dead end somewhere near Olympia in 1888, we have nevertheless seen en route more than enough evidence of an intimate friendship between the two women through most of the 1880s. Just how intimate, and just what kind of friendship was it? Two women sharing a flat, living together . . . on what terms? Of course we want to ask; it would be dishonest to pretend otherwise, whatever our mixture of motives, from scholarly curiosity to biographical prurience. But (as always) we are faced with that tantalizing gap between the textual traces that survive and the relationship as it was lived and (re)lived.

On November 8, 1885, Katharine Jex-Blake wrote to her friend Sellers. Her letter is full of all kinds of news: Mr. Waldstein's lectures on mythology ("I don't seem to get much out of [them]"), Max Müller's article in the new issue of *Nineteenth Century,* plus congratulations on Harrison's recent triumph in London: "It is most delightful to hear about your GA's lecture."[73]

Late-Victorian women's talk is a very foreign language indeed; "GA," "Grand Amour" (part of the same repertoire as the more common "GP," or "Grande Passion") is one of the trickiest foreign idioms of them all. The kind of relationship it connotes is comprehensible only against the background of nineteenth-century "rules" of female friendship and desire—which are not only impossible for us now to intuit, but were inevitably subjects of contest and debate at the time, especially as new forms of female independence and female sociality made their impact on patterns of personal, social, and sexual relations. Here Jex-Blake may be alluding to a reciprocal closeness between Harrison and Sellers, cast in a lighthearted, if overblown, shared argot; she may alternatively have had in mind a much more emotionally charged admiration on the part of Sellers, of which Harrison herself might have been (or might have affected to be) unaware; or again she might be hinting at a physicality that lay cloaked under an acceptably coy euphemism.

In reading her letter now (and maybe it would not have been so very different "then") we are caught in a classic interpretative schism. On the one hand, we may be tempted to fit Sellers and Harrison into the model of intense "romantic friendship" that is often taken to be a feature of nineteenth-century female relations, junior to senior. This was, so one standard argument goes, a socially approved and essentially asexual "sentimentality" that was displaced only in the aftermath of the studies of (in particular) Freud and Krafft-Ebing—which prompted women to redefine their own relationships, while encouraging observers to see those relationships in a new, sexualized light: nothing short of, in other words, the invention in the early twentieth century of the sexual "invert" or "lesbian."[74] On the other hand, we must always be confronted by the gnawing suspicion that such a linear development is simply far too neat, and palpably not up to the job of representing the nuances of real human friendships, passions, and affections, which were never wholly governed by changes (and changes there certainly were) in the discursive regime. At the same time, we cannot help but wonder whether our own construction of that Victorian model of "sentimental attachment" is no less than a willful (or self-censoring) attempt to deny its explicitly erotic potential—to hide from ourselves the sexual implications of late-Victorian female friendship.[75]

How crass a biographical project would it be for us now to attempt to decide precisely what emotions or what sexualities were involved in this relationship? ("Was Jane Harrison gay?" is a question that this book hopes to transcend.[76]) How crass, for that matter, would it be to attempt to fix Jex-Blake's rhetorical tone as gently teasing, guardedly jealous, willfully ironic, or collusively intimate—the touchstone of a confidence shared, the secret of Sellers's feelings for Harrison safe with Jex-Blake . . . ?

Which would be worse: naively to refuse to recognize the sexuality of such female relations, or equally naively to assume that "our lesbianism" is to be found, an exact match, in the other world of the late nineteenth century—a crudely modernizing sexual identity that must run against the distinctive grain of Victorian friendship?

Hope Mirrlees admitted no such doubts. By the time she came to work on her (never to be completed) biography of Jane Harrison, after Harrison's death in 1928, she had no trouble defining the relationship. Recording in her working notes some of her friend Alice Dew-Smith's recollections of Harrison (as always, it is hard to tell how much is Mirrlees, how much her informant, and how much Harrison), she wrote: "And she [i.e., Harrison] wouldn't discuss Mrs. Strong, & when she did, made excuses for her. She [Dew-Smith?] said that Mrs. Strong imitated Jane in everything. All her life Jane was tormented by people having *schwärmeries* [sic] for her";[77] elsewhere she remarks that "Jane was nearly driven mad by her GP."[78] Strong figures only very rarely in Mirrlees's voluminous biographical notes. When she does, it is for criticism—and precisely to be excluded from the story: "an unscrupulous adventuress" who "used people just to get on"; or else to illustrate Harrison's own magnanimity: "She would never join in the chorus of abuse of . . . Mrs. Strong."[79] Here, Sellers's relationship with Harrison is patronizingly cast as a *Schwärmerei,* a maddening schoolgirl crush; it was immature hero worship that we need not take particularly seriously, still less dwell on.[80]

But there is another aspect to this dismissal of Sellers's "GP." Mirrlees was, as we shall see in the chapters that follow, deeply bound up in the coded games of literary sapphism in the 1920s and 1930s; her own relationship with Harrison, even if not necessarily itself lesbian (who knows? and what would count?), was constructed within a frame that took for granted the newly explicit discourses of female sexuality (and inversion) that characterized the early years of the twentieth century. She dismisses not just Sellers herself but also the old-fashioned, pre-Freudian naïveté of what she could already cast (correctly or not) as late-Victorian romantic friendship; almost as remote for her as it is for us.

How exactly Sellers and Harrison themselves would have defined their relationship of the 1880s, we do not know; nor do we know in what terms they would have *re*defined it, from a twentieth-century standpoint. By that stage they were distant enemies; a Grande Passion had become a Grand Quarrel.

CHAPTER SIX

Alpha and Omega

Among the autobiographical notes of Mrs. Strong, in a chapter headed "Germany," are the following two paragraphs. They are carefully honed, some of the most heavily reworked passages in the draft. Strong's emended or alternative wordings are shown here in single square brackets, her still-legible deletions are shown in double brackets:

> In London, during these teaching years, I made acquaintance [[who]] with another personality who, in a manner very different from Sir Charles Newton, [[even induced me to]] fanned my desire to study archeology. For here, preceding me, was a woman actually making for herself a career on the lines, more or less that I desired to pursue. [[True the advice she gave me]] Her example, which endorsed my ambitions, was stronger than the advice she gave me. I was, to her understanding [views], totally unsuited for such career [unfit for so high a calling as her own], unfit for scholarship, incapable of lecturing. [[Discouragement did not discour . . . daunt me but it [*sic*] react upon my feelings towards her. For that and other more personal reasons]] The lack of generosity, [[and]] if not of insight, shown by such discouragement [[was a factor]] helped to open my eyes to flaws in that over-emotional character, strained [[hyster]] to the point of hysteria and instability? For that and presently more personal grounds of [[discontent]] discord a friendship which had begun with admiration on my part and gratified acceptance of admi-

ration on hers terminated [[finally]] eventually in a complete breach.

Those were the days of the Victorian New Woman—a creature daring but overestimating her daring, breaking conventions [[by]] but carrying the wreckage [[attached to]] dangling at her skirts. One type, frankly plain, exaggerated her lack of feminine charm, became aggressively masculine; the other far from renouncing power of fascination applied it [[as [illegible] opportunity chiefly]] where she could on callow youths chiefly and younger women. My wider background and underlying common sense saved me betimes from the net. Peace be to those pioneers. They [illegible] a path for the independent self reliant capable girl of today, attractive still.[1]

The name of Jane Harrison is not mentioned here (nor anywhere in this autobiographical account—except in the cryptic note "?short while with Miss H?" that we have already seen); but there can be little doubt, as Thomson concluded in *Mrs. Arthur Strong,* that Harrison is the referent—and the target.[2] It amounts to a wide-ranging attack on her one-time teacher and (flawed) role model, who was not only mean-spirited, unstable, and discouraging, but also (to follow through the implications of the second paragraph) a destructive temptress of the young, a Siren and a wrecker—a pioneer maybe, but the kind of trailblazer whose own example is best forgotten. At the same time it is a complex piece of self-defense, as Strong (from her vantage point of the 1940s) grandly distances herself from the aspirations of late-Victorian women and lays claim to a maturity of vision, even in those early days, that made her immune to the treacherous attractions of her seductive teacher.

What drove Strong, at the very end of her life, to cast her relationship with Harrison in these terms we cannot now reconstruct in any detail. She writes of a friendship that terminated in a "complete breach"—referring to professional animosity and, obliquely, "more personal grounds of discord." From Harrison's side there is even less information, though it is compatible (so far as it goes) with Strong's account. Hope Mirrlees, after noting how "Jane said she was nearly driven mad with her GP," went on to say (curtly), "Mrs. Strong tells people there was a terrific bust-up."[3] Even through this wall of reticence we can clearly detect a very fiery end to the friendship.

So when did the "bust-up" take place? We have seen Harrison and Sellers enlisted in the same cause (supporting Dörpfeld) in 1891, and in early November of that year Harrison could at least trail Miss Sellers's name in the *Pall Mall Gazette* as someone who was ready to step into her lecturing shoes,[4] but something had certainly happened (or was in process) by 1895. In that year Harrison's review in the *Classical Review* of Sellers's translation of Furtwängler's *Meisterwerke* (as *Masterpieces of Greek Sculpture*) is significantly double-edged in its praise where it is not gratuitously and personally critical: too many Germanisms, she chides, for English elegance ("Germanisms abound and sometimes issue in complete obscurity . . . a stern set must be made against writing Germanized English"); too much gush and too little critical perspective ("She has undertaken it as a confessed enthusiast, accepting her author's view *en bloc;* the translation is all aglow with eager championship, and indeed only the devotion of an ardent disciple could have carried her with such brilliant success through a task veritably Herculean.") It is impossible that the review could have been written by one who still saw the translator as an "eager champion" of *herself;* it is easy to see that Sellers's loyalty and "ardent devotion" might itself be at issue.[5] The split must have come between 1891 and 1895.

Gladys Scott Thomson comes close to hinting that Vernon Lee was in some way involved in the breach.[6] Lee (whose real name was Violet Paget) was one of the most outrageous intellectual celebrities of the late nineteenth and early twentieth centuries. Though she is now more often referred to than read, an obligatory cultural footnote to the history of the period, during her lifetime (1856–1935) she was, as she set out to be, one of the most famous women in Europe: terrifyingly prolific author (of more than forty books); notorious art critic (she had a famous quarrel with Berenson, who claimed she had stolen his ideas); gadfly novelist (not yet thirty, she took on the whole Pre-Raphaelite movement in *Miss Brown,* a "very nasty" satire on an artist's relations with his model); uncompromising nonconformist (she was a militant pacifist in the Great War); wizard storyteller (try her ghost stories); glamorous and stylish lesbian (queen of the Parisian Left Bank, the lesbian flagship of the early twentieth-century world); friend, close enemy, and determined correspondent of almost "everybody" (William Morris, Henry James, H. G. Wells, the Burne-Joneses, Natalie Barney, the Humphry Wards, Bernard Shaw, Edith Warburton, Walter Pater . . .)[7]

Lee was English, though for most of her life she was based near Florence—with (to follow the standard biography) her almost equally idiosyncratic mother, a father who spent most of his time in the garden (one long-staying visitor was apparently surprised to be told that the "man . . . about the garden" was Mr. Paget), and her half-brother Eugene who, after Oxford and the start of a career in the diplomatic service, spent eighteen solid years in bed, nursed by his mother and half-sister, the victim of an undiagnosed condition (a German doctor who pulled off the miracle cure in 1893 hinted at "auto-suggestion").[8] Not surprisingly, whenever the money allowed (and, of course, she makes the usual complaints of poverty[9]), she traveled through Europe, with frequent visits to London, where she met both Harrison and Sellers. She was another of the young women who clustered around Charles Newton—and it was at dinner *chez* Newton in July 1886 that she first met Sellers (Harrison she had encountered some years before). It wasn't a particularly auspicious start: in her first letter home after that occasion, Lee misspelled Sellers's name and took a trenchantly independent view on the young lady's renowned beauty ("a learned young lady who two years ago, when she acted in the Greek play, was hailed as a pro-

digious beauty, which she isn't"[10]). But by 1887 Lee was displaying a photograph of "the beautiful Greek scholar . . . on the little
drawing room chimney piece" (see illustration 2, Chapter 2) and
was planning to stay with her for a few days in Cambridge.
Visits to Florence followed, as we have already seen, and in 1893
Lee and Sellers shared a London apartment for a while. Part of
the trouble may have been connected with this stormy flat-
share: "I spent a night at Eugénie Sellers," Vernon Lee wrote
later (spelling her name correctly by now), when the sharing arrangement had come to an end, "whom I appreciate all the more
that we are not housekeeping together; her housekeeping is of
the most sketchy and consists less of ordering food than of general complaints at the heartlessness of servants."[11]

But it was not domestic disputes of this kind that Thomson
had in mind when she wrote of "fireworks" between the two of
them in London—"amid the blaze of which the figure of Jane
Harrison as a third party can also be seen."[12] This three-sided
quarrel, still faintly traceable through the archives of both Lee
and Strong, was about Art and its Interpretation, not about
housekeeping. Specifically it was about Vernon Lee's dislike of
the style, theory, and content of Harrison's *Introductory Studies in
Greek Art,* published in 1885. The aim of this book, as Harrison
stresses in the Preface, was "to express the secret of the beauty
and the permanent vitality" of Greek art. "Why, when Egypt
and Assyria and Phoenicia are dead, is Greece alone untouched
by time, vital for ever?" The answer (which borders, we must admit, on circularity) lies in its "largeness and universality which
outlives the individual race and persists for all time"; a quality
she defines, with a good deal of help from Plato, as "Ideality."
The core of this book is a chapter on Pheidias and the Parthenon marbles—illuminated by her reading of Greek philosophy
("What is expressed but undefined in Pheidias becomes clearly
articulate in Plato"). It was explicitly based on her teaching in
the British Museum.[13]

Vernon Lee would have none of this—for reasons we shall

now explore. It is worth reviewing her objections, and the surrounding storm, in some detail: they have never before been written into the Harrison story, and they make a considerable difference to it. As we shall see in Chapter 8, the standard mythology of Harrison's career emphasizes D. S. MacColl's attack on her approach to the visual arts (dramatically fired off in 1887, as part and parcel of his critique of her lecturing style) as an intellectual turning point; it was this unexpected attack that is said to have prompted her "conversion," that is, her shift from art history to the study of ritual and myth.[14] In fact MacColl's criticisms cannot have been as unexpected as they are often painted. Vernon Lee had made some of the same points, with a similar degree of intensity, at least a year earlier.

We enter the story at that dinner party "at Mr. Newton's," where Sellers and Lee first met.[15] The main topic of conversation between the two women was (no prize for guessing) Miss Harrison. Something had apparently been puzzling Lee—and she took the opportunity of raising it with Sellers, whom she must have discovered (if she didn't already know) was one of Harrison's closest friends. It was all to do with a letter that Lee had written to Newton when *Introductory Studies* first appeared. In it she had told Newton exactly what she thought about the book *and* had asked him to pass her criticisms on to Miss Harrison herself. That being so, she had been puzzled, "when Miss H. came to Florence, at her curious manner in seeming neither moved nor annoyed by [the] strictures"; in fact she said nothing about it at all. At the dinner, Sellers was not particularly concerned or surprised at Harrison's silence (she might, like us, have seen that Newton could all too easily have chosen to forget this unenviable favor demanded of him). But later she began to fret—both about Harrison's odd behavior ("I well know Miss H's excessive reserve—yet I could not see its 'raison d'être' on this occasion") and about the criticisms that Lee had raised of her approach to art.

She could not put her mind at rest immediately (for Harrison was away, traveling in Russia and Germany). But as soon as Harrison returned, she "asked her straight out about the letter" and discovered what had happened: Newton had never so much as mentioned it. She wrote immediately to Vernon Lee, on October 16: "It seems that she has never seen it or even heard of it—probably some mistake of dear old Mr. Newton. She is naturally rather vexed about it—so I determined to tell you all about the matter at the risk of being thought very troublesome—but I believe you will be glad to know the truth."

Lee *was* glad, she claimed (and particularly glad to have received a letter from Miss Sellers, whom she had not seen since the dinner).[16] But the matter didn't end there: for, of course, Lee was still anxious to make her views known to Harrison, and Sellers quickly came to see that she should be defending her teacher and friend. After thanking Sellers for her efforts and confessing to a slightly wobbly memory (had she specifically asked Newton to show Harrison the letter, or only implied that he should communicate the gist of it?), Lee's reply goes straight onto the offensive: "I was in a state of wild fury," she explains; " . . . I burned to tell Miss Harrison or anyone else what I thought of her book. I did not write to her because, 1stly the attitude she assumed in the book seemed to me to make all argument quite vain, it being my strong conviction that despite her great ability and classical knowledge, she had no instinct for art of any kind and a want of knowledge of other art besides that of antiquity (wherein I proved quite right, for she was utterly ignorant of Tuscan sculpture) and could consequently not see the very basis for my remarks. 2dly that I had not seen her or heard of her for four years, and considered our acquaintance utterly lapsed."[17]

Lee had turned up the emotional pressure; and Sellers was now implicated more deeply than perhaps she would have wished. She responded immediately to answer one point only:

Harrison had not been "indignant" about the letter to Newton; Lee had completely misunderstood; Harrison was only concerned that her behavior had seemed strange—and, besides, would have liked to see the letter, because "however adverse your criticisms may have been she would have considered them valuable."[18] At this stage in the correspondence some letters are missing; but the issues (and "that letter") were still being debated when Sellers wrote to Lee on January 16, 1887.[19] Between October and January, Lee must have laid out her objections to Harrison's book (particularly its reliance on Plato) in some detail. For it is "Platonism," and Harrison's use of Plato particularly in her chapter on Pheidias, that Sellers now sets out to defend in the eight pages of the letter:

> I confess I feel roused when you accuse Plato (or is it only Miss Harrison? it seems to me like both) of cut and driedness. Poor old Plato—my difficulties with him have been quite of a different kind—the gorgeousness of his thought and imagery often bewilders me so that it prevents me almost from understanding . . . I gather you mean he is narrow, or that those are narrow who apply those particular theories of the Phaedrus to art—but it seems to me that the theory is just wide enough to include all great art—and the rest is rightfully shut out. That the metaphors in which Plato clothed his thought are foreign to modern taste, or that his conception of the 'other world' of beauty is crude, and will be modified by modern thought, does not prevent to my mind the intrinsic truth and absolute satisfactoriness of the main conception. Plato, nor anyone believing in the theory, does not imagine that nature should not be studied, since it alone is powerful to awaken the artistic faculty.

We do not know exactly what Vernon Lee's objections were. Harrison had argued in *Introductory Studies* that the greatness of Pheidias, his eternal "vitality," could be understood in terms of the Platonic theory of Ideas (or Forms): that the great artist captures more than individual examples of beauty in the world around us, he captures something of the form of Beauty itself—transcending, rather than replicating, nature. From Sellers's letter in reply, and from what else we know of Vernon Lee's writing on art at this period of her career, we can infer that Lee had attacked the inappropriateness of Plato's vision as a general model for art, while defending the importance of the observable natural world against the almost mystical realm of "Ideality." That, at any rate, would be a predictable enough line from a critic who just a few years earlier had been preaching the "simplicity" of art, and its capacity for giving pleasure that had emphatically nothing whatsoever to do with transcendence, mysticism, poetry, or deep psychology.[20] For Lee, it was all a question of the plastic (not the Platonic) form of sculpture, of the color and line as it existed on the canvas—not of some woolly metaphysical Ideality beyond or behind the work of art itself.

Sellers defended the intellectual basis of Harrison's arguments, but she also defended her as teacher and friend. In the same letter to Lee, she wrote about her own "discovery" of Greek art and the subsequent influence of Harrison:

> For years, even after my 'discovery' of the Elgin marbles I was a terrible materialist—and pictures and statues seemed to me pleasant things to look at, and that was about all. It is to Miss Harrison's teaching solely at first, that I owe having even thought that their mission might be quite other than to amuse me. Indeed I owe such a mighty debt to Miss Harrison for this, not to say that she has been one of my kindest friends in more material ways, that I always feel somewhat ashamed when I reflect how lukewarmly I took her part when I spoke with you in the summer. I foolishly thought you were simply annoyed with her about that unfortunate letter—but afterwards I understood you were opposed to her for the very principles of her work and teaching—and this is really a matter of great regret to me.

If Thomson found these letters in preparing her memoir of Mrs. Strong, it is not hard to imagine how and why she might have suspected that any "terrific bust-up" between Harrison and Sellers could well have had something to do with Vernon Lee: the combination of fervent loyalty, intellectual antagonism, and the most famous lesbian in town could, after all, explain almost anything. But, in fact, it cannot have been the main cause of the breach. For all the significance that the dispute deserves (and I shall return to it when I come to discuss the role in the Harrison mythology of MacColl and *his* attack on her art criticism), it happens years too early to account for the end of the friendship. We do not know how peace was restored between the women (after January, I have found no securely dated letters until September 1887), but restored it was: Harrison and Sellers continued as intimate allies until at least 1891; Sellers and Lee went on to develop a friendship that (apart from quarrels over housekeeping) lasted for the rest of their lives.[21] The final bust-up must have come later.

Traces of it are preserved, perhaps, in a strangely cryptic letter sent from D. S. MacColl to Sellers in November 1891. MacColl and Sellers had been on friendly terms ever since Harrison had engineered their meeting in 1886,[22] and a cluster of nearly thirty of his letters to her, the majority written between 1889 and 1891, is preserved in Strong's papers. Many of them tell the usual (day-to-day) kind of story: invitations to tea, lectures, and dinner; the return of loaned books ("rather dishevelled in the keeping; but if she is going to the binder that does not matter so much"); apologies for staying too late; jokes about Dörpfeld ("Old Dörpfeld, I am sure, would rouse the archaeologist from a deathbed to attend a six hours lecture," he wrote after she had been ill in Greece, remembering, presumably, the lecture *he* had attended with Harrison).[23] But one particular letter stands out. MacColl's style is characteristically a mixture of the engagingly blunt and tantalizingly encoded. Never more so than on November 29, 1891.[24]

"My only difficulty about meeting you as you desire," he starts, "is that it would leave you under a mistaken impression, so I trust you will have the justice to read this first, since it is quite inadmissible to write such a letter as you, without reading the reply. To comply with your request simply, would place me in a quite false dilemma either putting another person in the wrong, or myself, and I cannot consent to either interpretation." Out of this (to us) baffling opacity, something does shortly emerge: the "another person" is a woman. "Your first point is to call me to account for the action towards you of a lady with whom I am proud to be on terms of friendship. But as that gives me no right or claim whatever to control her actions to others or her friendships, it would clearly be as great an impertinence for me to interfere in such a matter, as it would be for me to criticize, say, your actions to other people, or, I may add, as it would be for the world or any part of it to criticize her friendship for me, in which I am unable to see anything absurd." What the "action" was he does not state—except to indicate that Sellers has completely misunderstood its intention: "It is clear you have written under a complete misconception, it being quite impossible that she should have meant to convey to you by anything she said what you have taken her to mean. Indeed I should hardly be writing now, if you had not indicated that you did not yourself believe in the insulting suggestion you make." He closes the letter with an agreement to meet Sellers ("as you propose," though this letter can hardly have failed to make her decidedly less keen on the proposal) and some half-hearted apologies for not being in touch sooner.

There is a very narrow dividing line here between (on the one hand) admitting that we simply cannot decode the circumstances of this letter at all and (on the other) finding it self-evident that MacColl's "another person" and the figure lurking behind the obviously unpleasant message is Jane Ellen Harrison. Should we simply accept that (for all our researches, our prying into their correspondence) these are people whose lives we can know only in the very smallest degree, and that most of what they did, felt, or argued about on most days of their lives is utterly lost to us, and that letters like this have more possible referents than we could even begin to imagine? Or are we entitled to think that we *do* know these particular biographical subjects well enough; well enough, at least, to have few doubts that MacColl's "lady with whom I am proud to be on terms of friendship" (well known, at the same time, to Sellers) was bound to be Miss Harrison?

Let's suppose, for the moment, that it was. In that case, the letter may merely chart a temporary rocky patch in a continuing friendship; nothing more significant than that. (Certainly there were other rocky patches: a letter from MacColl to Sellers on December 25, 1890, complains over three pages that *she* (i.e., Sellers) had complained that he had broken a confidence entrusted with him.[25]) Or it may be testimony to the "terrific bustup." If so, it dates the breach between Harrison and Sellers more firmly. In January 1891 (when we know them to have been working on the same side, if not exactly together, on the Dörpfeld controversy) MacColl had written to Sellers in Athens: "I picture Athens crowded with eminent Oxford dons turned Pausaniacs, each with a copy of Harrison and Verrall under one arm, and Schuchardt (is it?) under the other"; surely a neat (as well as a tactful) image of personal harmony to picture the learned traveler clutching his Harrison's *Monuments and Mythology* in one hand and Sellers's translation of *Schliemann's Excavations* in the other.[26] And there was no sign of any change, so far as the *Pall Mall Gazette* was concerned, in the first week of November 1891, when Sellers was still accorded her place in Harrison's intellectual entourage. By November 29 the personal harmony had disappeared. But MacColl's letter does not leave us much the wiser about the circumstances. We have an "action" (on the part of Harrison), a "misconception"(on the part of Sellers), insults (fired off, received, or invented: "it being quite impossible that she should have meant to convey to you by anything she said what you have taken her to mean"), and friends caught in the middle, conscripted by both sides. But what terrific bust-up was ever not composed of just those elements?

Even if we cannot reconstruct the details, the obviously stormy conclusion to the friendship of Harrison and Sellers is crucial in their (auto)biographical tradition. For the ill feeling, the rage and hurt that marked its end must have been important factors in writing that friendship *out* of our histories, in excluding each woman, never to be mentioned, from the authorized version of the other's life. *Damnatio memoriae,* modern style. In the next chapters, we shall see first what happens if we try to write them in again, what difference that *re*insertion might make to our understanding of Harrison and Sellers as ancient historians and art historians. Then we shall explore other factors, apart from the terrible final quarrel, that might be at work in keeping Sellers out of the story of Harrison. We shall end up pondering the tricky exercise of reading an archive.

CHAPTER SEVEN

Ancient Art and Ritual

The absence of Jane Harrison from the published work of Eugénie Strong (and vice versa) has passed, so far as I can tell, entirely unremarked. After all, with the exception of her early translations (Furtwängler's *Masterpieces*, Schuchhardt's account of *Schliemann's Excavations*, and Pliny's *Chapters on the History of Art*), Strong's work is firmly focused on Rome, Harrison's equally firmly on Greece. Such has been the strength of the territorial divisions in the study of ancient art, that no one has ever seriously expected to find Greek Harrison making an impact (whether acknowledged or not) on Roman Strong.

On the other hand, as soon as you have seen how closely they were once associated, it is impossible not to be struck by the similarity of the methods and approaches that underlie their work; it is hard not to feel (as we have already noted) that Strong in some sense "[did] for Rome what Harrison had done for Greece." *Of course* she did, we might now add. This was no mere coincidence, not just a consequence of some turn-of-the-century zeitgeist. Strong's work shares features in common with Harrison's precisely because they worked together, as pupil and teacher and as friends, over nearly a decade, through the 1880s and into the early 1890s. Strong's *Apotheosis and After Life*, like most of Harrison's writing, is founded on a commitment to reading visual images as part of an argument about ancient culture and religion more generally; scratch the surface of her polemic against the woeful neglect of Roman artistic production in comparison with the Greek genius, and you find a radical attempt to see Roman ideology through (and as constituted in) its images. It amounts to a manifesto: "that," to use Harrison's words "the story which art has left us should [not] remain unread."[1]

I want to take the connection between Harrison and Sellers a little further: beyond the broad similarities of approach that confirm the influence of one on the other, to a much more precise idea of what Sellers might have learned from Harrison, and (more crucially) how she might have learned it. Pedagogy is about process as much as it is about subject matter and skills. Inevitably teachers teach their pupils not only *what* they themselves already know but also *the way* that they themselves learn, and the latter (the process) is even more important than the former (the content) in defining scholarly influence and genealogy. In this chapter I want to explore how Sellers learned (to learn) from Harrison.

In doing that, I shall not be focusing on the possible changes in the aims and content of Harrison's work over the period in which she was teaching and collaborating with Sellers. (There is quite enough on that subject in Chapter 8.) I shall concentrate instead on recapturing the encounter between student and teacher that is central to the experience of learning: the class, the tutorial, the supervision, the lecture, the pieces of work set and handed back. These nuts and bolts of everyday teaching and learning are usually lost to us among the more imposing ruins of past intellectual life: the published books, the self-justificatory memoirs, the institutional histories. Even when we know (from lecture titles or examination syllabuses) what people claimed to teach, we can hardly ever discover what that meant on the ground, what kind of exercises were set, what answers were expected, what comments were given in return. In Harrison's case, however, we can do rather better—not just by reexperiencing those famous lectures but (thanks to some unpromising scraps of paper preserved in the Newnham Archive) by actually stealing a glimpse into the kind of teaching that went on in the flat in Colville Gardens, London (W), where Harrison entertained her chosen pupils.[2]

As we have seen, the style of Harrison's public lectures prompted a variety of responses, from admiration to revulsion. Sellers attended many of them; for some she acted as secretary and business manager, sold the tickets, and encouraged the adulation. There can be no doubt that Sellers learned from Harrison's example, whether imitating, modifying, or rejecting the model; no doubt that she (and her friends) measured the success of her own lectures against those of her teacher's: "I prefer them to Miss Harrison's . . . for she is always so desperately patronizing" was the verdict we already noted from the loyal Violet Buxton.[3]

Harrison's lectures of the 1880s also formed the basis of her early books, explicitly so in the case of *Introductory Studies* ("The chapter on Pheidias . . . contains the gist of what during five years of archaeological teaching at the British Museum I have constantly tried to enforce"[4]) and probably in *Myths of the Odyssey* as well. It is hard not to read either of these volumes without sensing the ghost of a lecture behind them: the diverting quotes from poetry, the consistent use of the first person plural, the lecturing tropes ("To continue"; "Next let us turn to the beast-god on the left"; "This brings us back to the Egyptians."), and the occasional flashes of irony ("Was there no hope for the art of Egypt?"). But quite how far they preserve the overall character or the exact words of the original deliveries (themselves different each time, we may guess) is impossible to know. Even the preserved lecture aids (the lists of key terms to be projected through the magic lantern) are not so transparent as they once were. What point did she actually make with her list of Athenian virtues ("self-sufficiency, greatness of spirit, discretion, Reverence & grace")? Was it fed to the audience straight? Was it held up for admiration? Was its simplicity questioned? Or did it depend on what kind of audience it was? A prompt for a lecture, rather than a guiding text? For all the detailed descriptions, the lantern slides, the resulting books, the sense of atmosphere, the public éclat, it is almost impossible now to reconstruct the *teaching* at the heart of those great lecturing occasions.

Paradoxically we can say more about Harrison's private teaching than about her public performances; more about her methods with those small groups of pupils who met for instruction behind the closed doors of 45D Colville Gardens than with the vast audiences that gathered in museums and provincial lecture halls. It was this Colville Gardens flat[5]—written up for all it was worth—that provided the backdrop for the interview with Miss Harrison, published in the *Pall Mall Gazette* in 1891: "The very air breathed antiquity," enthused the reporter. "There was a fine photograph of the Parthenon on the wall; over an etching of a Burne-Jones picture a piece of mummy cloth was hung; there were strange vases and pots; and books and pamphlets innumerable . . . Two ladies bent together over a book of daintily coloured plates, lost in admiration of something I was presently called upon to admire."[6] Miss Harrison and Miss Lathbury (though it might equally well have been Miss Harrison and Miss Sellers) at work. We may suspect that they were putting on a good act for their gullible visitor; maybe sending him up.[7] For a normal day's work in Colville Gardens (when the press wasn't watching, that is) was a far cry from the gushing, weak-at-the-knees, aestheticized "admiration" that our roving reporter suggests. A much more hardheaded, and at the same time much more ambitious, program of teaching and learning is captured by the dog-eared, faded, and (at first sight) uninspiring collections of notes, exercises, and syllabuses stored up in the Newnham Archive.[8]

The published syllabuses of Harrison's courses for the University Extension Society in the late 1880s and the 1890s, combined with a hand-written prospectus for a group of ladies studying by correspondence at about the same time, make it absolutely clear that at that period her teaching stood for more than art "appreciation." Side by side with routine admonitions to the students to buy the essential textbooks, to get out to the museums to see the original works of art, to have their work handed in on time, and to use their brains ("In God's name I beg of you to think," runs her motto), she lays out a program for the scientific study of myth-and-art, art as myth, myth as art:

> First mythology will be dealt with everywhere, not so much as a product of poetical fancy clothed in elaborate ritual form—a possible view of the later forms of myths, though educationally of less value—but as an object of scientific enquiry . . .
>
> Mythology becomes not merely a matter for artistic contemplation but for serious study: in itself it is the best evidence of the organic growth of an ancient nation and its historical examination calls us to exercise to the utmost the faculty of discrimination.
>
> Further, special stress will be laid upon the study of *Mythography* ie *Mythology as expressed in Art.* Here too, the Monuments studied will be regarded not merely or chiefly as beautiful illustrations, but as original sources for scientific use.
>
> . . . Art criticism will find but a small place.[9]

The link in her teaching between art history and the study of myth and religion was not in itself quite so novel as has often been imagined; at least, as we shall see in the next chapter, a similar link had been established in the new classical archaeology papers in Cambridge from the moment they were introduced in 1879. What was revolutionary (and proclaimed as such by Harrison and her admirers) was her method of teaching the subject. The *Women's Penny Paper,* interviewing Harrison (the woman who "has shown herself the equal of men in a path untrodden almost by women") for its issue of August 24, 1889, singled out her teaching practice: "In classes she has a method of her own. She teaches by personal examination of objects." She herself wrote of her 1890 series, "Athens: Its Mythology and Art": "The Class will be conducted by a new method of problem photographs, lent to the students and to be discussed and explained by them."[10] Her priority here (apart from ensuring that she got those expensive photographs *back* from the students[11]) was to teach interpretation, method, and argument—as is laid out in the instructions she gives to her correspondence students: "State what you believe to be the subject and meaning of 1. The whole design, 2. Each figure. In every case state what you base your opinion on."

A few of these "photograph tests" survive in the Newnham Archive, along with some of Harrison's comments on the work submitted. Most striking is a faded sheet of paper labeled "Miss Marshall" (a correspondence pupil in 1888–89 who also attended University Extension lectures);[12] attached are three photographs: (a) a vase painting, showing Zeus brandishing his thunderbolt at a large winged monster with a double serpent tail;[13] (b) the fragments of (the right side of) an archaic limestone pediment from the Athenian Acropolis showing a three-headed monster with serpent's tail; (c) a "proposed restoration" of the complete pediment, showing a large male figure in the center of the pediment attacking the three-headed monster shown in photograph (b), and, to the left, a fight between a figure in a lion skin and another serpent-tailed monster (Triton). Miss Marshall was asked to "Explain c with the help of a"; that is, to elucidate the reconstruction with the help of the vase painting. It was, in fact, an extremely up-to-the-minute (and complex) exercise. This now famous piece of archaic architectural sculpture (we call it the "Bluebeard pediment"—from the blue beards of the monster's heads—and have decided to restore it rather differently[14]) had just been discovered in the years 1888 to 1889. Harrison herself had seen the first couple of fragments of the Bluebeard when she was in Athens on her trip with MacColl and reported it in her survey of recent Greek archaeology in the *Journal of Hellenic Studies* for 1888.[15] The rest of the monster had been excavated the next year, and very soon afterward the first reconstruction of the whole pediment (as reproduced by Harrison) appeared in the *Athenische Mittheilungen* of the German Institute. It placed Bluebeard in one corner, attacked by Zeus in the center, with Triton in the other corner, being dealt a death blow by Heracles.[16] Like all reconstructions of these Athenian archaic pediments, it was a pretty desperate attempt, cannibalizing other fragments from the Acropolis excavations that seemed to match well enough to fill the vacant spaces. Zeus' central role in the conflict was justified, and the problem of Bluebeard's identity was "solved"[17] by reference to a hydria in Munich, where the god is shown dispatching a winged, serpent-tailed, bearded creature commonly identified as the monster Typhon. Harrison has found an illustration of this pot[18] (it was not actually illustrated in the article accompanying the restoration) and is effectively asking her pupil to retrace the steps of the restorer's argument.

This scrap of paper with its faded photographs is a rare document in the history of scholarship. It takes us beyond the published syllabus, directly to the task set for the pupil by the teacher. Here (and in the other surviving photographs that imply a similar agenda) we can see what Harrison did with her students, Sellers among them, and we can begin to sense what difference that teaching might have made.[19] It is not just a question of looking hard at individual images, nor a question of turning the discoveries of only yesterday (almost literally) into the teaching exercises of today—though that must have made it all the more exciting. What underlies these exercises is the idea that visual imagery is embedded in the cultural and religious history of the ancient world; that "art" is inseparable from the semiotics of ancient culture in its widest sense, and that there were skills of visual interpretation to be learned.

Harrison provided, no doubt, a firm guiding hand in this

difficult learning process; too firm for some, we might guess. "Explain c with the help of a" doesn't leave much room for debate or doubt, for raising awkward questions about whether the monster in "a" provided any justification at all for seeing Bluebeard as Typhon and killing him off with (a reconstructed) Zeus. And Harrison's comments on her pupil's answers (sadly, I have not been able to find them for this particular exercise) also adopt a tone of magisterial certainty: "Top centre figure certainly Heracles," she writes in response to another of Miss Marshall's photograph exercises. "Lion skin allows of no doubt. Object in hand not a [illegible] rather a [illegible] . . . You need never be surprised to see Athena attending Herakles any more than with Theseus."[20] But magisterial or not, they must have taught Miss Marshall (as Miss Sellers only a few years before her) that ancient art not only meant something but that, with "the right instinct of thoroughness & method,"[21] its meaning was recoverable.

It is, then, relatively easy to reinsert Harrison into Mrs. Arthur Strong's intellectual narrative, to find a place for the impact of her teaching in much of her pupil's writing. It is easy partly because there is no particularly powerful alternative narrative to challenge. The intellectual biography of Mrs. Strong is (as I write) a relatively open field. There are few vested interests in the story of how she came to rewrite the story of Roman art or to forge new links between the history of Roman religion and its visual representations; few vested interests because few people today would claim to be very interested in the intellectual roots of this unfashionable, fascist-sympathizing, sometime Assistant Director of the British School at Rome.

It is a different question (and a good deal trickier) if we try to define a place for Strong in the intellectual story of Harrison, and to ask how the story of the pupil might make a difference to our story of the teacher. This is largely because the long-established, authorized version of Harrison's life does not easily admit new members to its cast of significant characters. In particular, as we shall see in the next chapter, Harrison has been conscripted into "the story of Ritualism" as figurehead and focus of a Cambridge movement in the history of religion. This has left little place either for Harrison's (London) period as an art historian or for following the work of that early period through into her later "Ritualist" classics, *Prolegomena* and *Themis*. At the very least, Strong's art-historical story serves to remind us that there could be ways of understanding Harrison's work that are not simply in terms of the development of Ritualism and her development as a Ritualist.

One of the things that this Ritualist story has occluded is the fact that Harrison never ceased to be a historian of images, that all her major writing on Greek subjects was founded on the analysis of sculpture and (vase) painting, at least as much as on the discussion of literary texts. You need only glance at the pages of *Themis* (her most explicitly "sociological" production) to understand what I mean; for there as much as anywhere Harrison is constantly interrogating the visual remains of the ancient religious world, always at work as an iconographer, an interpreter of what she could *see*. Time and again, her major claims about the collective origins of the mysteries of the god Dionysus, and her interpretation of his rituals, are founded in visual evidence: more than one hundred and fifty "figures" (from a modern African initiation dance to ancient coins, Minoan sealstones to Attic vase painting) are analyzed and compared.

Harrison's procedure can be seen clearly in her discussion of the famous Minoan painted sarcophagus from Hagia Triada.[22] Why, she asks, do two of the obelisks shown on one of its sides appear to be sprouting leaves? What's the connection between the obelisks, the battle axes, the bird, and the sacrificial bull? "What does it all mean?" she wonders. Plato mentions a bull sacrifice in his Atlantis—where the blood of the animal actually touches a pillar (but no trees). Suppose you bring into the argument a group of (much later) coin types from Ilion? Some of these show a sacrificial cow in front of a pillar, others show the animal hanging on a tree. This *must* be the same kind of ritual as on the sarcophagus (and in Plato), and so on. . . .

Never mind that the conclusion of all this (accompanied by yet more visual parallels) is a characteristically unbelievable assertion about vegetation cults (the object is "to bring the *mana* of the bull in contact with the mimic trees . . . Tree and pillar and obelisk are all substantially one . . . All trees tend to be sacred . . . but above all fruit trees"). Never mind the fact that such flights of fancy tended to go down badly with most reviewers ("What she writes, for example, about the scenes on the Hagia Triada sarcophagus illustrates her deficiency on both these points [namely, knowledge of prehistoric Aegean culture and of Egypt and the Near East]. With the conventions alike of Egyptian and of Aegean artistic representation in mind, she would not have ventured to spin so much of her explanation of those scenes out of her inner consciousness; and if she had paid more heed to Western Asia than to Central Australia . . . she would have hesitated rather than hastened to find a representation of 'rain-making' with a gourd-rattle on a Dipylon sherd at Athens," scolded the *Times Literary Supplement*.[23]) The important point here is the method, the emphasis on visuality and on inferences drawn from the juxtaposition of significant (visual) parallels. In the next chapter I shall show how closely linked archaeology and the history of religion were in the late nineteenth century; how predictable it might seem that details of iconography should be a central element in the analysis of myth. But Harrison is doing something more. Her analysis of the Hagia Triada sarcophagus is another case (and you will find them throughout her work) of "explaining c with the help of a"; she taught her students what she had learned herself: to explain by visual comparison.

Even with *Themis* in 1912, we are much closer to those early days in the sitting room of 45D Colville Gardens, and to Miss

Marshall's (and Miss Lathbury's and Miss Sellers's) "problem photographs," than we usually (let ourselves) imagine. Or to put it the other way round, the lessons in Colville Gardens prompt us to see *Themis* afresh, not simply as a Ritualist tract or a Durkheimian exploration, but as a study in art history and archaeology.

CHAPTER EIGHT

Hellas at Cambridge

So far I have concentrated on the more or less *auto*biographical reasons for the separation of Harrison and Strong in our intellectual traditions, and in our storytelling. Whatever the cause of the "terrific bust-up," it gave each woman good reason to forget the other, to write the other out of her own version of her life. It is no surprise, in fact, that we have to work hard to piece together a relationship, for on both sides it was meant to be forgotten. I want now to explore the absence of Mrs. Strong from the story of Miss Harrison in a different way, returning to the question of how our myth of Harrison is constructed. This chapter will focus on the so-called Cambridge Ritualists. In almost all recent writing Harrison's intellectual career has been understood in terms of her relationship with this particular "movement": when did she become a Ritualist? what was her first truly Ritualist work? how important was her contribution to Ritualism? I shall be daring to challenge the very existence of the Cambridge Ritualists, at least in the (capital R) sense in which that title has come to be used. And I shall be arguing, at the same time, that Eugénie Strong (and a good many other significant influences on Harrison's career as well) has been written out of the Harrison story precisely because she could not be conscripted into the story of Ritualism. Scholarly mythology has made Harrison and Ritualism virtually coterminous. For "biography of Harrison" read "story of Ritualism" (and often vice versa); anything that will not fit neatly into the narrative of *Harrison as Ritualist* has tended to be forgotten.

Let's start where we began this book, with Gilbert Murray, for Murray has an even bigger part to play in (the construction of) the story of Harrison than the first Harrison Memorial Lecture at Newnham might suggest. Inevitably he is as much a part of her mythology as he was one of its creators. The first published biography of Harrison was explicitly based on the letters that she sent to Murray and his wife, carefully preserved by their recipients. As we have seen, she contrived to burn all of his letters to her, but one side of the correspondence remained intact, and it was this version of Harrison's relationship with Murray that provided the narrative frame for Jessie Stewart's *Jane Ellen Harrison: A Portrait from Letters.*[1] But Murray is still more deeply embedded in the Harrison story than even that would suggest—largely through his role as a Cambridge Ritualist.

One of the central planks of Harrison's work was, as we have noted, the primacy of ritual in the interpretation of Greek myth and religion: "My belief is," she wrote in her introduction to *Mythology and Monuments of Ancient Athens* in 1890, "that in many, even in the large majority of cases *ritual practice misunderstood* explains the elaboration of myth."[2] I am not concerned here with exactly what she meant by this; the meaning is in fact much more elusive than the simplicity of the slogan might suggest.[3] But it is a claim that, in various forms and in various elaborations of its own, underlay much of Harrison's work on Greek (and other) culture for the next thirty years. ("I would here record my conviction which I hope to establish in another connection that the widespread legend, Don Juan, arose from a fertility ritual," she teased, in a footnote to her *Epilegomena* in 1921.[4]) And in general, it is a claim echoed over the same period, more or less loudly, by a number of other classicists and archaeologists, mostly working in Cambridge and many of them good friends of hers (and of each other). Murray himself (Professor of Greek at Oxford between 1908 and 1936, though in close touch with Cambridge colleagues, staggeringly prolific translator of Greek tragedy, and equally tireless campaigner for all the best liberal causes[5]) wrote an "Excursus on the Ritual Forms Preserved in Greek Tragedy" to be included in Harrison's *Themis,* and apparently never swayed from the view that the plots of Greek drama could be explained by the Dionysiac ritual that was their origin.[6] Francis Cornford (Laurence Professor of Ancient Philosophy at Cambridge from 1931 to 1939, translator and commentator on Plato, author of one of the most famous books on Thucydides ever written, as well as of *the* most famous satire on university politics, *Microcosmographia Academica*) also contributed a chapter to *Themis,* "The Origin of the Olympic Games"—and the title of one of his many books, *The Origin of Attic Comedy,* hints (to those in the know) at his interest in ritual as the origin of the central institutions of Greek culture.[7] To a greater or lesser extent you could see similar concerns in the vast multivolume *Zeus* of A. B. C(ook), whom we met in Chapter 1 as part of the warm-up routine at Murray's Memorial Lecture,[8] and even maybe, traces at least, in J. G. Frazer's founding tracts of (classical) anthropology—from the ever-expanding, multi-edition *Golden Bough* to his not much trimmer commentary on *Pausanias.*[9]

There is no doubt that these writers knew each other (we have a tantalizing reference, for example, to a Hebrew class comprising Harrison, Frazer, Cook, and Cornford—which must have been a daunting assignment even for their hand-picked tutor, the Regius Professor of Hebrew at Cambridge[10]); and there is no doubt also that they made a difference to each other's work—sometimes choosing to celebrate their mutual influence. Preface after preface joins in the chorus of goodwill, the parade of friendship and mutual self-congratulation: "My debt to Miss

Harrison is great and obvious";[11] "It was Sir James G. Frazer who first advised me to put together in permanent form the materials that I had collected . . . Most of this book has been perused, either in manuscript or in slip, by Miss J. E. Harrison . . . Other helpful criticisms have reached me from Mr. F. M. Cornford";[12] "The hypothesis . . . would never have occurred to me if I had not had in mind Professor Murray's theory of the 'ritual forms' in Tragedy. My debt to him is, therefore, great . . . Two friends have given me much help: Miss Jane Harrison and Mr. Arthur Bernard Cook."[13] Obituary notices, too, chime in (though not always in exactly the tone their subjects would have liked): "He came much under the influence of Jane Harrison. In the long run her influence doubtless helped his development, which needed a sharp emancipation from orthodox aims and methods, but its immediate effects were not altogether good, for he was too much dazzled by her rather slapdash brilliance, and she encouraged his instinctive tendency to equate soundness with dulness," carped D. S. Robertson, writing of Cornford in the *Cambridge Review* just after Cornford's death.[14]

At the same time, it is clear that all these writers were as different as they were similar, and sometimes very different indeed—in reputation, interests, and scholarly allegiances. Never mind the distance that, in most respects, separated Frazer from the others,[15] Cornford came increasingly to specialize in philosophical theory, Murray was (as his position at Oxford indicates) a "literature man," and Harrison left the others behind when she diverted into Russian studies in the 1920s. Besides, if there was a "party line" shared by some, it did not extend very far or last very long. Murray's *Four Stages of Greek Religion* (for all its expression of gratitude to Miss Harrison) was in fact an explicit attack on Harrison's views on the classical Olympian deities (which she saw as pale and uninteresting shadows of their primitive precursors): "She has by now," wrote Murray in his Preface, "made the title 'Olympian' almost a term of reproach and thrown down so many a scornful challenge to the canonical gods of Greece, that I have ventured on this attempt to explain their historical origin and plead for their religious value."[16] Back-handed compliment, friendly badinage, in-group irony perhaps, but certainly not the sign of a group with a single, shared stance. Nor did they speak of themselves in such terms. "The Cambridge Ritualists" was not *their* coinage, and it would have been a strange title for them to choose. "The ritualist is, to the modern mind, a man concerned perhaps unduly with fixed forms and ceremonies, with carrying out the rigidly prescribed ordinances of a church or sect," wrote Harrison in *Ancient Art and Ritual*.[17] That is not what they were about at all.

But recent studies have provided our Ritualists with a much firmer identity. Historians of classical scholarship, at least since the 1960s, have liked to give them a capital *R* and to make them a bona fide club, with members paid up and card-carrying: the "Ritualists". The history of this nomenclature is (inevitably) murky. The invention of Ritualism in this sense was a discursive process, not a momentary origin: it is not so much a question of when, or by whom exactly, the title was first applied to Harrison and friends, but of how (in what contexts, and for what reasons) the descriptive adjective, *ritualist* became gradually reinterpreted and reread as an identifying slogan. And much the same complexity of origin (and use) underlies their alternative titles, the Cambridge Group or Cambridge School. These are sometimes deployed as convenient synonyms for the Ritualists; sometimes they seem to be the precursors of the other term; on still other occasions, they are used as a means of retaining the idea of a "group," while weakening the link with any particular theoretical position on the role of ritual.[18]

What *is* clear is that Cambridge Ritualism has become a thriving scholarly industry, spawning books, articles, and conferences: *The Cambridge Ritualists Reconsidered* (proceedings of "The Cambridge Ritualists: An International Colloquium,"

April 27–30, 1989, at the University of Illinois, Urbana-Champaign);[19] *The Cambridge Ritualists: An Annotated Bibliography;*[20] "Some Letters of the Cambridge Ritualists";[21] *The Myth and Ritual School: J. G. Frazer and the Cambridge Ritualists;*[22] and so on. Much of this scholarly energy has, in fact, been devoted to deciding who was, or was not, to count as a member of the group. "Clarity departs," writes Robert Ackerman, "when one considers whether to regard A. B. Cook as a full fourth 'member' of the group. I count him as such, but I recognize that reasonable people can differ on this . . . Two others, A. W. Verrall and J. G. Frazer, were never members but in different ways were significant intellectual presences."[23] Shelley Arlen has similar problems, choosing to see Harrison, Murray, and Cornford as "the closely knit group," while "Cook's role in the Ritualist group was more subtle."[24]

The reason why "reasonable people can differ" is, as I have already suggested, that there never was such a group in the terms that Ackerman and others imply; these Cambridge ritualists (small *r*) were never, and certainly never called themselves *"the Cambridge Ritualists."* There was simply no club for them to be members of. In emphasizing this point I am not, of course, arguing that it is necessarily illegitimate to categorize these writers in terms they would not have dreamed of themselves. Just because *they* didn't write under the banner of Ritualism, doesn't necessarily mean that *we* shouldn't use the word. Intellectual and artistic movements have regularly (and often usefully—think of mannerism) been identified retrospectively. Historians have an obligation to use their hindsight to do precisely that: to identify structures, allegiances, and common ways of thinking that would never have been apparent at the time. That is, after all, what history (the history of scholarship as much as any other variety) is *for.*

The problem is not so much with the modern invention of Ritualism, as with how that category is put to work once invented, and particularly with the constant slide in most modern discussions from Ritualism *as an intellectual process* (as *ideas*—in the air, debated over tea and dinner, reargued, refuted, and refined) to Ritualists *as a group of individuals* with a shared intellectual program and a common manifesto. Of course, these boundaries will always be slippery. It is impossible, now as much as ever, to know exactly what makes the difference between academic collegiality (sharing coffee breaks, swapping notes and drafts) and being members of a "movement," between being (just) friends and being written into the history of scholarship forever labeled as such. You need only reflect for a moment on how our own academic practice and politics might eventually be corralled into the intellectual history of the late twentieth century to see the point. For we know *as actors* what we often enough choose to forget *as historians:* that allegiances (and patronage) are crosscut; that shared theories do not necessarily make a "movement"; that intellectual and personal harmony sometimes are (but are sometimes not) coterminous.[25] In the case of Ritualism, to talk so consistently, as modern scholars do, of "membership" and "group" glibly concretizes and personalizes the fleeting, complicated, overlapping intellectual processes and relationships that (if anything) constitute the "movement," at Cambridge or elsewhere. It is to turn the history of ideas into biography and into a series of biographical puzzles, and at the same time it risks turning biography (with all its necessary untidiness, its shifting and contested categories) into the history of a single idea.

But rather than simply dismiss it, I want to explore the myth of the Ritualists a little further: first (and briefly) by looking at the "evidence" that seems to sustain the idea of a close, intimate, and defined group of scholars working under the same intellectual banner, then by following some of the implications of this construction for how the life of Jane Harrsion is written—whom and what it must exclude.

Although, as I stated so firmly, the so-called Cambridge Ritualists never referred to themselves as such, support for the idea of a Group (or, if you like, a School) has sometimes been drawn directly from the words of Gilbert Murray himself. "You are quite right in emphasizing the 'group,'" he wrote, "—Jane, FMC, me and, I think, A. B. Cook. She had the power of making us feel that we were all working in common and not considering who should have credit for what."[26] On another occasion, he writes:

> We were a group, and we did help one another very much, but I am not sure that your catalogue of the contributions each of us made is much to the point. About the Group: do you remember what I said about Jane always looking out for the religion—or new light on religion—that was behind a ritual or an art form etc. Well, I think that was common to the Group and was what annoyed the 'sound scholars' so much. We were—perhaps foolishly—young. We expected to find a great light which our elders had not seen. FMC was always looking for it in his Pre-Socratics, and finding it; I was the same in Euripides; JEH was doing it everywhere. We all wanted to see what things 'really meant'; we were not content with merely construing or cataloguing them. ABC was a great help to us, but not one of us. I think my successor here, E. R. Dodds, is of our sort.[27]

These passages, in Murray's hand, serve as ammunition in many of the debates about the Ritualists' membership: Cook in or out? Well, half in, but not fully paid up, "a great help . . . but not one of us." However, quoted at length (which they are usually not), they undermine, rather than support, the fiction of the Ritualist club. Murray is certainly claiming a shared outlook, but it is hardly based on ritual. It's the youthful radicalism of a bunch of like-minded friends that he celebrates, not any party line about the priority of ritual over myth. That is, of course, how E. R. Dodds gets in on the act ("our sort") and how the much more serious and agressively scholarly ABC doesn't (quite). Dodds had nothing whatsoever to do with theories of ritual and myth, and even less to do with Harrison, Cornford, and Cook. But he was Murray's successor at Oxford, a man

Murray liked and equally a champion of radical causes inside and outside Classics—someone he could see as a fellow traveler.[28]

Murray is also writing with very long hindsight, as the inclusion of the much younger Dodds in his roll of honor hints. In fact these words are drawn from letters Murray wrote in the 1950s when he was nearly ninety (which may explain his stress on the youthfulness of the group; Harrison was, after all, fifty by the time she got to know Murray). Far from contemporary comments on his relations with Cornford and Harrison, these are the musings of a very old man about the now distant past. Nor are they unprompted: both these passages are drawn from letters to Jessie Stewart, Harrison's first biographer. They are responses to her sending him a draft chapter entitled "The Group" (it finally appeared under the title "A Triad of Scholars"), in which she argued for "a close mental intimacy . . . between Jane and her two scholar friends"—with "Jane" of course at the center, pulling the strings. Though she puts little emphasis on Ritualism as such, she certainly envisages a collaborative project under Harrison's direction (she writes of her "assigning tasks" to the others).[29] What did Murray think of this analysis, she wanted to know. Could she conscript him in its support?

Broadly speaking, as we have seen, he was happy to go along with the idea. Indeed, even if it had not been put into his head, he *might* have put it in very much those terms himself; we do not know. All the same, very shortly afterward a friend wrote to Stewart, in another context, reminding her of Murray's suggestibility: "He is very old and can't be bothered and agrees to almost everything that is expected of him."[30] It is hard not to suspect that, bombarded with letters, queries, and draft chapters from an enthusiastic biographer of a friend who had been dead for twenty-five years, Murray found it easiest to go along with it all, politely adding a few personal reminiscences. Were you a "Group"? she demanded. Whatever that meant (and it could have meant many things), how could he have said no?

I shall return in the next chapter to the construction of Jessie

Stewart's biography of Harrison, to her vested interest in the Harrison legacy, and to her conflict with her rival biographer, Harrison's pupil and friend Hope Mirrlees. For the moment, let me suggest that it was Stewart, writing in the 1950s—albeit enlisting the compliant support of grand old Murray—who first chose to turn the productive encounters of Harrison and friends into a much more formal "group of which Jane was the forerunner in age and inspiration." It only waited for a theoretical gloss (in the form of ritualism reinterpreted as "Ritualism") for a fully fledged academic movement to be invented.

We may choose, then, to doubt the *reality* of the Cambridge Ritualists (at least in the strongly defined sense in which the term is normally used). Nonetheless, real or not, the Ritualist movement has come to provide the context for assessing the importance of Jane Harrison and the development of her writing. It is not only the heroizing Stewart who has placed her at the center of this particular stage, pulling the strings of Murray, Cornford, and (maybe) Cook. Gender here has worked to Harrison's posthumous advantage. We might have predicted quite the reverse: that among the serious business of male scholarship, Harrison would have been represented as the eccentric old dear who made the tea while Murray and Cornford got on with the men's business of *thinking;* that she would have been written out of the intellectual story in the same way that Rosalind Franklin is written out of the discovery of (Crick and Watson's) DNA.[31] True, we find some blustering from the likes of L. R. Farnell, who found "the writings of Jane Harrison, the leading woman scholar of the time . . . marred by a spirit of feminist propaganda,"[32] and even Lloyd-Jones occasionally trivializes her female susceptibility to "seductive theories," regretting how "the light-heartedness and playfulness that make her letters to Gilbert Murray so delightful could spill over into silliness and sentimentality."[33] But generally, Harrison, as a woman among men, is inescapably made to stand "at the heart of the group (in more than one sense)," and it is through her, and her relationships and entanglements with the others, that modern critics articulate the structure of the group as a Group.[34] For better or worse, for supporters and critics, it is she who defines Ritualism; she is the social and the intellectual driving force behind the whole enterprise, "the acknowledged leader of the Group,"[35] "the undisputed center of the triad."[36]

And it is Ritualism (or so it easily seems to follow) that defines her—and all too "naturally" turns the study of Harrison into a Ritualist teleology: How can you plot the growth of Ritualism through her work? How far can you spot the seeds of future Ritualism in this or that piece of *juvenilia?* When did she become a Ritualist?

Inevitably, all kinds of genealogies are canvassed. Had she read Robertson Smith's *Religion of the Semites,* with its emphasis on "ritual institutions"? And if so, when? Or was she already working along Ritualist lines by the time Robertson Smith's book appeared?[37] And so on. But the answer to the question of when exactly it was that she "became a Ritualist" has often focused on the traces of her argument with D. S. MacColl. As we saw in Chapter 5, MacColl wrote her a letter early in 1887 sharply criticizing her flamboyant lecturing style. The immediate result was an emotional recantation on her part, extravagant pledges to mend her ways—followed by an almost instant return to just what she had been doing before: the power dressing, the histrionic voice, and the showy audiovisual aids. But the letter (not to mention the arguments that presumably followed it) contained other criticisms too, which were aimed at Harrison's whole approach to the history of art. The "MacColl incident" was, in the words of one of the standard accounts of Harrison's early career, "the watershed after which everything is new and different." Up to that point she had been committed to an "aesthetic" approach to the visual arts, to Platonic Ideality and to an admiration for the classical perfection of the age of Pheidias.

Then came a complete academic change of direction, as she turned increasingly, under his influence, to the origins of Greek culture and to the study of folklore, religion, anthropology, and ritual. It was nothing less than an academic rebirth—into Ritualism; "a *rite de passage,* a death and rebirth, which she would come to understand in *Themis* as the paradigmatic Greek religious ritual." *Themis,* of course, was still fifteen years away. But significantly (so this story goes), just three years after MacColl's intervention, in 1890, she published *Mythology and Monuments of Ancient Athens,* with its famous phrase about *"ritual practice misunderstood":* it was "the first book of the Cambridge Ritualists."[38]

Scratch the surface of this tidy account of Harrison's Ritualist conversion, and you will find it a good deal less tidy than it seems at first sight. Even the most enthusiastic modern historians of Ritualism recognize the slight awkwardness of making *Mythology and Monuments* "the first book of the Cambridge Ritualists,"—for in 1890 Harrison had neither moved back to Cambridge nor, so far as we know, even met Murray or Cook (still less Cornford, who was only sixteen at the time).[39] Besides, we saw in Chapter 6 that MacColl was not the first person to attack Harrison's theory of art; the previous year Vernon Lee had fired off her attack (via Charles Newton in the first place; later, and more successfully, via Eugénie Sellers) on *Introductory Studies,* taking issue—like MacColl—with its oozing Platonism. If there is a shift in Harrison's approach around this period, it was not simply the result of the intervention of a single critic in a single letter.

But was there a decisive shift at all? That turns out to be a trickier question than it seems. It is much harder to demonstrate a change of attitude and approach than the usual neat stories of intellectual development would have us believe, much harder to know how to recognize an intellectual change (or continuity, for that matter) than we would perhaps like to imagine. It is certainly the case that some of Harrison's early writing strikes a pose quite different from the anthropological tone of her later years. In 1884, for example, our soon-to-be champion of primitive Greece had this to say of the new Cambridge collection of plaster casts of ancient sculpture, which were temporarily sharing their gallery with some exotic ethnographica: "There is, or should be, a limit even to the modern mania for *origines*. A mere accident of space has placed under one roof with the Greek gods and goddesses a collection of prehistoric and anthropological specimens . . . I do hope . . . that no unfortunate undergraduate will think himself bound to begin his studies in Greek art with a course of Fiji islanders."[40] It is also true that *Mythology and Monuments* does offer what we may take as a clear Ritualist sound bite, the first she ever coined—at any rate in so uncompromising a form. If you are searching for the beginning of (Jane Harrison's) Ritualism, this is not an implausible choice.

Yet attentive readers of her very first book, *Myths of the Odyssey in Art and Literature,* can make an equally good case for pushing the origins of her interest in mythology and ritual a good deal further back—to the very beginning of her career, before ever MacColl or Vernon Lee came on the scene. Never mind the gushing references to "pure taste" and "well-balanced emotion" as the rewards of careful archaeological study.[41] Here already, in 1882, are clear glimpses of several of the distinctive hallmarks of her later work: an interest in the history and development of myth, and a commitment to seeing visual images as a medium for the *construction* of myth (it is a crucial—and disconcertingly modern—tenet of *Myths of the Odyssey* that vase painting does not merely illustrate the mythic narratives of literature but itself plays an active role in mythic production: "We shall see again and again that the ancient artist was no *illustrator* in the modern sense of the term."[42]). She even occasionally betrays a sense of the ritual origins of a variety of Greek cultural forms (as when she relates vase images of women on swings to the rituals of the Attic festival Aiora[43]). Conversely, those who suggest that Harrison moved away from her highly aesthetic approach to art in the late 1880s under the direct inspiration of MacColl must be surprised to discover that the book she coauthored with MacColl in 1894, *Greek Vase Paintings,* is the most explicitly *aesthetic* book she ever wrote: "An art so perfect as that of the best Greek vases can never be stationary long," enthused MacColl in his part of the introduction; this is a far cry from the voice that reputedly advised Jane Harrison to give up enthusing and get down to comparative folklore (and so on to Ritualism).[44] Meanwhile, as late as 1912, in the Introduction to her most anthropological *Themis,* Harrison herself (whose interest in the primitive was always more theoretical than practical) takes a sideswipe at "savages" who "save for their reverent, totemistic attitude towards animals, weary and disgust me, though perforce I spend long hours in reading of their tedious doings."[45] How ironically she meant this, we can only guess.[46]

You can play endlessly with continuities and discontinuities in the work of Jane Harrison (as in the work of almost any scholar). Is, for example, the notorious *Introductory Studies* really the high point of her ("preconversion") aestheticism, as most modern critics (not to mention Lee and MacColl) have seen it? Well, yes—if you go by the main chapter on the classical genius of Pheidias, and by her expressed aims laid out in the Preface: to explain "why from the contemplation of Greek art . . . we derive not merely an impression of the senses, but also a satisfaction that abides and an impulse to growth, moral and intellectual"; "to express this secret of the beauty and permanent vitality of Greek work."[47] But must it not strike us, then, as rather odd that a good half of the book is devoted to the art of Egypt, Assyria, and Phoenicia? Is that merely for contrast—to demonstrate even more clearly the abiding genius of the Greeks, by comparison with their Eastern predecessors? Is it even more simply a reflection of the balance of the British Museum collections, on which the book was based? Or is this already a sign of her interest in origins, the beginning of a trend that would develop in *Prolegomena* and *Themis* into a preoccupation with what came before (as she was then to see it) the lifeless perfection of classicism? But at the same time, maybe she did not abandon "classicism" quite so radically as we are led to believe. When she wrote in the *Edinburgh Review* of 1897 of the "qualities which we expect from Greeks" as "dignity, restraint, good taste" and referred to "the pure Hellenic strain, with its instinct for rationalism," had she forgotten that she was, by then, well on the road to being a Ritualist, with a healthy distrust for the shimmering surface of Greek rationalism?[48] Was this simply a hurried piece of writing in which she slipped thoughtlessly back to her earlier assumptions? Or did admiration of the Greek genius still seem an appropriate line to adopt on some occasions, for some audiences?

Of course, we can play these games endlessly. Personal intellectual histories *(lives in writing)* are never reducible to neat and straightforward teleologies. Writers can never entirely discard their old ideas. After all, books are there (and read) long after their authors may think they have changed their mind; and audiences demand to see the old favorites in print, to "hear" them again. The more famous (and the more read) you are, the harder it is to escape what you used to write. Besides, new ideas are always provisional, always being "tried out," testing the boundaries of their own implausibility (as when Harrison wonders about explaining the story of Don Juan as an attenuated fertility ritual[49]); and they always seem better, more appropriate, more convincing in some contexts than others. How you talk about Greek art (now or then) to the local Rotary Club is quite different from what you say at a professional seminar; what you write for a popular encyclopedia is radically different from what you write for an academic journal (at least, you would be a rhetorical failure if it were not). New ideas enlarge your repertoire; they don't necessarily change the tune. Ritualism, and Harrison's growing concern with primitive origins, added new players to her repertoire of arguments, but that is not to say that she always wrote, spoke, or thought in Ritualist mode.

Prizes in writing the *history* of scholarship, however, usually go to those who plot the Big Ideas, to those who chart the origin and growth of Grand Theory, its genealogy and influence—not to those who celebrate the untidiness, vacillations, and day-to-day provisionality of the (real) life of the mind. Most intellectual histories find it hard to incorporate the fact that many academics are influential precisely because of the conceptual *disorder* they leave in their wake. No surprise, then, that Harrison's intellectual story has been trapped in the (late twentieth-century) invention of Ritualism, which has in turn acted to occlude the many other factors at work in Harrison's ideas and writing. Obviously, Ritualism found no place for Mrs. Strong in the Harrison story; she was, after all, in the "wrong" subject and, for most of her life, the "wrong" town (not to mention the fact that she and Harrison finally parted company just after *Mythology and Monuments,* with its first clear Ritualist statement, appeared). But Ritualism has prompted some even more glaring omissions. It pays only lip service, for example, to Harrison the Durkheimian—even though an equally plausible (if, in my terms, equally crude) version of her intellectual development could be told as a story of her growing commitment to *social* and *sociological* theories of religion, prompted by her reading of Durkheim. It is instructive, in fact, as well as slightly disconcerting, to read the anthropologist Evans-Pritchard's account of Harrison, Murray, Cornford, and Cook. Never mentioning the words Ritualism or Ritualists at all, he discusses their work as a classic example of the influence of Durkheimian theory on English studies of religion.[50]

But there is another context for Harrison's work that is repeatedly overlooked: I, too, have been concentrating on Harrison among her *friends,* but this is to forget Harrison in her *Fac-*

ulty.[51] The Ritualist story, in other words, turns a willfully blind eye toward the institutional background of Ritualism, and particularly toward the focus and range of the new subject of archaeology as it was taught in Cambridge from the early 1880s to just after the Great War (when Harrison left Newnham for Paris). The prominence usually given to Harrison's argument with MacColl in 1887 and her supposed "conversion" to Ritualism implies a major shift in the subject matter of her work— from art history and archaeology to folklore and the history of religion. That is certainly a huge change of direction in our terms—in the terms of the territorial boundaries that have operated within British and American Classics since the Second World War. But if we stop for a moment to wonder what was meant by the discipline of classical archaeology in the late nineteenth and early twentieth centuries, we shall find that it was not then the major shift that it seems to us, and we shall also find that Harrison's apparently distinctive combination of interests (of ritual, archaeology, visual images, and religious theory) found a precursor, maybe indeed its origins, in the archaeology section of the Classical Tripos at Cambridge. It is worth taking a closer look at the detail.

After years of infighting, the Cambridge Classical Tripos was radically reformed in 1879. What had been a course (in Cambridge jargon) of just one "Part," testing little more than the student's ability to translate into, and out of, Latin and Greek, was now divided into two. Part I remained heavily linguistic; the optional Part II offered students the chance to take papers in the various subdisciplines of classical learning. For the first time (in what was called Section D of the new Part II) classical archaeology was on offer to Cambridge students as a major component of their degree. The precise content of the examination took some time to settle down, and the first few years of the new Tripos saw numerous minor changes in the scope of the archaeology papers. But overall this course looks strikingly different from what *we* would define as classical archaeology, and at the same time it is very close indeed to almost all the interests of Jane Harrison.[52]

The first year that the new archaeology examination was set (1883), there were five individual papers that students choosing this option were required to take: Paper 1 concentrated on the history of art; Paper 2 on history of religion ("Describe the election, duties, and dress of the *flamen* and *flaminica,*" asked one question; "Give an account [a] of the rites and ceremonies, and [b] of the myth, to which the above passage [Pseudo-Vergil, *Ciris,* 13–34] refers," demanded another); Paper 3 concentrated on two special sites (the Parthenon in Athens and the Forum Boarium in Rome); Paper 4 was concerned with the antiquities of everyday life ("Describe the different fashions of wearing the toga which prevailed at different periods of Roman history. Explain the term *umbo* and *balteus* as applied to the Roman toga."); finally, Paper 5 was a general essay on all subjects covered by Section D ("The relations of art to religion, and the influence exercised by one upon the other, in Greece between Ol.70 and Ol.90: with especial reference to the art of Pheidias"). By the next year, the individual papers had been given specific titles: "History of Art," "Mythology and Religious Usage," "Olympia and the Palatine" (the special sites had changed), "Antiquities," plus the final general essay. And so it went on, with some fine-tuning: significantly perhaps for us, in 1888 Paper 2 was given the new title "Mythology and Ritual," and it changed again in 1890 to "Myth, Ritual and Religion."

The questions that were asked (and so, we presume, the teaching through the year) matched these titles. "Compare the cults of the Greek chthonian and celestial deities" and "How far is it possible to distinguish between the religious rituals of the Homeric poems, and those of historical Greece?" ran two of the questions in "Mythology and Ritual" in 1888; in the same year one of the topics for the general essay was "Traces of Totemism

in Greek legend and custom." Three years later, in 1891, the essay paper gave the undergraduates the option of writing on "The
stage in the Greek and Roman theatre at various periods," which
must have prompted a good deal of heated argument against (or
possibly for) Dörpfeld and his female "partizans."

The main point I am making here is very simple. Harrison's
supposed conversion from art to the history of religion (a conversion we have already had cause to question) simply does not
make sense in the context of late nineteenth-century subject
definitions—which (at least in Cambridge) saw religion, mythology, art, and antiquities as constituent parts of the same
subdiscipline, classical archaeology. This was no "watershed" after which "everything was new" but an exploration around different aspects of the same subject. It is also hard not to be struck
by the prominence of ritual in these archaeology papers. There
may be no explicit reference here to the *priority* of ritual in explanations of myth, there may be no examination question that implies a specifically Ritualist agenda in that sense, but Cambridge
classical teaching was already explicitly putting myth and ritual
side by side in 1888; it was not a big step to suggest that ritual
came *before* myth. Paradoxically, perhaps, Ritualism as an idea
owed its origins to the apparatus of Classical Tripos and the institutions of the Cambridge Faculty as much as it did to any
dangerous feminism on Harrison's part or the self-conscious (and
self-congratulatory) radicalism of Murray.

It is now very hard to know exactly whose influence lay behind the particular definition of classical archaeology adopted at
Cambridge (it is interesting to find J. G. Frazer's name among
the first group of examiners, but there is no reason whatsoever to
suppose that he had anything to do with designing the course).
It was not, in any case, an especially maverick definition for a period that could see the purpose of archaeology as "to collect, to
classify, and to interpret all the evidence of man's history not already incorporated in Printed Literature." Those, in fact, are the

words of (none other than) Charles Newton, from the opening pages of his once famous, but now largely forgotten, essay "On the Study of Archaeology"; first delivered as a lecture in Oxford in 1850, it should count as one of the inaugural moments for the academic discipline of archaeology in England.[53] Newton went on to discuss the different spheres that properly belonged to archaeological endeavor, from the history of hieroglyphics to the customs "still surviving among the peasantry in remote districts," from Christian iconography to the history of carpentry. For the archaeologist's motto, he proposes: "HOMO SUM, HUMANI NIHIL A ME ALIENUM PUTO."[54] This amounts to the history of culture in its broadest sense. And it is as the history of *classical culture in its broadest sense* that archaeology was first established in the Cambridge Classical Tripos.

When Harrison returned to Cambridge from London in 1898, it was the archaeological option in Section D of the Tripos that she taught. Although she herself had not taken these papers when she was a student (they were first devised in precisely the year, 1879, in which she finished her course at Newnham), she would almost certainly have been familiar with the debates about the new range of subjects that were to be taught (and specifically about the question of what was to count as "archaeology"). Then, when she went to London, it was with Charles Newton and his all-encompassing "cultural" view of the subject that she first systematically encountered archaeology. Even if later (as we have seen) she was to credit her archaeological training to her German masters, it was Newton's (and Cambridge's) distinctively *British* understanding of archaeological knowledge that was to frame almost all her subsequent work—from ritual to vase painting, Pheidias to totemism. Harrison the Archaeologist captures the historical specificity of her work so much better than Harrison the Ritualist.

CHAPTER NINE

Pandora's Box

Every biographer of Jane Harrison (and so every student of Ritualism) is obliged sooner or later to visit the Archive of Newnham College, where most of the surviving "raw material" on the life of Harrison is preserved. In the course of this book I have tried to offer alternative views of Harrison, using Eugénie Sellers, in particular, to open up a perspective from London (via Girton). Even so, the footnotes still contain more references to the Harrison Papers at Newnham than to any other single source of information. Inevitably. But this material at Newnham—to be precise, twenty-five boxes of different shapes and sizes labeled "Harrison"—ought to seem more puzzling and to raise more questions than it usually does. It is, in fact, much less raw than most investigators ever (let themselves) imagine. For what we call the Harrison Papers contains nothing at all left, given, assembled, or bequeathed by Jane Harrison herself. Harrison, remember, destroyed her papers when she left Cambridge in 1922. It was a histrionic bonfire, maybe (which surely didn't destroy quite the "all" that the story suggests; no one ever destroys *all* their papers), and it was certainly another form of self-dramatizing display. But it partly explains the peculiar and tricky character of the documents assembled under her name. These comprise a series of donations from Harrison's friends, colleagues, and pupils, of letters, papers, and mementoes. Some were written by Harrison herself (notably the collection of letters to Gilbert Murray, which—as we shall see—formed the basis of Jessie Stewart's *Jane Ellen Harrison: A Portrait from Letters*); many others are more tangential, but deemed by their donors to have some connection with J. E. H. All were gratefully accepted by a young Cambridge college looking for an iconic heroine. No college, least of all Newnham (busy throughout the first half of the twentieth century inventing its own history and mythology) could afford to pass up the reflected glamour of Jane Ellen Harrison.

Most of the papers in the collection are less concerned with Harrison herself than with the construction of "Jane Harrison" as a biographical subject and with competing claims to authority over her memory. Who is to control the Harrison tradition? Which of her friends, letter after letter insistently disputes, can be trusted to write the biography? Who has the nerve? ("I - *couldn't do justice* to the life without writing about very intimate things which Jane wished forgotten.") Or who might be cajoled into writing? ("Would V. de Bunsen take it on, in part or in whole?") And who must be stopped? ("I should have to know a great deal about her [Lady Trudy Bliss] before allowing her to have a finger in the pie.")[1] It is a striking illustration of the complexities of power at work around the biographical subject, who (even dead) is appealed to as the ultimate source of biographical authority ("Jane would simply have *loathed* it"[2]) but is meanwhile dismembered (and reinvented) in the competition for authority among those proposing rival versions of her life.

The Harrison Papers, then, form an archive already tinged by postmodernism, irrevocably committed to the decentering of any unitary subject—a multiplicity of biographical narratives that are made visible in the very urgency of their policing and in the cacophony of voices claiming themselves to be the single authorized source. But within that cacophany we can see the domi-

nance of two women (and, as I shall show, one of them in particular) who are the archive's creators, whose versions of Harrison's
life their archive is effectively designed to impose on all who
consult it, and whose own biographies (as I shall now briefly
sketch them) are also embedded in the collection. It is not "raw"
material at all, or only in the very limited sense that most of it
remains unpublished.

The two women are Jessie Stewart and Hope Mirrlees, both
close friends of Harrison herself. Stewart (born Jessie Crum) was
a student at Newnham between 1897 and 1901. Her undergraduate career started inauspiciously, with an undistinguished
"Second Class (third divison)" in Part I of the Classical Tripos
(presumably, like Eugénie Sellers and many women students at
the time, she was defeated by the translation tests in Part I), but
she was rescued by Harrison (who had returned to the college in
1898), took up classsical archaeology for Part II, and toured
Greece with Harrison over Easter in 1901. It was the kind of
personal tuition that most students (even then, when hand-
picked pupils might expect to be nurtured in ways inconceivable now) could only have dreamed of: a week's guided tour
round Athens with Harrison, then on to Dörpfeld's *Peloponnes-
Reise* (still with Harrison, but Hilda Lorimer came too, just
graduated from Girton and now a student at the British School
at Athens[3]), and all the time there was plenty of opportunity to
quiz these luminaries (with whom she was now on first-name
terms) about what she was seeing ("Interviewed Wilhem [i.e.,
Dörpfeld] . . . about a relief," she wrote in her travel diary, "J.
wants it to show transformation of hero into Dionysus.") Unsurprisingly, perhaps, she finished with a First in her summer examinations: "my first First," as Harrison called her, neatly sharing the intellectual honors between teacher and pupil.[4]

Miss Crum basked in this academic glory for only a short
while. Less than a year after her final exams, she married the
Reverend Hugh Stewart, then the chaplain of Trinity College

(who later moved to St. John's as Fellow and Dean, and was University Reader in French from 1922 till his death in 1944) (illustration 8). She still remained close to Harrison: they shared a Newnham and Cambridge social life; Stewart continued to make Harrison's lantern slides; while Harrison, ever ironically, negotiated her relations with Stewart's new family (she longed, she wrote after the birth of a baby, for "a sight of the mother—babies are all very well but mothers are very much better").[5] But they seem never to have been quite so close again as they had been during their trip to Greece and the triumphant success that followed it; Harrison, as we shall see, looked for a new favorite elsewhere. The rest of Stewart's life was filled with all those activities usually hidden and forgotten under the title "don's wife," like having (five) children, campaigning for women's suffrage, supporting her old college, "making cardboard armour for the Greek play,"[6] running the local music festival—and, of course, *biography*. As we shall see, the memory of her teacher was to become one of her lifetime projects. But that was not all. Between them, Jessie and Hugh Stewart played a major part in framing our vision of late nineteenth- and early twentieth-century Cambridge and its cast of characters. Hugh was instrumental in "orchestrating the legend" of (Professor of Latin) J. E. B. Mayor.[7] Jessie constructed the first book-length biography of Jane Harrison, and after his death, she turned her husband's life and *his* version of *their* Cambridge into the (carefully sorted) Stewart Papers, now deposited in the Cambridge University Library. The Stewarts wrote themselves into (local) history as Cambridge people; it will come as no surprise that Stewart's Harrison is written up as a *Newnham* don and a *Cambridge* celebrity.

Hope Mirrlees had also been at Newnham reading Classics, from 1910 to 1913. While growing up in Scotland ("descended from Scottish royalty on her mother's side," as she herself must have boasted[8]) she had originally planned a career in theater and

Fig. 8.   All dressed up, Hugh Stewart chats with Hope Mirrlees
at the Newnham College Jubilee party, 1921.

even begun a course at the Royal Academy of Dramatic Art—
but had soon given up acting to go to Cambridge and learn
Greek. This late start may explain why (like a number of students at that date, not necessarily the least able) she sat no formal Tripos exams; it certainly did not prevent her becoming the
next favorite of Jane Harrison. The world that Harrison and
Mirrlees shared at Newnham is one that is almost impossibly
hard for us to understand. The surviving notes and letters in the
Newnham Archive range from a brusquely businesslike style to
an archly intimate argot. On the one hand, Harrison arranges
teaching for Mirrlees and makes appointments for her to meet
her supervisors and to attend lectures, in the usual manner (now
as much as then) of the Director of Studies writing to her student. "Just to tell you," she jotted on a postcard at the end of one
university vacation, "that I shall not be back quite at the beginning of term. I suggest that you try Professor Housman on Horace—go the first time & see if you get anything from him."[9]
Even on the occasion of a broken engagement, Mirrlees received
a classic "teacher's" letter from Harrison: some conventional
words of good advice, quickly moving on to business as usual
and the reading she should be doing for next term. ("Thank you
for writing to tell me about yr engagement. I *am* relieved it is
ended—for tho' 'pedestrian love' is a good & great thing—it is
not quite enough I think on which to climb the steep stair of
marriage. Anyhow I am truly glad we shall have you at Newnham next autumn . . . We must scheme out a course of work before term begins—but for the present you have enough in the
Odyssey."[10])

On the other hand, many of the letters between Harrison and
Mirrlees adopt a quite different rhetorical style, constructing a
shared fantasy world populated by a variety of cuddly toys,
bears, and sea creatures. Harrison referred to herself as the "Elder
Walrus," to Mirrlees as the "Younger Walrus"; letters of invita-
tion, of condolence, of best wishes in illness were issued in the

name of "the Bear" (who lived in "the cave"; that is, Harrison's Newnham room)—"The Bear (his temperature is lower but he is still *very* weak) sends Mr. Velvet Brown with his compts [compliments] to stay with you till you are better," wrote Harrison to Mirrlees on one occasion, at the same time (presumably) as she sent her some new stuffed animal, "Mr. Velvet Brown," for company.[11] On another occasion Harrison, writing in the name of the Bear (this note, like several others, is signed with the pattern of the constellation Ursa Major) invites Mirrlees to join her for dinner and some student theatricals: "I desire that my young Wife [i.e., Mirrlees] do dine in Hall tomorrow with my elder Wife [Harrison] and go to the young ladies' Revue. I desire that my elder wife do not dragnet my younger wife the whole evening. She is *not* a comic cut she is my young Wife. Given in the Cave—in the presence of Mrs. Mutz and the Glass Horse."[12] It is now extremely difficult to reconstruct what kind of closeness the use of this extraordinary argot reveals, or conceals; impossible to know quite how strange (sinister, erotic, or merely "normal") it seemed to their other Newnham friends. (Were they *all* writing to each other like this? Did they read anything particular into Harrison's addressing her student in terms of conjugality, albeit obliquely, and through the mouth of a stuffed toy? Did they even know about it?[13]) But this was certainly the start of a continuing friendship that was to frame both their lives until Harrison's death in 1928. What kind of friendship, we shall discuss later.

When Mirrlees ceased to be a student at Newnham, she continued to live (more or less) with Harrison. She was intermittently resident in Cambridge between 1913 and the early 1920s, and also traveling. Just after leaving Newnham she went to France and Italy, for example, with Karin Costelloe, a college friend who was shortly to marry Adrian Stephen, brother of Virginia Woolf; through Karin's mother (the Mary Costelloe who had been part of the "aesthetic trio" tramping round Italian art galleries and had now married Berenson), she was probably introduced to Mrs. Strong at the British School at Rome.[14] In 1922 she and Harrison left Cambridge permanently, going first to Paris, where they had earlier spent some idiosyncratic working holidays (see ill. 9)[15]—then returning to London in 1925, where they shared a flat for the last years of Harrison's life, on Mecklenburgh Street on the edge of Bloomsbury. During this final period, Harrison (now in her seventies) and Mirrlees worked together on a translation of the Russian *Life of the Arch-Priest Avvakum,* a religious autobiography of a fanatical Russian nonconformist, as well as on an illustrated *Book of the Bear,* also a translation (of bear stories) from Russian.[16] (At this point it is hard not to feel some nostalgia for the writer of *Prolegomena* and *Themis*—impossible books that they are.) Meanwhile, in dedications, thanks, and acknowledgments they paraded their mutual debts, as publicly as the Ritualists had once done. In 1921 Harrison dedicated to Mirrlees her last book on Greek religion, *Epilegomena:* "To Hope. In remembrance of Spanish nights and days," referring—if to nothing more—to a shared Spanish holiday in 1920, followed (deliciously arcanely) by four lines of verse in Persian, on the purity of the human spirit when freed from the "dust of the body."[17] Mirrlees reciprocated in 1923 with the dedication of a novel: "To Jane Harrison. μάλιστα δέ τ' ἔκλυον αὐτοί." You would not have needed an immense knowledge of Greek to spot the reference here. It is a quotation from Homer's *Odyssey,* book 6, line 185. Odysseus, just after his arrival in Phaeacia, is speaking to Nausicaa, praying that she

---

Fig. 9. Jane Harrison and Hope Mirrlees in Paris, 1915. The photograph was sent as a postcard by Harrison to Gilbert Murray, July 2; it was taken, so she claims to Murray on the reverse, "hurriedly in the Tuilleries by a strolling bear." The message scrawled around the outside of the picture is in typical Harrison idiom, a story of her confrontation with French bureaucracy, full of multilingual puns and playfully obscure literary references.

I was living peacefully and - music-al with my pieces till I tried catling to you!

The official Báurpayos has a consuming passion for this photograph. In fact, as the 'Caveated Banquet' used to say kil re grise de mes bottines — small wonder! — see left-foot!

will one day receive her heart's desire, marriage: "For nothing is greater or better than this, when two people keep house together, man and wife, a great grief to their enemies and joy to their friends; μάλιστα δέ τ' ἔκλυον αὐτοί / while their own fame is unsurpassed." For "man and wife" read "Jane and Hope"?

Mirrlees was in her early forties when Harrison died in London, of leukemia; for the next fifty years (until her own death in 1978) she lived partly on the reputation of being Jane Harrison's closest companion and partly as a rather well-connected and avant-garde writer. She was in fact much closer to Bloomsbury and other intellectual scenes than a single visit to Europe with one of the Woolf's future in-laws would on its own suggest. Virginia Woolf's correspondence and diaries include some typically acid (though maybe insightful) glimpses of Mirrlees, at the same time suggesting quite a degree of closeness between them. In 1919, after Mirrlees had been to stay, Woolf wrote (in a mixture of spite and generosity): "Her stockings matched a wreath in her hair; every night they were differently coloured; powder fell about in flakes; and the scent was such we had to sit in the garden. Moreover, she knows Greek and Russian better than I do French." A few years later she summed up Mirrlees to Lady Cecil, in a similar (if marginally more generous vein): "She is her own heroine—capricious, exacting, exquisite, very learned and beautifully dressed."[18]

To see Hope Mirrlees only in the context of Jane Harrison, as the "daughter" Harrison found in later life,[19] as merely the obsessive hagiographer of her closest friend and teacher, is to underrate her. She is one of those writers forever on the brink of being "discovered" (in the 1990s as much as in the 1920s); the subject of enthusiastic reviews in all the right places, of critical appreciations that proclaim her talent ("What Joyce has done for Dublin and Eliot for London, Hope Mirrlees has done for Paris"[20]), she never quite makes it. But however we choose to judge her (and like all such forgotten writers, she is an uncomfortable challenge to the arbitrariness of literary fame—quite *how* good can we allow her to be?), her published work makes a difference to our understanding of her relationship with Harrison and her long-attempted life history of her friend.

Mirrlees's published writing includes poetry, fiction, fantasy, and biography (though not, of course, of Harrison). In 1919 the Woolfs' new Hogarth Press produced an elegant Bloomsbury-style edition of her self-consciously modernist poem *Paris*.[21] Crammed with different typefaces, variant line spacing, large and small capitals, prose and musical score interspersed with verse, it is an evocation of the city, much in the style of Joyce or Apollinaire:

> I want a holophrase
> NORD-SUD
> ZIG-ZAG
> LIONNOIR
> CACAO BLOOKER
> Black-figured vases in Etruscan tombs
> RUE DU BAC (DUBONNET)
> SOLFERINO (DUBONNET)
> CHAMBRE DES DEPUTES
> Brekekekek coax coax we are passing under the Seine
> DUBONNET

run the first few lines of the book of some twenty elegant pages. A poetic cityscape. But not just any city. As I have already noted, Paris in the early years of the twentieth century was the lesbian capital of the Western world ("Paris Lesbos," as it was affectionately known). It was a city whose very name could be a shorthand for sapphism; the city of Gertrude Stein, Natalie Barney, Una Troubridge, Alice B. Toklas—and later, we shall wonder, of Jane Harrison and Hope Mirrlees.[22] Significantly, the first line of the poem ("I want a holophrase") is an allusion to Harrison's discussion of early language in *Themis,* while its end is marked by the very same diagram of the constellation—Ursa Major, the Bear (aka the Big Dipper)—that signed off several of the notes and letters written by Harrison to Mirrlees, "in the name of the Bear."[23]

If any readers detected a lesbian resonance in Mirrlees's poem (as did Woolf herself, who called it "very obscure, indecent and brilliant"[24]), they would have found ample confirmation of their suspicions in her first novel, published in the same year: *Madeleine: One of Love's Jansenists.* It tells the story of a young girl (Madeleine) living in Paris in the seventeeth century and obsessed by the figure of the famous Mademoiselle de Scudéry, self-styled sapphist, biographer of Sappho, and center of a renowned literary salon.[25] In the course of the book Madeleine rejects her young lover Jacques, though in the end she is horribly disillusioned with her female idol. Uncompromisingly difficult (and much more impenetrable than my brief summary suggests), it turns on the nature of desire, the conflict between "the meaningless drip of circumstances" in the outer world and the *reality* (paradoxically) of the inner world of fantasy. Virginia Woolf privately was unimpressed and, one suspects, found it baffling (except that it was "all sapphism . . . Jane and herself"[26]) but still managed to give it a low-key, pat-on-the-back review in the *Times Literary Supplement:* "It is well worth while to read this difficult and interesting novel."[27]

Two other novels quickly followed. *The Counterplot,* published in 1923 (dedicated to Jane Harrison), is a study of the life of a woman of "literary temperament" within an upper-class family. Again issues of Life, Art, and Representation dominate; this time she uses the device of a "play within a novel" to capture the "subconscious desires" of her heroine—the play (which fills the last hundred pages of the book) performing "the function that Freud ascribes to dreams."[28] And in 1926 came *Lud-in-the-Mist,* a strange fantasy of magic and faeries—yet again testing the boundaries of imagination and reality (with a good deal of Platonic allegory taken for granted). After Harrison's death, this flow of books slows down. There are a few more poems published (now much more "traditional"[29]) and, in 1962, a stylishly flamboyant biography: *A Fly in Amber: Being an Extravagant Biography of the Romantic Antiquary Sir Robert Bruce Cotton.* The biography she never managed to write of Harrison.

The Foreword to *A Fly in Amber* hints at some of her other literary connections. She warmly thanks Mr. T. S. Eliot "who has read three redactions of the book (he calls it 'Penelope's web'!) and without whose encouragement I might have lacked the heart to finish it." Conventional enough gratitude toward an editor, perhaps, but the words both reveal and disguise a much closer friendship between Eliot and Mirrlees. Having met him through Virginia Woolf, she had been friends with Eliot since the time of his first marriage ("one of the few of Eliot's friends who took trouble with Vivienne"[30]), and in 1940 Eliot moved in to lodge for the rest of the war with Mirrlees, her mother, and her aunt (in Woolf's words, "domesticating with Hope Mirrlees: spiritually, of course"[31]). Eliot became a household pet, ingratiated himself with the aunt by smuggling her a few cigarettes (she was not allowed to smoke), and sat down to get on with the *Four Quartets.* Over dinner he must have been treated to a fund of stories about Jane Harrison, her wit, charm, greatness, and intellectual brilliance; hardly a surprise, then, that we find him prominently listed among famous admirers of Harrison's work—he probably didn't have much option.[32]

Friend of the Woolfs and Eliot, walk-on player in many of the literary memoirs of the period (we shall see shortly how she enters those of Antony Powell). It is only a hair's breadth, the arbitrariness of biographical boundaries, that keeps her from "the Bloomsbury Group" or its close penumbra; in the twenties in Paris and London, Harrison and Mirrlees could have seemed a perfect (or perfectly plausible) Bloomsbury pair.

*　　*　　*

To return now to the Harrison Papers. The majority of these were collected and given to the Newnham College Archive by either Stewart or Mirrlees; very many of the "Harrison" documents are in fact *their* letters, written by them or to them, and often from one to the other; literally hundreds tell the complicated thirty-year story of the attempts and counterattempts by each of them to write a biography of Harrison. It is, as we shall now see, a story of competition, hommage, enthusiasm, rebuttal, perseverance, bad temper, and bad faith. It is hard not to sympathize with both Mirrlees and Stewart as they discover the duplicity, the inactivity and disloyalty of the other; and as they both discover the horrible truth—that most of the world (even most of the world *in Cambridge*) was not half so interested in Harrison, nor half so eagerly awaiting her biography, as they were themselves. At the same time, as you explore box after box of letters (alternating outrage, indignation, and embarrassing optimism about the success of their projects), it is hard not to find all these squabbles faintly and repetitively absurd. The overcommitment of both these women, for over half their lives, and with no apparent trace of humor about the whole enterprise, seems almost demeaning. Were it not for the fact that the Harrison mythology is embedded in, and largely formed by, these long and tortuous squabbles, we would be tempted to pass them quickly by. In what now follows, summarizing thirty years of biographical activity in just a few pages, I try to capture something of its obsessive (and slightly ludicrous) spirit.

The story starts very soon after Harrison's death, when Mirrlees proclaimed her intention to write her friend's life.[33] But by the early 1930s, this had already become a joint enterprise between Mirrlees (taking the "personal" side of Harrison's life) and Stewart (dealing with the "intellectual" history). To begin with, their letters are touchingly optimistic. In the spring of 1932 Mirrlees wrote confidently of the arrangements: "I feel so relieved and pleased about Jane's 'Life'—it's a lovely plan,"[34] and only a few months later some actual work on the project was in prospect: "Suddenly this morning," wrote Mirrlees to Stewart just after Christmas 1932, "I decided to put my other book aside & start right off on Jane's—& I am now full of it! . . . I'll start on the 'frame' of her life, if you will do her writings & then we can compare notes—don't you think that will be best."[35]

But the optimism did not last long. Their first problems arose over Harrison's letters. True, the contents of her own filing cabinets had been obliterated on her departure from Cambridge (though Mirrlees doesn't miss the chance of gaining the advantage and pointing out that Harrison had actually shown her most of the material as it was being destroyed: "At the time that she was tearing everything up she used to show me anything she thought would amuse me"[36]). But there were still all her letters to Gilbert Murray, which he (or rather his wife) had kept safely stored away. It was these that prompted the first signs of dispute. Murray himself was quite happy that Mirrlees and Stewart should use them in any way they wished. At first, they were obviously a great help, passed back and forth between the two writers: "I am finding them invaluable for the Life—they throw so much psychological light and bring her back so. I am not finished with the batch you sent."[37] But how exactly were they to be used? Murray's wife had her doubts about publishing them *in extenso,* as did Mirrlees; not quite so sickeningly coy as the "Walrus" letters, they were nevertheless full of pet names, private jokes, and bizarre academic enthusiasms—and there was a strong chance that they would look very silly if exposed to public view. ("I am beginning to understand Lady Mary's point of view—people would giggle."[38]) Besides, no one could quite decide what format would be the best for publishing them. Should they be kept entirely separate from Mirrlees's narrative of Harrison's life and given to Stewart to dress up as a piece of academic history? ("I told him *you* would edit them with an archaeological Introduction."[39]) Or did they deserve to be included in the main story? Everyone had a slightly different, and firmly held, view. ("Professor Cornford is strongly opposed to two volumes—he thinks the letters should be incorporated in the Life."[40])

Meanwhile, of course, the letters themselves were becoming a terrible liability, a precious cargo that had to be guarded not only against enemy action (in fact, they went to Mirrlees's solicitor and the safekeeping of a bank for much of the war) but also against all kinds of other, more mundane losses, which were the all too likely consequences of their being handed round from author to author. ("I don't understand how it can have happened," flapped Mirrlees over a group of letters that had apparently gone astray, "I have never looked at the letters since Prof. Murray first lent them to me after Jane's death."[41]) When Stewart did finally publish her selection of these letters in 1959 in *Jane Ellen Harrison: A Portrait from Letters,* it was (as she remarked in the Preface) twenty-five years since she had first got her hands on them— twenty-five years of grumbling dispute.

Nonetheless some work on the joint project continued through the thirties, or at least the brave words continued: "At present I am redoing some of the nineteenth century part—*before* her return to Cambridge. Then I shall launch out on the years covered by the letters."[42] It wasn't until 1943 that there was the first major explosion. On March 17, 1943, Victoria de Bunsen (another of Harrison's first generation of Newnham students and—as the *College Register* mysteriously records her—"traveller to Babylon") wrote to Stewart as follows: "Hope M. suddenly turned up here [illegible] all in a *furore* of excitement and bluster—& dumped *on me!* the notebooks in which she had collected the information about Jane (in the first few months I imagine after her death). She announced she wished to 'wash her hands of it.'"[43] Not *entirely* wash her hands of it, as it turned out. Within a fortnight she was writing to de Bunsen to beg the return of the notebooks ("In the mean time, I think I had better have my own materials back again. They are very *intime* & I think I had better have them back."[44]) But not before the other Harrison friends had had time to chew over the story and to wonder what Mirrlees had actually been doing for the last decade or so: "What an amazing creature Hope is! Why didn't she give in her hand long ago instead of waiting 16 years? Hasn't she written *any*thing? I thought she did at least make a beginning."[45]

Stewart, for her part, obviously decided to patch up some sort of compromise with Mirrlees. But by now Mirrlees was greeting any suggestion for completing the work with quite inappropriate solemnity and suspicion, seeing treachery in every change, however inadvertent it might have been. At the end of August 1943, she sent to Stewart what amounted to a summary of negotiations up to that point, in a distinctly formal tone. It all reads more like international diplomacy than correspondence between two friends interested in producing a biography of their teacher—who had been dead now for fifteen years:

> I was much interested in your letter giving me an account of your new plan. The alternatives that you & I discussed together were, if I remember right, as follows:
>
> (1) That G.M. [Gilbert Murray] should do the whole thing
>
> (2) That G.M. should write a substantive account of her work, & that I should do the life
>
> (3) That I should do the whole thing & that you should help me in the collecting & elucidating of the material for the part about her work. But that we should not start till I had finished the book I am working on at present.
>
> Therefore, as I say, what you suggest is a *new* plan. But I think it is a good one . . . Certainly an account of the work during her great period, illustrated by her letters to G.M, & related to what other scholars were doing in the same and kindred subjects would make a most interesting & valuable book. And if this is what you intend to do, you most certainly have my 'blessing'. *No-one* is more suited to the task than you are.[46]

From this point on, Stewart pressed ahead with different versions of her "new plan" to build some kind of memoir around the Murray letters (this was essentially the germ of the book that was to appear in 1959). Mirrlees's recurring theme, by contrast, was that only she was qualified to write about Harrison *as a person*—and yet that was a subject of such intimacy that she could not possibly put pen to (public) paper (or at least not yet). "The problem of what to say & what to leave out," she mused in the midst of the negotiations in 1943, "is a very difficult one. And my inability to solve it is one of my principal reasons for wishing to abdicate. Jane was extremely reserved about her own past. She had weathered a great many storms, & I think wanted them forgotten . . . And yet, if one omits them, the life looses [*sic*] what she would have called its 'pattern' . . . perhaps your idea of a sort of memoir is the best."[47] And she repeated the point a few months later: "I *couldn't do justice* to the Life without writing about very intimate things which Jane wished forgotten. So that is that—*final* decision."[48]

"Final," of course, didn't literally mean *final.* But even when Mirrlees had written something (*finally* in 1950), she could only parade its inappropriateness for immediate publication: "And, by the way, I have now *finally* decided that my two chapters would not fit into any frame. They deal with Jane's spiritual problems & emotional adventures. I still hope that *some day* I may write her biography—but *not at* present."[49]

Stewart meanwhile busied herself with the letters, at the same time looking round (as quietly as she could, no doubt) for a candidate to replace Mirrlees in writing a "life." By 1946 her son-in-law George Thomson (Professor of Greek at the University of Birmingham, Marxist, and author of *Aeschylus and Athens*), had come up with a suggestion: R. F. Willetts, his new young lecturer, just returned from three years with the army in Burma and looking for a research project. For a few months there was a flurry of activity and debate. Was Willetts the man for the job, to suit all the vested interests? Was there any chance he would pass the Mirrlees test? ("Now with regard to Mr. Wilkins [*sic*]. Before anything can be done or thought of, I should like to know *definitely* whether you *know* that he *wants* to write a study of Jane and her work."[50]) What material should be handed over to him? (Not the *intimate* notes, of course[51]) What was his brief to be? Stewart by this stage realized that she would have to bow to Mirrlees's view of her own privileged intimacy with Harrison: "One point is to me crystal clear that you alone can do the personal life & you have got it all there, waiting to be brought forth—I do not see why you should tell the Secret. 'Pourquoi rompre ce glorieux silence?' Her emotional development need certainly not be gone into by Mr. W."[52]

Willetts seems to have been keen enough on the whole idea to start with; he took away some of the material and there were plans for a visit to Mirrlees.[53] But his enthusiasm quickly waned. Maybe he was anxious to get back to his real interests of Crete and the Gortyn Code.[54] But, at the same time, it wouldn't have taken a smart man long to realize that this was a nightmare project, impossible to complete to the satisfaction of all those who thought they had a right to be satisfied by it, much more likely to blight than to advance a young man's career. As he faded into the background, he became merely another cause of reproach between Mirrlees and Stewart: "Who on earth is to write the biography? The young man you proposed before was a complete frost," carped Mirrlees several years after Willetts had disappeared from the scene.[55]

Mirrlees produced nothing for publication herself, but she gradually consolidated her position as "Harrison's closest friend" and, as such, the arbiter of anything written about her by anyone else. In 1946 (eighteen years after Harrison's death) Stewart sent Mirrlees the first full manuscript of what she had written around the letters to Gilbert Murray. Mirrlees's response (and it is a response that was to be replayed in a series of variations over the next thirteen years) was to sympathize with the difficulty of the task, to damn with faint praise, to quibble at any number of minor errors (especially those that cast Harrison in anything other than a saintly light), *and* to keep her finger very much in the pie: "I have now read all of your MS," she writes on this first occasion, "—many thanks for allowing me to do so, It has, I am sure, the makings of a *very* nice book, but I do agree it needs pulling together."[56]

These delaying tactics were matched by a repeated insistence that what Stewart was writing was *not* a "life" but an account of Harrison's work, and that a "life" remained to be undertaken— preferably by herself: "Yes I hope some day to write a memoir."[57] It was with this in mind, no doubt, that Mirrlees advocated "*The Making of Themis* or something like that"[58] as the title for Stewart's book, presumably not an attempt, consciously at any rate, to consign the whole project to oblivion (though that would surely have been its effect), but to remind writer and reader alike that this was not the personal history (that only Mirrlees was qualified to write).

Stewart persevered through all this, writing and rewriting. But if Mirrlees damned with faint praise, for at least a decade no publisher (Cambridge University Press, Oxford University Press, Blackwell, Gollancz, Hogarth . . .) offered any praise at all—or, despite repeated approaches and powerful intermediaries, seemed remotely interested in publishing it. Stewart engaged an agent who kept her optimism up, often quite falsely. "I have had a very nice letter from Leonard Woolf," he wrote in May 1954, introducing Woolf's comments on the manuscript— which were not in fact "nice" at all, but devastatingly critical: "It is a great pity that it is so incoherent . . . I'm afraid it is so obscure that it is out of the question to make a book out of it." And he went on (in an absolutely classic faux pas) to suggest handing it all over to his old friend Hope Mirrlees: "I feel that she would be quite capable of taking the material and making something of it."[59] That was, of course, out of the question, but the agent did trawl up another potential author who might have been able "to lick [the] MS into shape":[60] Lady Trudy Bliss (semiprofessional biographer and wife of the composer Sir Arthur Bliss). But after almost a year of procrastination, and in the face of Mirrlees's refusal (according to Stewart) to help with any material at all, she turned the project down ("I am sorry," writes the agent in March 1955, "to learn of Lady Bliss's final decision about the book."[61])

There was little more encouragement from friends and colleagues in Cambridge or outside. Stewart eagerly sent her manuscript around the academic glitterati—and (notwithstanding a few pockets of lingering enthusiasm for Harrison) received a series of gloomy responses: "Jane Harrison was a wonderful woman," wrote the Master of Jesus College in kindly tones, before delivering the usual blow, "but I fear she does not lend herself to a memoir that will appeal to a wide enough public to attract any publisher."[62] Even Gilbert Murray himself was by this stage confessing to others that he thought the project hopeless[63]—although, to Stewart, he tried to put the best possible interpretation on the resounding lack of interest: "She suffers from being a pioneer," he soothed;[64] her once radical ideas were now so "proved and accepted" that no one could work up much interest in them any longer ("just as now no one wants to make a speech advocating Woman Suffrage [*sic*]").[65] Harrison today may have become one of the most glamorous figures in the history of Classics, a female icon and intellectual radical; in the 1950s her fame was at a low ebb.

Eventually, and on unfavorable financial terms,[66] Jessie Stewart found a publisher for her *Jane Ellen Harrison: A Portrait from Letters,* the small Merlin Press. ("I am distressed to hear that you are publishing at your own risk," wrote Mirrlees on November 2, 1957, criticism now masquerading as concern.) George Thomson wrote a short introduction, celebrating Harrison's openness to new ideas. "Will he keep it clear of politics?" Mirrlees had written, on hearing of the plan to enlist this particular well-known Marxist into the team. ". . . To expound Jane's theories as incipient communism is really *very* misleading."[67] (In fact what he wrote was fulsomely hagiographic and sadly apolitical.)

Inevitably, publication did not put an end to the disputes and rivalries. It quickly became clear (to Mirrlees) that Stewart had not actually shown her everything that was to go into the final version (Stewart's not entirely convincing defense was that Mirrlees had simply forgotten the details of what she had been shown.[68]) When Mirrlees first read the published book and came across Stewart's story of Harrison's relationship with Francis Cornford (which went beyond their academic collaboration to suggest that she had been in love with him and tortured to the point of breakdown by his marriage to young Frances Darwin), she fired off her well-known, and often quoted, tirade: "But, oh Jessie, how *could* you have put in some of the parts of the 'Francis and Frances' chapter? They were *certainly* not in the version that you showed me. I am *horribly* distressed that this has been published. Jane would simply have *loathed* it."[69]

But equally characteristic of Mirrlees's investment in the Harrison story is the first part of this letter, before its angry eruption: "Your manipulation of that huge undigested heap of letters is masterly, & your comments & explanations are inserted so unobtrusively & helpfully . . . But in two of the extracts that you cite there are touches that mar the portrait physically ie Bunny Garnett's description of her manner as rough and Virginia Woolf's delusion that she *stooped.* Her manners were noted for their *suavity* and her straight back was her pride."[70] Mirrlees never let an opportunity slip to remind anyone who would listen that *she* was the guardian of the Harrison legend in all its forms.

Ostensibly, then, Mirrlees had lost the battle. By a combination of sheer perseverance and the alibi offered by Murray's letters, Stewart wrote not only the first substantial account of Harrison's life but also a memoir of her life that decisively broke through the constraints that Mirrlees believed she had imposed on it. Mirrlees was simply *too late,* we cannot help but think—as she vainly fantasizes yet again (just a few months after the appearance of the *Portrait*) on her own planned contribution to the legend: "A little memoir of Jane is beginning to form up in my mind."[71]

But within the archive itself the victory looks rather different. For it is the figure of Mirrlees, not Stewart, who dominates the Harrison Papers—thanks in part to her own obsessive collection of Harrison memorabilia (it was she, for example, who must have squirreled away the syllabuses from Harrison's teaching in the 1880s); in part to the almost equal obsession of Jessie Stewart, who seems to have filed every single carping letter from her rival; but most of all thanks to the carefully preserved preliminary manuscripts of the biography Mirrlees was always intending (not) to write.

Archives entice and seduce: the temptation of letters locked away out of the public domain is irrististible—not to mention the sheer immediacy of the yellowing pages, the illegible handwriting, the crossing out, the scribbles, the illicit pleasure of reading what we believe we were never meant to see, of reaching what we take to be the "biographical source." Anyone who goes to the Newnham Archive in search of unpublished material on Jane Harrison is richly rewarded—by Mirrlees's biographical drafts and notes (subtly different versions, reworking the same material with just the slightest variation) and by the records she carefully wrote of the interviews she had conducted with Harrison's friends. There are well over a thousand pages, and I have often necessarily quoted from them in the preeceding chapters, as they are the only "source" for large parts of Harrison's career. As we might expect, the tone of all this material (written, or so I guess, at various periods over the fifty years between Harrison's death in 1928 and Mirrlees's own in 1978) is insistently and explicitly hagiographic, sprinkled with eulogies that make even Murray's words of praise look restrained: from cloying idoliza-

tion ("Jane's conduct was always magnificent but it was not necessarily prompted by charity. Nor was it prompted by principles. It was simply that she could not act otherwise," or "As
usual without hesitation, without self-congratulation, she an-
swered the call of duty") to the ludicrous search for star quality
in Harrison's idiosyncratic and self-glamorizing aestheticism
("When I knew her she was always put beside herself by the pic-
torial value of washing hung out to dry").[72] But there is also a teleology, a powerful interpretative framework and a significantly
personal agenda at work in these manuscripts of the unfinished
biography. It is a personal agenda (often unrecognized as such)
that has found its way into many of the accounts of Harrison's
life that have drawn on the Archive.

We do not know the exact nature of the relationship between
Harrison and Mirrlees. What they said to each other, still less
what they did, behind the closed doors of Harrison's Newnham
room, of their Paris apartment, or of their flat in Mecklenburgh
Street, we cannot hope to reconstruct—any more than we were
able to pin down the nature of Eugénie Sellers's "GP" for Miss
Harrison. It is certain enough, however, that the relationship between Harrison and Mirrlees was not the same as that between
Harrison and Sellers. For all kinds of reasons, but not least because times, language, and culture had changed since the 1880s.
As most histories of sexuality insist, by the time of the Great
War, the powerful discourse of—intimate, but not essentially
erotic—female friendship was on the wane, to be replaced by a
much more "explicit" discourse of lesbian inversion and the parade of specifically lesbian options in language, clothing, and
lifestyle. I have already raised a number of doubts about the
simple linear development implied in that story of "paradigm
shift." But paradigm shift of some kind there certainly was—at
the very least the change in the *discursive world* in which they
lived (with its new way of *talking* and *writing* about female affection) must inevitably have affected the attitudes and experience

of Harrison and her friends. Exactly how it affected them is quite another, and much more difficult, question: histories of sexuality will always be a treacherous guide to what people "really" did (or thought) in private, and few scholars have stopped to ask how, for those who live through it, such paradigmatic change in discursive practice affects individual experience. But it is beyond doubt that, in the years after the war, Harrison and Mirrlees operated against the background of a very different female sexual culture from Harrison and Sellers in the 1880s; their partnership was inevitably represented and interpreted differently (by themselves and by observers). That, of course, is a long way from saying that we *know* that Harrison and Mirrlees were, in our terms, gay. We do not.[73]

What we do know is that Mirrlees was talked of in ways that pointed to her homosexuality. Antony Powell's memoirs recount one such classic anecdote: the day after VE-Day in 1945, at a slightly incongruous lunch party, he and his wife entertained Mirrlees along with the Czech military attaché Colonel Kalla. Over drinks, Kalla got up and, eyes staring, advanced slowly and purposefully toward Miss Mirrlees. Love at first sight, they assumed; Kalla was about to leap on her. "Hope Mirrlees, whose emotions so far as known were orientated towards her own sex, seemed to share our fears. A look of absolute terror came into her face. She straightened her somewhat dumpy figure in readiness for the final pounce." Of course, in these urbane memoirs, there was a happy ending: Kalla was only trying to remove an earwig that had settled on her scarf.[74] But it is the assumption of Mirrlees's emotional (and sexual) preferences that gives the story its edge. And it was an assumption shared by others. Gertrude Stein (in a nice reversal of the usual hierarchy) dubbed Harrison "Hope Mirlees' [*sic*] pet enthusiasm."[75] Virginia Woolf cast Harrison and Mirrlees together as a sapphic pair. We have already noted her judgment on *Madeleine:* "all sapphism . . . Jane and herself"; in 1925 she wrote to a friend about a party given by

Karin Stephen (Costelloe): "Hope Mirrlees arrived half an hour early (do you admire her novels?—I can't get an ounce of joy from them, but we like seeing her and Jane billing and cooing together)";[76] likewise, a couple of years earlier, she had written to Molly MacCarthy of her visit to Paris: "There I shall stay a few days & meet Jane Harrison & Hope Mirrlees who have a Sapphic flat somewhere, while Leonard returns."[77] Woolf clearly saw their relationship as an erotic one.

She would, of course. And these letters had their own agendas, in presenting Woolf as the canny commentator on human frailty, knowingly "modern," a wry cynic when it came to the ambitions, motives, emotions, and sexualities of others. But, in her comments on *Madeleine,* Woolf also spotted how Mirrlees (and I shall suggest Harrison too) encoded their relationship within the terms of literary sapphism. *Madeleine* is not simply a story of a young girl's erotic obsession with an older woman; Mirrlees explicitly writes Harrison into that tale, using (for example) a quotation from *Art and Ritual* ("Art springs straight out of the rite, and her first outward leap is the image of the god") as the epigraph to her final chapter (entitled "The Rape to the Love of Invisible Things"). And, as we have seen, the Greek dedication of *The Counterplot* conjures the relationship of Harrison and Mirrlees in strikingly (striking for those who knew Greek, at any rate) conjugal terms, matching the memory of (shared) "Spanish nights and days" in the dedication "To Hope" of Harrison's *Epilegomena.* Even their decision, as two women, to move from Cambridge to *Paris* effectively encouraged their relationship to be read as lesbian. For that is what Paris meant.[78]

This is a complex game of sexual/literary coding, and it is hard to pin down exactly what is implied by each reference, by each cleverly deployed quotation. That was no doubt the intention. After all, Mirrlees's novel are very largely *about* the contested boundaries of Art and Life, and she will not be caught out by any crude reading of her text. All the same, if we set the material in the Newnham Archive against the background of Mirrlees's published work and literary reputation, we will find it easier to understand the logic of her refusal, reluctance, or un-willingness to complete her biography of Harrison. We cannot explain exactly *why* she did not complete it (and no document could ever tell us that). But we can now see much more clearly the problems that any biography of her friend would have posed for her: the problems of explicitation, which a biography would always risk. Unwilling to write her own intimacy *out* of the story, but unwilling to write it *in* either; caught on the knife edge between Bloomsbury-style exposure and the alternative rhetoric of reticence. Hence (as we have seen) her constant claim to a unique right to speak of Harrison's private world—and, at the same time, her constant refusal to do so; her repeated parade of the intimate secrets she knew but could not say, the things that Harrison had told her but that she could never make pub-lic. Or at least not yet.

We can also understand more clearly the overall direction of her biographical notes. Amid all her apparently unconnected jottings, the aides-mémoires on persons and places earmarked for a place in the never-finished product ("The Impressionists," "Cambridge society in the seventies," "Discarded Theories," "The Poetry Jane's Mother Read," "Jane's Income"), Mirrlees's notes and draft biography of Harrison saw the life of her subject in terms of a particular end, a defining goal: the final period of happiness that Harrison enjoyed with Mirrlees, the glorious years of their life together. This was the perfect safe haven that followed Harrison's much more stormy course in early life: frus-trated passions, disappointments, a whole series of relationships (with men) that were to bring only tragedy and trouble. This is what forms the broken narrative of the notebooks as well as the more coherent story line of the various biographical drafts. First there was her undergraduate love for her supervisor, S. H. Butcher, who reciprocated her affections but turned out all along to have been engaged to another and nearly broke her heart: "The great overshadowing event of her Newnham years was her tragic passion for Henry Butcher . . . He was already engaged to Miss Trench . . . to whom he was devoted. This did not prevent his falling in love (I gather) also with Jane."[79] Then came her turbulent intimacy with D. S. MacColl (a dreadful *crise,* but what kind of *crise,* Mirrlees repeatedly asks).[80] Next, just after her return to Cambridge, there was possibly an engagement with R. A. Neil, a classicist at Pembroke College, but this was ended by his sudden death. "She felt his death terribly . . . he wanted to marry her, & . . . she had decided to accept him."[81] Tragedy upon tragedy.

Finally came the attachment to Francis Cornford that was more than hinted at by Stewart.[82] In Mirrlees's notebooks, the whole story is flagged by scribbles and erasures (in the heading of the pages, in fact, she has ostentatiously scored out the title "The Cornford Letters," so we read just "The C—— Letters": *damnatio memoriae?*[83]). Pages and pages follow, barely coherent, sewing together quotations apparently from Harrison herself ("the most beautiful happiness I have ever known") and allusions to her other disastrous passions ("it was more and more imperative I should be separated from the man"—hence the "friendship with —— [Cornford]"), all combined with narrative reconstructions of Mirrlees's own ("[She] thought of suggesting they should marry, but just then gossips began to talk and things at Newnham became a little difficult for her"). And in the end, emotional disaster came again: Cornford married Frances Darwin, the daughter of one of Harrison's college contemporaries. Harrison had first introduced the couple; many (including Frances) thought she had pushed them together. Even so, she barely survived the shock of the desertion. Mirrlees again, once more interweaving the words of her heroine: "Gradually [she] feels more and more that his heart is elsewhere & that she is only a duty. 'I had had the foolish dream that love of one woman need not diminish the closeness of friendship with another' . . . 'I had come back from Death . . . just to find the man I always called my 'Rock of Ages' slipping away from me.'"[84]

What she writes of these relationships is frustratingly allusive, But the discretion in which the stories are elaborately cloaked, far from concealing the underlying agenda, calls attention to the untold narrative of the intimacies and emotional battlegrounds that (we are left in no doubt) formed the frame of Harrison's life. ("One episode the key to JEH's life—indiscreet to mention—*wd* cripple her work—She would have hated it published"[85]). At the same time Mirrlees's vast documentation, her concealed knowledge, is meant to reassert her own culminating importance in (and knowledge of) Harrison's life.

There are many versions of a life; that has been one of the main arguments of this book. Mirrlees's story is a significant version of Harrison's biography, written by one of her most intimate friends and drawing undoubtedly (though probably less directly than it is made to appear) on conversations she had had with Harrison herself. But it is only one version among many, the construction of an individual with an almost full-time, and deeply personal, investment—over fifty years—in (not) telling the story. Mirrlees must be as loaded a witness of Harrison's career as she is a privileged one. If it is easy for us to forget that simple point, it is precisely because Mirrlees was committed to making her story the authorized version, the only possible story (not) to tell. And at the same time, it is precisely because the archival resource (the Harrison Papers) that dominates research on Harrison, the collection to which all must turn in (re)writing her life, is so much Mirrlees's creation that it forces its readers into collusion with her vision of her subject.

To some extent, no doubt, all archives present the same pleasures and problems. No archive is neutral; every document saved is always saved *by choice,* and every choice is a loaded one. That is one reason that archives are so interesting: who saves what, and why, always counts. The case of the Harrison Papers, however, is peculiarly extreme. For all the input of Stewart, it is the testament of a woman who made her career out of Harrison's memory, and who was committed to defining herself as Harrison's true partner and soul mate.

The model that Mirrlees offers of Harrison's emotional progress through life could not have failed to be an extremely influential one, all the more so for its not being published. It certainly left its mark on Stewart's *Jane Ellen Harrison* over the thirty years in which they together fanned the flame of Harrison's memory. (Stewart's trouble was partly that she learned the Mirrlees lesson all *too* well . . .) It also underlies the sub-Freudian, pyschosexual biography by Sandra Peacock. Savor, for example, the following: "Although she loved him desperately, she knew that the strongest bond between them lay in their mutual interest in each other's work"; "Although Jane had a very sensual element in her nature that could not escape unnoticed, she also possessed extraordinary self-control. Such control exacted an enormous psychological cost."[86] Lines like those could almost have been written by Mirrlees herself.

The Mirrlees model is also inscribed at the heart of more strictly "intellectual" history. The idea that Harrison's life could be structured as a series of emotional struggles (with men) has become inextricably connected with the story of Ritualism, and with modern scholarly reconstructions of her role as Woman at the center of the (male) Group.[87] We have already spotted Ackerman referring to her position "at the heart of the group (in more than one sense)"; see now how that pun on "heart" can be played out:

> Miss Harrison was, in every period of her adult life, always connected in a deeply emotional way with some male scholar of (supposedly) superior philological attainments who acted as a technical adviser and, just as importantly, as an essential emo-

tional support. First it was the art historian D. S. MacColl, and then Francis Cornford, with both of whom she seems to have been in love. There were as well older men with whom she was likewise close, although probably not in love: as an undergraduate it was her teacher A. W. Verrall (to whom *Prolegomena* is dedicated), in her first year back at Newnham R. A. Neil; and then there were A. B. Cook and, preeminently, Gilbert Murray, both younger men, to both of whom she was deeply attached. And of course each of these men, in his own way, returned her affection . . . In one sense, then, the reason for the group's coming-to-be was that Jane Harrison had a need for making passionate intellectual friendships.[88]

In one sense an analysis of this kind cannot fail to be true— and would be true (in some form or other) of every one of us, both now and then. How, after all, could you write an intellectual biography that did *not* reflect on the interrelationship of friendship, affection, sex, and ideas? The sense in which it is true, however, is vastly outweighed by all the senses in which it is dangerous fantasy. I am not only referring to the practically meaningless certainty with which the emotions of Harrison and her contemporaries are categorized, much as membership of the group had been categorized ("love" for MacColl and Cornford, "closeness" but "not love" for Verrall, and so on),[89] and I am not only referring to the crude way in which Harrison's gender informs the explanation (as Ackerman effectively admits, the work of no male scholar would be so clearly cast in terms of his emotional or sexual attachments). I am referring also, in a much more radical sense, to the inadequacy of this whole model for our understanding Harrison's intellectual development—for the simple reason that it fails to recognize its own origins in the very myth that it propagates. That is, the model that claims to isolate "passionate friendships" as the explanatory force behind Harrison's work and career is a model that is generated directly out of the self-defined "passionate friendship" that lies (hidden) at the heart of the Harrison tradition: the friendship with Mirrlees.

We do not know the "truth" of Harrison's involvement with these men, or the "truth" of her distress when (for example) young Cornford went off and got married. Nor could we ever hope to. After all, not even the survival of Harrison's own letters would guarantee a single authoritative account to be preferred over any other stop. Distress never comes in just one version, and the sufferer may well be the worst guide. But we *can* trace the origins of our preoccupation with that particular way of telling the life of Harrison. Mirrlees's legacy to all modern studies of Harrison has been to make these men (and their accompanying distress) crucial, with only Mirrlees left at the end. No wonder there is no room in this story for Miss Sellers.

CHAPTER TEN

Epilegomena

For almost forty years after the "terrific bust-up" in 1891 there was no contact at all between Miss Harrison and (as she was to become in 1897) Mrs. Arthur Strong; at least, I have found no trace of any.[1] But when, after her death in 1928, an appeal went out for the Jane Ellen Harrison Memorial Fund, sponsored by some of her best-connected friends, Strong responded with a check for a guinea (£1.05, roughly $1.70).[2] A carefully chosen amount, we must assume: certainly not generous, but not the kind of meanness that would attract attention either; almost the regulation sum (so you can tell from the list of contributors) for those who wanted to pay their proper respects while being careful not to upstage Harrison's very closest companions and colleagues.

In all, more than one hundred seventy people contributed a total of £458 16s 8d (roughly £458.83, or $743). Hope Mirrlees and her mother put in twenty pounds between them; Dörpfeld remembered his old "partizan" with one pound; Paul Valéry came up with the standard guinea, as did the historian G. M. Trevelyan and various classical colleagues (Janet Bacon from Girton, W. E. Heitland, D. S. Robertson); the Murrays and the Cornfords each produced ten pounds. For every single one of these contributors there must have been a different connection with Harrison, a different story of her life. What memories would André Gide have mustered, as he sent off his ten pounds? Or Roger Fry his five? And what of those who were emphatically missing, intentionally absent, from this list of well-wishers? The Harrison story is as much a story of antipathy as of devotion: of those who winced at her showpiece lectures, those who found her scholarship frankly sloppy, those who simply couldn't stand this self-promoting, chain-smoking *woman*.[3] As one of her old pupils ventured: "Plenty of people in Cambridge . . . would have gladly given her hemlock."[4] Harrison's enemies have their own versions to tell.

But, enemies or not, Harrison remains the most famous female classicist there has ever been, an originary and radical thinker, a permanent fixture in the history of scholarship. So crucial is she to our own understanding of why we think (about Greek culture and religion) as we do that it is hard to believe quite how *dispensable* she seemed in the decades that followed her death—certainly, as Stewart found when she trawled round the presses of England, not worth publishing a book about. The scorn for Harrison in the 1940s and 1950s, the faint praise that damned any interest in her as touching (but misplaced) loyalty, now seems little short of ludicrous.

Mrs. Strong, by contrast, has no place in the pantheon. For all the razzmatazz of her years in Rome, the praise and honors and unbeatable connections (even as she was dismissed from her post at the British School, she was hailed by a former prime minister as the most "distinguished woman scholar" in the world), her fame has not lasted. This book has suggested a variety of reasons for her eclipse: an awkwardly warm relationship with Fascist archaeology (if not fascism); an expatriate death in the middle of a war zone (effectively precluding a memorial service's launch into posterity[5]); perhaps even her messianic commitment to Roman culture, when scholarly fashion was increasingly tending toward the Greeks. But more than anything, it is the absence of pupils—not just to promote her memory but to fight over it. Reputation, inevitably, is in the hands of those who spread it, and those who have some stake in the spreading. Many brilliant minds are entirely forgotten. Mirrlees and Stewart, and their rivalry commemorated in the Harrison Papers, not only ensured that (and how) Harrison was remembered but also ensured that she came to seem *worth remembering*.

There are signs now of the beginnings of interest in Mrs. Strong, a few flickers at least: a dramatization of her letters, a promised biography, a share in the spotlight of this book (though, significantly perhaps, not a share in its title). Will any or all of this, in the end, make her, too, seem *worth remembering?* I simply do not know.

Lifelines

JANE ELLEN HARRISON

1850   Born, September 9, Cottingham, Yorkshire

1867–1870   Attends Cheltenham Ladies' College

1874–1879   Studies Classics at Newnham College, Cambridge

1880   Teaches for one term at Oxford High School

1880–1898   Based in London
     1882   *Myths of the Odyssey in Art and Literature*
     1883   Perfomance of *The Tale of Troy*
     1885   *Introductory Studies in Greek Art*
     1887   *Alcestis* in Oxford
     1888   Visits Greece with D. S. MacColl and others
     1888   Applies for Yates Chair of Classical Archaeology, University College London
     1890   *Mythology and Monuments of Ancient Athens,* with M. de G. Verrall
     1894   *Greek Vase Paintings,* with D. S. MacColl
     1896   Applies for Yates Chair of Classical Archaeology, University College London

1898–1922   Based at Newnham College, Cambridge (Research Fellow and College Lecturer in Classical Archaeology)
     1901   Visits Greece with Jessie Crum (Stewart)
     1903   *Prolegomena to the Study of Greek Religion*

1910–1913	Teaches Hope Mirrlees as a student at Newnham
1912	*Themis: A Study in the Social Origins of Greek Religion*
1913	*Unanimism*
1921	*Epilegomena to the Study of Greek Religion*

1922–1926	Based in Paris
1924	*Life of the Arch-Priest Avvakum,* translated with H. Mirrlees
1925	*Reminiscences of a Student's Life*

1926–1928	Based in London
1926	*The Book of the Bear,* translated with H. Mirrlees
1928	Dies, April 15; Gilbert Murray gives first Harrison Memorial Lecture, October 27

EUGÉNIE SELLERS (*Mrs. Arthur Strong*)

1860	Born, March 25, London
1867–1879	Lives in Spain and France; convent schooling
1879–1882	Studies classics at Girton College, Cambridge
1882–1883	Teaches at St. Leonard's School, St. Andrews, Scotland

1883–1897	Based in London and, later, Munich
1883	Performance of *The Tale of Troy*
1885	"Short while with Miss H[arrison]"
1891	Studies at British School at Athens; translation of Schuchhardt's *Schliemann's Excavations*
1892	Studies at German Archaeological Institute in Rome
1895	Translation of Furtwängler's *Masterpieces*
1896	*The Elder Pliny's Chapters on the History of Art,* edited with K. Jex-Blake
1897	Marries S. Arthur Strong

1897–1909	Based in London and Chatsworth
1904	Death of S. Arthur Strong; appointed Librarian at Chatsworth in his place
1907	*Roman Sculpture from Augustus to Constantine*
1909	Appointed Assistant Director and Librarian of the British School at Rome

1909–1943   Based in Rome

1910   Elected Research Fellow of Girton (holds fellowship *in absentia*)

1915   *Apotheosis and After Life*

1925   "Retirement" from British School at Rome; retirement dinner in London, continues to live in Rome

1943   Dies, September 16

Notes

1. Prolegomena

1. Quotation is from G. Murray, *Jane Ellen Harrison: An Address,* 4–5. The details of the appeal are preserved in Harrison Papers, box 20; see below, Chapters 2, 10.
2. Murray's comment: letter to Jessie Stewart, May 1, 1928 (Harrison Papers, box 21); for Virginia Woolf's patronizing description of the occasion, which in fact took place in the (hardly out of the way) St. Marylebone Cemetery, Finchley, North London, see *The Diary of Virginia Woolf,* ed. A. O. Bell (Harmondsworth, 1979–1985), 3: 181.
3. Reprinted in the *Newnham College Roll Letter* 1929, 51.
4. Murray's text was published by the college. The terms of the endowment were that the lecture should be "on any subject that would interest Jane Harrison" (Murray's would have fitted this bill perfectly); the lectures still take place at Newnham, now in alternate years.
5. Stewart, *Jane Ellen Harrison: A Portrait from Letters* xiv; Mirrlees to Murray, October 30, 1928 (Harrison Papers, box 21).
6. Peacock, in *Jane Ellen Harrison: The Mask and the Self,* tries to piece together the events of Harrison's childhood, largely drawing on Harrison's own autobiographical memoir (reprinted in *Arion* 4, 312–346). She makes it a lurid account of a wicked stepmother, extreme fundamentalist Christianity, and underprivilege. In fact Harrison's classical education and the choice of Cheltenham La-

dies' suggests a very different interpretation. The family was neither poor nor philistine; her little brother, after all, was—as the
memoir informs us—sent away to school at (expensive) Harrow.
Like it or not, Harrison's story must be a story of privilege.

7. Eight students were admitted in the first year, eight in the second,
twenty-two in the third, and thirteen in Harrison's year. In 1875
the college moved from makeshift accommodations in the center
of Cambridge to Newnham Hall (now Old Hall on the college's
present site). For an account of its early history, see R. McWilliams Tullberg, *Women at Cambridge,* (2nd ed. (Cambridge, 1998),
chaps. 4 and 5.

8. Paley (Marshall), *What I Remember,* 20–21; the remark, I am
afraid, must have been as blandly meaningless in the 1870s as it
would be now.

9. For details of Harrison's examination performance, see Peacock,
Jane Ellen Harrison, 54. The intricacies of the nineteenth-century
Cambridge system of marking and exam classification are baffling
even to those of us who are familiar with the (still pretty strange)
modern versions. In 1879, women sat the examinations only
through the goodwill of the examiners, who "unofficially" informed them how they ranked (within three main classes: first,
second, and third). From 1882 the women's results were officially
published (separately from the men's)—although women could
not formally receive a Cambridge degree until 1948.

10. For these quotations, see Murray, *Jane Ellen Harrison,* 10–15.

11. Essays on these and other subjects are collected in her *Alpha and
Omega.* The quotations are taken from "Homo Sum: Being a Letter
to an Anti-Suffragist from an Anthropologist," *Alpha and Omega,*
80–115.

12. *Mythology and Monuments of Ancient Athens,* with a translation by
M. de G. (or Mrs. A. W.) Verrall.

13. For a basic bibliography of Harrison, see Stewart, *Jane Ellen Harrison,* 203–208; for the complete works, see Arlen, *The Cambridge
Ritualists: An Annotated Bibliography,* 19–79.

14. The final phase of her life and the growth of her interest in Russian are discussed in Peacock, *Jane Ellen Harrison,* 233–244. As
Peacock observes (and the bibliographies [n. 13] make clear), her
interest in things Russian had roots further back in her career; see,

for example, *Russia and the Russian Verb: A Contribution to the Psychology of the Russian People* (Cambridge, 1915).

15. The fate of the letters from Murray to Harrison first became an issue in 1932, when Jessie Stewart planned to publish part of the correspondence (see below, Chapter 9); for example, Murray to Stewart, November 14, 1932: "after she had gone it occurred to me to wonder what had happened to my letters to her" (Harrison Papers, box 11).

16. Such genealogies are inevitably murky, constantly contested. Versnel makes a brave attempt to disentangle the links between Harrison and Burkert in "What's Sauce for the Goose Is Sauce for the Gander: Myth and Ritual, Old and New," 25–95; so also does Burkert himself in *Homo Necans,* 29–34. But (as R. Buxton comes close to hinting in *Imaginary Greece* [Cambridge, 1994], 151–152) they succeed better in demonstrating the mythic intricacy of the history of the study of myth. For Gernet and the Paris School, see Di Donato, *Per una antropologia storica del mondo antico,* 255–263; Lloyd-Jones, "Jane Harrison 1850–1928," 29–72, pp. 60–62.

17. So writes G. S. Kirk in *Myth: Its Meaning and Functions in Ancient and Other Cultures* (Cambridge and Berkeley, 1970), 31.

18. All the same, it is worth reflecting on why it might be that Dodds remains largely silent about Harrison's contribution. She finds no place in his *The Greeks and the Irrational* (Berkeley and Los Angeles, 1951), even though the book was dedicated to Murray; and she is entirely absent (very missing) from Dodds's memoir, *Missing Persons: An Autobiography.*

19. An enthusiastic recent attempt to track Harrison's influence through modernist literature is Carpentier's *Ritual, Myth, and the Modernist Text: The Influence of Jane Ellen Harrison on Joyce, Eliot, and Woolf.*

20. T. S. Eliot, *Selected Essays* (London, 1951), 62: "Few books are more fascinating than those of Miss Harrison, Mr. Cornford and Mr. Cooke, when they burrow in the origins of Greek myths and rites." His graduate paper of 1913 ("The Interpretation of Primitive Ritual") survives in the Modern Archive of King's College, Cambridge (John Hayward Bequest); see P. Gray, *T. S. Eliot's Intellectual and Poetic Development, 1909–1922* (Brighton, 1982), 108–142, and R. Crawford, *The Savage and the City in the Work of T. S.*

Eliot (Oxford, 1987), esp. chap. 3. For further (more unexpected) connections between Eliot and the Harrison myth, see Chapter 9.

21. Gregory, *H. D. and Hellenism: Classic Lines,* esp. 117–118, 274. The lecturer was Rev. W. A. Wigram, canon of Malta.

22. *A Room of One's Own,* 19 and 79. Woolf's Newnham lecture took place on October 20, 1928, exactly a week before Gilbert Murray's address; the Girton version was given only the day before, on October 26 (*Diary of Virginia Woolf* 3: 199–201). For Vernon Lee's part in Harrison's story, see Chapter 6.

23. *Reminiscences of a Student's Life* was fashionably published by the Woolfs' Hogarth Press.

24. *Reminiscences,* 45. Helen Gladstone was a "friendly enemy" (*Reminiscences,* 46) of Harrison.

25. Ibid., 45–46.

26. Ibid., 54.

27. Ibid., 58.

28. For an analysis of such tropes, and for the "advent of theory in the reading of autobiography" (with its inevitable challenge to the truth claims of any autobiographical narrative), see P. Lejeune, *Le pacte autobiographique* (Paris, 1975), and J. Sturrock, *The Language of Autobiography: Studies in the First Person Singular* (Cambridge, 1993); Sturrock's formulation, that every autobiographer is "a contentedly guilty egotist," suits Harrison very well.

29. *Reminiscences,* 12–14.

30. It also underlies the joke of the archaeologist Sir Charles Newton (himself—like me, as it happens—from rural Shropshire, on the Welsh borders), that Harrison was "too North country"; quoted in a draft biography of Harrison by Hope Mirrlees, Harrison Papers, box 15; see below, Chapter 9.

31. Peacock, *Jane Ellen Harrison,* too often falls into the trap of taking Harrison's protestations *à la lettre* (for example, "She faced a serious struggle to overcome the handicap of her Yorkshire background," p. 43). It also catches (as the title indicates) Thomas W. Africa, "Aunt Glegg among the Dons or Taking Jane Harrison at Her Word," in Calder, ed., *The Cambridge Ritualists Reconsidered,* 21–35; surprisingly, even Lloyd-Jones (in "Jane Harrison") tends to paraphrase the densely ironic humor of *Reminiscences* into "straight" narrative. By contrast, Hope Mirrlees (whose complex

involvement in the Harrison story is discussed later) warns: "Her own pen, when writing about herself, is not altogether to be trusted. It is too facile & too objective for autobiography" (Mirrlees, Notebook, Harrison Papers, box 15). Mirrlees sometimes had powerful motives for wanting to believe her own version rather than Harrison's, and odd reasons for doing so ("too objective?"), but she was probably right all the same.

32. J. Clifford, "Hanging-Up Looking Glasses at Odd Corners: Ethnobiographical Prospects," in D. Aaron, ed., *Studies in Biography,* Harvard English Studies 8 (Cambridge, Mass., 1978), 41–56 (quotation on p. 44). Clifford offers one of the most powerful critiques of the idea of "coherence" that underlies most biographies.

33. Written lives are, by definition, battlegrounds—as most recent, and not so recent, writing on the theory of biography stresses. See, for example, E. Homberger and J. Charmley, eds., *The Troubled Face of Biography* (Basingstoke, 1988); M. Shortland and R. Yeo, eds., *Telling Lives in Science: Essays on Scientific Biography* (Cambridge, 1996), esp. 1–44; R. Whittemore, *Whole Lives: Shapers of Modern Biography* (Baltimore and London, 1989), 47–78 (for an account of Virginia Woolf's influential reflections on the subject). Harriet Waugh's *A Chaplet of Pearls* (London, 1997) is an elegant (fictional) exploration of the same range of issues. These theoretical discussions have, however, hardly made a mark on the practice of contemporary biographical writing, But see I. B. Nadel, *Biography: Fiction, Fact and Form* (London and Basingstoke, 1984), 183–205 (reviewing a variety of brave attempts to write biography "experimentally"); I. Donaldson, "Gathering and Losing the Self: Jonson and Biography," in I. Donaldson, P. Read, and J. Walter, eds., *Shaping Lives: Reflections on Biography* (Canberra, 1992), 1–20 (an exploration of the relationship between biographical theory and Donaldson's own practice as an editor of Ben Jonson).

34. This is a polemical allusion to D. Nokes, *Jane Austen, a Life* (London, 1997): "In this biography I have sought, so far as possible, to present each moment of Jane Austen's life as it was experienced *at the time,* not with the detached knowingness of hindsight. This is a biography written *forwards*" (p. 5; his emphases).

35. One of the sharpest discussions I have found of the difference that time and period make to (auto)biographical narrative (as well as

many other issues in the practice of life writing) is D. Lessing, *Under My Skin: Volume One of My Autobiography, to 1949* (London, 1995), 11–17; see also the astute observations in Sturrock, *The Language of Autobiography*, e.g., 204–205, 232, 256.

36. H. James, *The Aspern Papers* (New York edition, 1908), and W. Golding, *The Paper Men* (London, 1984), are probably the best known explorations of the essential immorality of archival/documentary biography; related questions are raised by Sturrock, *The Language of Autobiography*, 2: "Should we feel particularly bad when theorising about autobiography?"

37. These and other tensions, paradoxes, and politics of archiving are memorably explored in J. Derrida's *Archive Fever: A Freudian Impression* (Chicago, 1995; trans. from French, *Mal d'archive*, by E. Prenowitz).

38. Briggs and Calder, eds., *Classical Scholarship*. The necessary condition for an entry in this collection of the most famous fifty classicists is to be dead; apart from Harrison, the only woman included is Lily Ross Taylor.

39. Written by G. S. Thomson. Stephen Dyson is working on a new biography, provisionally entitled *Portrait of an Archaeologist*, and as I write, Alistair Crawford has launched an *Evening with Eugénie Strong*, a dramatized reading from letters written by Strong and others, evoking "life in academic Rome in the 1920s during the rise of Fascism" (performances so far in Rome, Wales, and Lambeth Palace, London).

40. Different versions of this "fame question" are usefully explored by J. Rodden, *The Politics of Literary Reputation: The Making and Claiming of 'St. George' Orwell* (New York and Oxford, 1989); J. Gasgoigne, "The Scientist as Patron and Patriotic Symbol: The Changing Reputation of Sir Joseph Banks," in Shortland and Yeo, eds., *Telling Lives in Science*, 243–265.

2. Mrs. Arthur Strong

1. *Elegie Romane* (Bologna, 1892), 25 (ll. 15–16): "a star's brightness she holds within her / Not just of her own skies, but the light of the whole world is Rome." (The poem, of which these are the last

two lines, reworks Ovid, *Tristia* 1.1—addressing the book of poems that is being dispatched to Rome, where its exiled master
cannot go; a neat joke for the epigraph of a book on ancient Roman sculpture.)

2. Thomson, *Mrs. Arthur Strong*, 9; all the quotations from the
speeches delivered on the occasion are taken from this book
(pp. 9–11), except where otherwise indicated.

3. The guest list and seating arrangements are preserved among the
Strong Papers (box 17).

4. So Lady (Lily) Rennell Rodd was (not very affectionately) known;
see J. Brown, *Lutyens and the Edwardians* (London, 1996), 160.

5. The sitting was arranged in a letter of W. Holman Hunt to
Sellers, September 17, 1888 (Strong Papers, box 15).

6. Some dug deeper than others: Frazer gave five guineas (£5.25, or
about $8.50); Evans, in the name of Lady Evans, two guineas
(£2.10, or about $3.40); both of them, as I have said, were signa-
tories of the appeal brochure). Trevelyan gave one guinea; George
Macmillan, a handsome ten pounds. It was such people as these
(who "retained the tradition of doing honour to scholarship") that
Harrison herself parodied as British Lions and Lionesses: "There
lived no Lion who could end his address without telling you that
it was the writing of Latin Prose that had made him what he was!"
(*Reminiscences,* 53).

7. The first quotation from Lord Oxford's speech is taken from an
(unidentified) press cutting (Strong Papers, box 17). "The beads
on her rosary of honour" is a light reference to Strong's Catholi-
cism (her mother was a French Catholic, who died when Eugénie
was eleven).

8. He had already made this error about their first meeting in his autobiography, *Social and Diplomatic Memories 1884–1893* (London,
1922), 196. Perhaps he had simply forgotten, or perhaps the story
of the Parthenon was just so much better than the (literal) truth.

9. Strong, laying it on thick to Lord Crawford and Balcarres on June
19, 1925 (Strong Collection, British School at Rome; hereafter,
BSR).

10. Thomson, *Mrs. Arthur Strong,* 102.

11. For Girton's early history, see McWilliams Tullberg, *Women at*

Cambridge, esp. chaps. 4 and 5. The phrase "Girton Pioneers" is taken from a college song (sung to the tune of *The British Grenadiers*) celebrating the first three Girton students ever to sit Tripos examinations in 1873: "Then let us fill a tea-cup / And drink a health to those / Who studied well and played well / As everybody knows. / May we fulfil the promise / Of Girton's earliest years, / Of Woodhead, Cook and Lumsden, / The Girton Pioneers." *Girton College Song Book* (Cambridge, n.d.), 8–9.

12. There is a letter of condolence on her failure in Mathematics from Lady Stanley, December 19, 1879 (Strong Papers, box 2). Note that the system of classification had changed in two respects since Harrison's day. First, a list of women's results were published in parallel to the men's (see Chapter 1, n. 9). Second, the precise rank ordering of students had been abolished; the three main "classes" of degree remained, now with a number of subdivisions, and within those division students were listed in alphabetical, not rank, order ("third class, third division"). Harrison's and Sellers's careers spanned other major changes in the Classical Tripos in Cambridge; for these see Beard, "The Invention (and Re-invention) of Group D: An Archaeology of the Classical Tripos, 1879–1984," and, for the wider context, Stray, *Classics Transformed: Schools, Universities, and Society in England 1830–1960,* 117–232.

13. For women's achievements in the Classical Tripos in this period, see Breay, "Women and the Classical Tripos 1869–1914." Part II of the Tripos (examining specialist classical subjects: philosophy, history, and so on) was first introduced in the examination of 1882—too late for Harrison; it remained an entirely optional extra, usually taken by only a small minority of students, until 1895.

14. Alfred Cooke, testimonial, June 20, 1883 (Strong Papers, box 2). Postgate regularly taught the Girton classicists; Sellers's work on his *Primer* (London, 1888), is discussed in letters to her from Postgate written on November 4, November 23, and December 5, 1888, and March 2, 1889 (Strong Papers, box 2).

15. Sellers to Vernon Lee (Violet Paget), dated January 16, 1886 (but, since they had not yet met then, 1887 must be meant), Vernon Lee Papers.

16. See E. Sharp, *Hertha Ayrton: A Memoir* (London, 1926), pp. 95 and

109 on sharing the flat; P. Hirsch, *Barbara Leigh Smith Bodichon: Feminist, Artist and Rebel* (London, 1998), 278–290, 315. Marks married her Physics teacher, Professor W. E. Ayrton, and is now best remembered for her invention of the "Ayrton fan" (used to keep gas out of the trenches in the First World War).

17. "I resigned, trusting with extreme recklessness to private coaching in London." Quoted in Thomson, *Mrs. Arthur Strong,* 21.

18. The banker and classicist; see Chapter 5, n. 23.

19. For the diplomacy that finally produced the appendix, see letters from Sellers to George Macmillan, October 3, 1890; January 27, 1891; February 16, 1891 (Macmillan Archive, 50/50, 14/155).

20. Correspondence between Sellers and Furtwängler over the translation and amendments is preserved in the Strong Papers, box 17, and in the Strong Collection, BSR; a letter from Furtwängler (March 14, 1894) suggests that the initiative for Sellers's translation came from him: "*Ist Ihnen ein Verleger Heineman [sic] in London bekannt? Er scheint Lust zu haben eine Übersetzung meines Buches zu veranstalten.*" ("Do you know a publisher called Heineman [sic] in London? He seems keen on producing a translation of my book."), Strong Papers, box 17. The letter (Sellers to [George?] Macmillan, October 10, 1895) is preserved in the Macmillan Archive, 16/244.

21. Originally published by Macmillan (repr. Chicago, 1968); the division of labor mirrors Harrison and Verrall's collaboration in *Mythology and Monuments,* a similarity underlined in the rhetoric and layout of their respective (Macmillan) title pages.

22. Letters by Sellers in the Macmillan Archive and the Strong Papers provide full background to the major dispute with Urlichs (who was then working in Germany on an edition of Pliny), and to the polemical leaflet he published and distributed among the "*Fachgenossen*" (Sellers to Urhlichs, December 10, 1896, Strong Papers, box 2).

23. Sellers in Furtwängler, *Masterpieces of Greek Sculpture,* ed. Sellers, 346–347; as she acknowledges, P. Wolters had already seen (in 1886) that it was a more significant piece of work than usually supposed, but he had not seen the closeness to Praxiteles. Because of its place in *Masterpieces,* there is a tendency to assume that the idea was Furtwängler's.

24. Lee, *Letters,* ed. I. Cooper Willis, 351–352; Strong to Sellers, April 23, 1895 (Strong Papers, box 2).

25. This and the other quotations are drawn from a letter from Harry Brewster (expatriate writer, based in Rome) to Ethel Smyth, May 16, 1896, reprinted in E. Smyth, *What Happened Next* (London, 1940), 139. Sellers's correspondence with the Berensons is collected in the Strong Papers, box 10, with further material in the Berenson Papers at the Harvard University Center, Villa I Tatti, Florence. Berenson himself could blow hot and cold about Morelli: "Berenson is here—very prosperous," wrote Arthur Strong (in Bayreuth) to Sellers, July 10, 1894. "His book is going into a second edition. He has now taken to speaking against Morelli, whom he calls 'disingenuous,' 'arbitrary' and 'unintellectual'" (Strong Papers, box 2).

26. D. C. Kurtz, "Beazley and the Connoisseurship of Greek Vases," *Greek Vases in the J. Paul Getty Museum* 2 (1985): 237–250; R. Neer, "Beazley and the Language of Connoisseurship," *Hephaistos* 15 (1997): 7–30. The distinctively late nineteenth-century radicalism of Morelli is captured by C. Ginzburg, "Morelli, Freud and Sherlock Holmes: Clues and the Scientific Method," in U. Eco and T. Sebeok, eds., *The Sign of Three* (Bloomington, Ind., 1983), 81–118. As letters in the Strong Papers, box 17, amply attest, Sellers also knew Jean Paul Richter well.

27. Strong Papers, box 2.

28. The school's mission was "to promote the study of Roman and Graeco-Roman archaeology in all its departments, and of palaeography . . . Every period of the language and literature, antiquities, art and history of Rome and Italy shall be considered as coming within the province of the School." It did not acquire a director or accommodation until 1900–1901. See T. P. Wiseman, *A Short History of the British School at Rome* (London, 1990), esp. 1–14.

29. Thomson, *Mrs. Arthur Strong,* 72

30. Strong Papers, box 17.

31. Wiseman, *A Short History of the British School,* gives an excellent summary of the Ashby-Strong years ("unpretentious" is his description of Mrs. Ashby; a very different—and engagingly malign—view is presented by Alistair Crawford in his dramatized

reading, *Evening with Eugénie Strong;* see also Thomson, who tactfully glosses over the final debacle in *Mrs. Arthur Strong,* 69–94.
32. Strong to Lord Crawford and Balcarres, June 19, 1925, Strong
Collection, BSR.
33. Agnes Sandys (of St. Hilda's College, Oxford), quoted in Thomson, *Mrs. Arthur Strong,* 73.
34. Striking for their characteristic (self-)hatred are the letters of
Ezra Pound: "If yr damn'd jew-run and usury-dominated rump
end of a government goes on monkeying with American mail TO
AMERICANS in Europe, a war of the U.S. ON England will before long be rather popular in the U.S.A.," Pound to Strong, February 5, 1938 (Strong Papers, box 15). There are many others
equally unworthy of quotation.
35. Quite how and by whom it was all transported to Girton (and
quite who decided which of the papers—mostly those that refer
directly to the British School—should remain in Rome) is not entirely clear to me, and is not recorded at Girton.
36. *La Chiesa Nuova* (Rome, 1923); *Times Literary Supplement,* for example, March 30 and April 6, 1933; April 18 and 25, 1936; July
30, 1938. Other work (on Roman art, St. Francis of Assissi, papal
patronage) is listed in Thomson, *Mrs. Arthur Strong,* 125–126,
and fully and more accurately in a bibliography Strong herself
compiled, published, and sent as Christmas presents in 1938
("Fascist era XVII," as she doubly dated it), Strong Papers, box
27.
37. Autobiographical notes, Strong Papers, box 15; Vernon Lee certainly refers to the possibility of Sellers's working on Italian material as early as 1887 (letters of Lee to Sellers, September 15, 1887,
and n.d. (1887), Strong Papers, box 16). Others, such as Thomson
(following Jocelyn Toynbee in her obituary of Mrs. Strong, *Antiquaries Journal* 23 [1943]: 188–189), identify her edition of Pliny,
which appeared in 1896 (still focused on Greek art, but a Roman
writer after all), as the break between Greece and Rome in
Strong's work—though, in fact, the Pliny edition goes as far as it
can (for an edition of a Latin author) to deny any interest in the
specifically Roman context.
38. *Girton Review,* Michaelmas Term, 1943, 14.
39. *Apotheosis and After Life,* 16 and 21;

40. See, for example, *Apotheosis and After Life*, 12: "It was the peculiar quality of Roman art as of Roman religion to be at the same time conservative and hospitable." Compare John North's discussion of religious "conservatism," "Conservatism and Change in Roman Religion," *Papers of the British School at Rome* 44 (1976): 1–12.

41. *Apotheosis and After Life*, lecture 1, 30–111 (quote on p. 75). I have (intentionally) "modernized" her expression but I hope not unfairly misrepresented her argument. There are plenty of other smart observations in this lecture; note, for example, the careful hedging in "the whole interest of *Roman sculpture or of sculpture at Rome*, whichever way you may prefer to put it" (p. 85, my emphasis).

3. Unanimism

1. Harrison, *Reminiscences*, 64–65; the story of Colvin's lectures is derived from the notes on Harrison's life made by Mirrlees (Notebook, Harrison Papers, box 15); it is repeated in Mirrlees's draft biography, box 15: "1878 In March goes to a lecture by Sidney Colvin on the excavations at Olympia. She told me that it was this that gave her the idea of taking up archaeology."

2. Quoted (from Mrs. Strong's own draft autobiographical notes, Strong papers, box 15) by Thomson, *Mrs. Arthur Strong*, 40. Postgate's letter (which admitted the "glamour" of archaeology): March 2, 1889 (Strong Papers, box 2). Postgate's underlying interest lay, we might suspect, not in deriding archaeology but in persuading Sellers to stick with language and literature (though 1889 was a bit late in the day, one can't help feeling).

3. Arthur Strong to Sellers, November 15, 1896 (Strong Papers, box 2); his emphasis. Sellers's masters in Germany included Wilhelm Dörpfeld, Ludwig Traube, and (above all) Adolf Furtwängler (Thomson, *Mrs. Arthur Strong*, 25–35).

4. Autobiographical notes (chapter heading "Germany"), Strong Papers, box 15 ("to practical purpose" is her correction for her earlier and more forthright formulation "to a career"); Arthur Strong, in a letter introducing Sellers to Salomon Reinach (March 1892), tactfully described her as "a pupil of Newton and Dörpfeld" (Strong Papers, box 2).

5. I have written about the archaeological revolution in Cambridge at this period in "The Invention (and Re-invention) of Group D" and (specifically on the foundation of the cast museum) in "Casts and Cast-Offs: The Origins of the Museum of Classical Archaeology." Jane Harrison was, in fact, corresponding with Waldstein (whom, according to Hope Mirrlees's draft biography, she had first met in Munich; Harrison Papers, box 15) at least from 1881, and was using letters of introduction from him in her travels around Europe; see the letters of Harrison to Waldstein in the Historical Archives of the International Olympic Committee, Lausanne, recently run to ground by Chris Stray; e.g., November 1 and December 31, 1881, Waldstein Papers, box 1.

6. A shared publisher would not today suggest any particular bond, but things were different in the world of late nineteenth-century "family" publishing houses. The Macmillan Archive (University of Reading) documents the close involvement of the Macmillan family (themselves major movers behind the British School at Athens and the Hellenic Society) with their authors; see also Henderson, *Juvenal's Mayor,* 28–34.

7. She cites the discussion in *Themis* of the Hagia Triada sarcophagus, in *Apotheosis and After Life,* 254 n. 6, and (on p. 255, n.8) Harrison's essay (including a discussion of *mundus*) in E. C. Quiggen, ed., *Essays and Studies presented to William Ridgeway* (Cambridge, 1913). For the list of donations, see Harrison Papers, box 20.

8. For her disputes with Ridgeway (Disney Professor of Archaeology in Cambridge, 1892–1926; Brereton Reader in Classics, 1907–1926), see Peacock, *Jane Ellen Harrison,* 213–215.

9. Peacock, *Jane Ellen Harrison,* 58; she is quoting the Notebook of Hope Mirrlees (Harrison Papers, box 15). Likewise, for that matter, there is nothing on Sellers in more strictly *intellectual* histories of Harrison's work; she is entirely absent from (for example) Ackerman, "Jane Ellen Harrison;" Schlesier, "Prolegomena to Jane Harrison's Interpretation of Ancient Greek Religion" (a German version, set in a broader context, is in Schlesier, *Kulte, Mythen und Gelehrte,* 123–192); and Lloyd-Jones, "Jane Harrison." Presciently, Chris Stray, in his review of Peacock's *Jane Ellen Harrison* in *Liverpool Classical Monthly* 16, no. 7 (July 1991): 103–111, sug-

gested Strong (among others) as offering a possibly illuminating comparison with Jane Harrison (p. 111, n. 37).

10. Thomson, *Mrs. Arthur Strong,* 24–25.
11. See below, Chapter 8.

4. Myths of the Odyssey in Art and Literature

1. This letter is quoted by du Puy's daughter, Gwen Raverat, in *Period Piece: A Cambridge Childhood* (London, 1952), 24.
2. Not yet *Sir* Charles; Newton was knighted a few years later, in 1887.
3. For what was *not* beyond description, see *The Times,* May 30, 1883, 10; May 31, 1883, 5; *Saturday Review,* June 9, 1883, 723–724; *Pall Mall Gazette,* May 30, 1883, 6; May 31, 1883, 4; *The Athenaeum,* June 2, 1883, 710; *The Graphic,* June 2, 1883, 546; *Vanity Fair,* June 2, 1883, 299.
4. *Pall Mall Gazette,* May 30. The place of this production in the modern history of Greek drama on stage is discussed in F. Macintosh, "Greek Tragedy in Performance: Nineteenth and Twentieth-Century Productions," in P. E. Easterling, ed., *The Cambridge Companion to Greek Tragedy* (Cambridge, 1997), 284–323 (esp. 292–294), and in E. Hall and F. Macintosh, *Greek Tragedy and the British Stage 1660–1914* (Oxford, forthcoming).
5. Very brief enjoyment, in fact: Leighton's peerage was formally confirmed the day before he died in 1896.
6. Vernon Lee to her mother, Mrs. M. Paget, July 2, 1883 (*Letters,* 123); "a superb decorator and a superb piece of decoration," she went on; more prosaically, S. Jones et al., *Frederic Leighton 1830–1896* (London, 1996), catalogue of Royal Academy exhibition, February 15–April 21, 1996.
7. That at least is the galaxy of artists involved in the production as recalled by Mrs. (Maud) Beerbohm Tree, "Herbert and I," in M. Beerbohm, ed., *Herbert Beerbohm Tree* (London, n.d., c. 1918), 18. But Mrs. Tree's memory may have added a few stars: the contemporary reviews that I have seen mention Leighton, Poynter, and Watts (a distinguished enough trio on their own)—backed up by G. Simonds, P. H. Delamotte, Henry Holiday, and Walter Crane, but not Burne-Jones and Millais.

8. Beerbohm Tree, "Herbert and I," 18.
9. These are the recollections of Elinor Paul (Ritchie), a friend of Harrison from Newnham, who played Andromache on the Greek nights. They come from a letter written by Paul to Mirrlees after Harrison's death, (Harrison Papers, box 9; dated "June 13," postmarked 1934[?], though apparently drawing on her 1880s diary). By the time of writing Paul looks back at the tableaux (now fifty years distant) with faintly patronizing, if fond, amusement: "I enjoyed it greatly for Jane and I used to spend hours at the B.M. where she was lecturing at the time looking at vases with Newton and Cecil Smith."
10. Paul quoted in Hope Mirrlees, Notebook, Harrison Papers, box 15; quite what irony was intended is unclear.
11. Mirrlees, draft biography, Harrison Papers, box 15. J. K. was part of the Stephen dynasty, cousin of Virginia Woolf; he starved himself to death in 1892.
12. See Chapter 2. This was the occcasion that Rodd (who played Eumaeus, the enslaved prince and swineherd—with "considerable dramatic talent," *The Athenaeum,* June 2, 1883, 710) forgot, or chose not to mention, when he spoke at the farewell dinner of having first encountered Mrs. Strong amid the columns of the Parthenon.
13. Mirrlees, Notebook (quoting Elinor Paul) and draft biography (Harrison Papers, box 15). A theme picked up in the *Vanity Fair* review, subtitled "When Freake Meets Greek, Then Comes the Tug of War" (parodying Nathaniel Lee's "When Greeks joined Greeks . . . ," a well-known quotation from *The Rival Queens*). In fact the young Cambridge ladies had plenty more sneers for their hostess: "[She always said] 'the demi-monde will come' meaning half the world" (Notebook); perhaps she was righter than they knew.
14. All correspondence connected with the theatricals is in Strong Papers, box 2 (except for the letter from Leighton, box 15).
15. Mirrlees, Notebook and draft biography, Harrison Papers, box 15, deriving from Elinor Paul's letter and diary (above, n. 9).
16. This reviewer, too, admired the ladies—and (like the contributor to *Vanity Fair*) spotted a Cambridge connection: "The number of ladies taking part in the chorus must have been beyond the re-

sources of Girton to produce." In fact, in 1883 the ladies of Girton were busy putting on their own Greek play, in Greek: Sophocles' *Electra.* This is described and illustrated by "a graduate of Girton," in "Greek Plays at the Universities," which appeared in *Woman's World,* a strikingly high-brow (and short-lived) women's magazine edited by Oscar Wilde. It is discussed by Edith Hall, "Sophocles' *Electra* in Britain," in J. Griffin, ed., *Sophocles Revisited: Studies for Sir Hugh Lloyd-Jones* (Oxford, 1999), 261–306, which will form a chapter in Hall and Macintosh, *Greek Tragedy and the British Stage.* A full photographic record of the production is preserved in the Girton College Archive.

17. Warr and Crane, *Echoes of Hellas.*
18. *The Athenaeum,* June 2, 1883.
19. *Pall Mall Gazette,* May 31, 1883, words echoed by the *Saturday Review,* June 9, which called Eumaeus "a picturesque homely figure"; either there was a common source (the program?) or this was journalistic plagiarism.
20. Traill's collected satires were issued under the title *The New Lucian: Being a Series of Dialogues of the Dead;* others set Lucretius together with Paley and Darwin, Lucian with Pascal.
21. H. D. Traill, "South Kensington Hellenism: A Dialogue"; "awfully clever" is the bravely ironic comment of Warr writing to Sellers, July 2, 1883 (Strong Papers, box 2).
22. These productions are discussed in Macintosh, "Greek Tragedy in Performance," esp. 290–294; Easterling, "The Early Years of the Cambridge Greek Play," Hall and Macintosh, *Greek Tragedy and the British Stage.* Contemporary overviews are given by the "graduate of Girton," in "Greek Plays at the Universities," and by Lewis Campbell, *A Guide to Greek Tragedy for English Readers* (London, 1891), 317–330.
23. The equivalence between Plato's school and their own had, in fact, never been lost on members of the Royal Academy (they had, for example, inscribed above the doorway to their Great Exhibition Room in Somerset House a parody of the words that were said to decorate the entrance to Plato's school: Plato had (according to Elias' sixth-century commentary on Aristotle's *Categories* 118.18) ἀγεωμέτρητος μηδεὶς εἰσίτω (No Entry for Those Ignorant of Geometry); the Royal Academy had οὐδεὶς εἰσίτω ἄμουσος (No Entry for the Un-Mused).

24. Strong Papers, box 2.
25. July 2, 1883 (Strong Papers, box 2).
26. Charles Newton, August 22, 1883 (Strong Papers, box 2).
27. Draft biography, Harrison Papers, box 15.
28. E. R. Lankester (one of the founders of modern zoology), June 6, 1883; the letter continued by (naughtily) inviting her to tea: "Pray come in a Greek dress & sandals & with a delicate touch of rouge—if you prefer it" (Strong Papers, box 2).
29. Draft biography, Harrison Papers, box 15.
30. Macintosh, "Greek Tragedy in Performance," is a good guide to this whole period, which is fundamental in the history of the reception of Greek tragedy.
31. This debacle is described by Hope Mirrlees, quoting a diary or letter of another would-be participant, Margaret Merrifield (Mrs. A. W. Verrall), draft biography, Harrison Papers, box 15. The Principal's objections make quite explicit the issues of erotics and gender that many of these (Greek) theatricals raised; they are touched on also in nineteenth-century fictional accounts of such performances; see, for example, E. Hall, "Greek Plays in Georgian Reading," *Greece and Rome* 44 (1997): 59–81, esp. 70–71; Easterling, "The Early Years of the Cambridge Greek Play."
32. P. de Cosson to Sellers, January 26 and February 29, 1884 (Strong Papers, box 2).
33. Todhunter to Sellers, March 9, 1884, a letter that lays out in some detail his own principles of theater production (Strong Papers, box 2).
34. Todhunter to Sellers, May 9, 1884 (Strong Papers, box 2).
35. She was originally to have gone, it seems, as one of Newton's own party, "an illustrious row of ten"; when she couldn't make it, he obligingly wrote to Todhunter to change her ticket to another day (Newton to Sellers, May 11 and May 13, 1886, Strong Papers, box 16).
36. *Daily Telegraph,* May 18, 1886, 5. As in *The Tale of Troy,* the cast had a sprinkling of professionals: the Beerbohm Trees (again) and Hermann Vezin; otherwise it was an intentionally amateur cast, including Mrs. Oscar Wilde.
37. There is a brief discussion in J. Stokes, *Resistible Theatres: Enterprise and Experiment in the Late Nineteenth Century* (London, 1972), 52–58; Macintosh, "Tragedy in Performance," 294–295; Marshall,

Actresses on the Victorian Stage, 97–98. The review in the *Telegraph* (n. 36), so critical of the acting, enthused about the set: "as fair a model as can be of the best known theatre on the Acropolis."

38. May 23, 1886 (Todhunter Papers, University of Reading, ms. 202/1/1 f. 327–330).

39. W. Courtney (n.d.) to Evelyn Abbott (Jowett Papers, Balliol College, Oxford); Courtney had been involved in the 1880 production of *Agamemnon* in Oxford and was the man behind the *Alcestis.*

40. Her lectures were noted in *The Times,* May 19, 1887: "a lady who has lately been giving in Oxford a successful course of lectures on Greek sculpture." Presumably this was a series of University Extension lectures.

41. *The Athenaeum,* May 28, 1887, 713. See also the letter of Todhunter with details of the sale, Todhunter Papers, University of Reading, ms. 202/1/1, f. 362–367.

42. Mirrlees, draft biography, Harrison Papers, box 15. The acting is described in a letter of Mrs. Sidgwick to her sister, Ethel Wilson, May 18, 1887 (copied for Hope Mirrlees, Harrison Papers, box 15); it continues, "Mr. Moberly & Ruth Woodhouse & Margaret Cornish . . . are rather shocked at the agony & grim Death . . . But the real life-tragedy is worse to see . . . for indeed Alcestises are in every corner of the land & the uncomforted heroines, whom all forsake & flee." This emphasis on "real life-tragedy" may or may not allude to Harrison's tragic non-affair with S. H. Butcher; see below, Chapter 9.

43. *Cambridge Review,* May 25, 1887, 345–356; *The Athenaeum,* May 28, 1887, 712–713.

44. Time chart, Strong Papers, box 15.

45. Jex-Blake to Sellers, n.d. (1887), Strong Papers, box 2.

46. The story of the Cambridge show (and its close connections with classical archaeology) is elegantly told by Easterling in "The Early Years of the Cambridge Greek Play."

47. Mirrlees, draft biography, Harrison Papers, box 15. The Helen of Troy whose performance Waldstein wished to improve was either Mrs. Beerbohm Tree (in Greek) or Miss Sellers (in English); as Harrison appeared only in the Greek version of the play, it was more likely the former.

48. I discuss his career (briefly) in "Casts and Cast-Offs," 9 and 14,

and (at greater length) in "The Invention (and Re-invention) of Group D."

49. Newton's transformation of the classical galleries of the British Museum is discussed by I. Jenkins, *Archaeologists and Aesthetes: In the Sculpture Galleries of the British Museum 1800–1939* (London, 1992), 168–195; his career (with a particular emphasis on Asia Minor) is detailed by B. F. Cook, "Sir Charles Newton KCB (1816–1894)," in I. Jenkins and G. B. Waywell, eds., *Sculptors and Sculpture of Caria and the Dodecanese* (London, 1997), 10–29; see also the obituary by Sellers herself (in French), *Revue Archéologique,* 3rd series, 25 (1894): 273–281. For Newton as "the tempter" of Sellers, see autobiographical notes, Strong Papers, box 15, quoted by Thompson, *Mrs. Arthur Strong,* 22.

50. Cook, "Sir Charles Newton," 17.

51. June 12, 1883 (Strong Papers, box 2); not that the photograph (even with the jewels) was quite the triumph they'd hoped it would be (above, n. 26).

52. August 22, 1883 (Strong Papers, box 2).

5. Introductory Studies in Greek Art

1. Her story, that is, according to Hope Mirrlees (draft biography, Harrison Papers, box 15).

2. Harrison, *Reminiscences,* 64 (and above, Chapter 3).

3. The Mallesons were a notable family of philanthropists; for their widespread connections, see Malleson, *Autobiographical Notes and Letters.* Harrison later traveled to Germany and Italy with Mabel.

4. Many of the series were University Extension lectures, the late-Victorian equivalent of our own continuing education programs. She also had a strong line in boys' public schools, archly recorded in *Reminiscences,* 54–55. For an alternative view of one of these occasions, see *The Wykehamist* 217 (March 1887): 131—a respectful account of her "most interesting" lecture on "Hellenic Vases," "illustrated by a magic lantern."

5. *Pall Mall Gazette,* November 4, 1891, 1.

6. Murray, *Jane Ellen Harrison,* 7. Cornford's recollection was published in the *Newnham College Roll Letter* 1929, 72 (and is quoted by Stewart, *Jane Ellen Harrison,* 20). The collection of lantern

slides is, in fact, extremely varied—including photographic images (from the Parthenon to bullfights) as well as hand-colored transparencies.

7. Harrison, *Reminiscences,* 63.

8. Violet Buxton to Sellers, March 2, ?1892 (Strong Papers, box 2).

9. A. Dew-Smith, *Newnham College Roll Letter* 1929, 6. Arthur Sidgwick, writing a testimonial for her application to the Yates Chair of Archaeology at University College in 1888 (Harrison Papers, box 18), probably thought it wise to make a preemptive strike against the predictable criticism: "[She] successfully avoids that common danger of lecturers who have the gift of speech . . . a tendency, namely, to high flown and overloaded phrases: her style is at once forceful, stimulating and unpretentious."

10. Alice Dew-Smith notes, in a diary entry dated "Friday Nov. 11, 1898," copied by Hope Mirrlees (Notebook, Harrison Papers, box 15): "Went to JEH's lecture—which was very full—on Delphi. The slides all went wrong & put her out very much."

11. See Borland, *D. S. MacColl,* and below, Chapter 8. All biographers of Harrison have tracked down the MacColl connection. Mirrlees and Jessie Stewart independently made (multiple) copies of selections from the MacColl Papers (now in Glasgow University Library). These (more or less accurate) copies are now lodged in the Harrison Papers, box 8 (Mirrlees; recopied into Notebook, box 15) and box 22 (Stewart).

12. December 15, 1920 (Strong Papers, box 13). For Strong's uncompromising reply, see her letter of December 20, box 13.

13. So runs one of Harrison's (melodramatic) replies to "that fatal letter" from MacColl, February 6, 1887 (MacColl Papers, H157; copy, Harrison Papers, box 22, and Mirrlees, Notebook, box 15). The whole incident is discussed (and, I shall be arguing in Chapter 8, inflated) by Ackerman, "Jane Ellen Harrison," 223–225; Peacock, *Jane Ellen Harrison,* 70–74.

14. Harrison to MacColl, MacColl Papers, H156 (copy, Harrison Papers, box 22, and Mirrlees, Notebook, box 15), dated "Saturday" (1887).

15. Katherine Raleigh had been an undergraduate at Newnham, reading Classics from 1883 to 1886 (though she took no university examinations); she later worked as secretary for the Hellenic Soci-

ety and the British Schools in Athens and Rome, as well as translating works by J. P. Richter into English (another link between this group and the Morellian revolution; see Chapter 2). At Newnham she is best remembered as the founder of the (still thriving) Raleigh Music Society.

16. This is the recollection of Miss Lilias Ramsay, quoted by Thomson, *Mrs. Arthur Strong,* 20. Sellers also taught Lilias's sister, Agnata Ramsay, who as an undergraduate at Girton famously outranked all the men in the Cambridge Classical Tripos in 1887 (and was even more famously depicted in a *Punch* cartoon, dressed in gown and mortar board entering a *first class* railway carriage marked "FOR LADIES ONLY" (*Punch,* July 2, 1887, 326). Agnata's finest hour was swiftly followed (in 1888) by marriage to the Master of Trinity College, Henry Montagu-Butler.

17. Autobiographical notes, Strong Papers, box 15.

18. See J. Sutherland, *Mrs. Humphry Ward: Eminent Victorian, Preeminent Edwardian* (Oxford, 1990); quotation on 201; P. Adams, *Somerville for Women: An Oxford College 1879–1993* (Oxford, 1996), 7–19. The Wards' excuses for nonpayment follow the predictable pattern (July 7, 1889: "I am too ashamed of myself about this cheque. It all comes of my having mislaid your letter," Strong Papers, box 16), but prompt payment or not, they were a useful celebrity connection, and Sellers called on them for testimonials when she applied for (or considered applying for) a lecturing post at Royal Holloway College in 1887 (Mrs. Humphry Ward to Sellers, n.d. (1887), Strong Papers, box 16).

19. The tableaux are described by young Dorothy Ward to Sellers, May 5, 1887 (Strong Papers, box 2).

20. Harrison to Miss Marshall, February 19, 1890 (Harrison Papers, box 9).

21. The apparent lack of interest on the part of the press is discussed in two letters to Sellers: from Lionel Johnston, November 6, 1885 and from Humphry Ward, November 10, 1885, (Strong Papers, box 2). Mackail's carefully polite reply (October 25, 1885), with Sidney Colvin's (October 28, 1885), is in Strong Papers, box 2. Leighton's flamboyantly illegible refusal (November 2, 1885) hides in Strong Papers, box 15.

22. October 28, 1885 (Strong Papers, box 2).

23. December 15, 1885 (Strong Papers, box 2).

24. In the 1880s psychical research was almost as fashionable as Greek theater: see C. Creighton to Sellers, January 29, 1885 (Strong Papers, box 2). The visits to the Alma-Tademas apparently start in 1887: L. Alma-Tadema to Sellers, November 20, 1887, and April 8, 1888; A. Alma-Tadema to Sellers, December 15, 1887 (Strong Papers, box 2).

25. Sellers to Lee, dated January 16, 1887 (but see below, Chapter 6, n. 19), Vernon Lee Papers; on the portrait, see Newton to Sellers, May 7, 1889 (Strong Papers, box 16). Hope Mirrlees predictably casts *Harrison* as Newton's special friend: "I always think that he had a great *tendresse* for Jane." (Notebook, Harrison Papers, box 15; a longer version of the relationship between Harrison and Newton is included in Mirrlees's draft biography, Harrison Papers, box 15.)

26. Postgate to Sellers, November 4 and November 23, 1888 (Strong Papers, box 2).

27. For an account of this election, see Calder, "Jane Harrison's Failed Candidacies for the Yates Professorship."

28. Postgate to Sellers, November 23, 1888 (Strong Papers, box 2). On Farnell, see Henderson, "Farnell's Cults." The damning of Waldstein is reported by Calder, "Jane Harrison's Failed Candidacies for the Yates Professorship," 51.

29. Despite the signed document, Calder ("Jane Harrison's Failed Candidacies for the Yates Professorship," 59) reaches the bizarre conclusion that prejudice against women played almost no part in the decision; Lloyd-Jones ("Jane Harrison," 34) apparently agrees: "no injustice . . . was done."

30. Smith to Sellers, February 3, 1889 (Strong Papers, box 2). "Of course," Smith's letter goes on, with more than a hint of the exclusivity that marked such allegiances, "she may not really belong to Miss Harrison's circle, but the odd thing is after the first meeting I had an instinctive feeling that she did though I did not definitely remember her face."

31. Harrison to MacColl (dated only "Wednesday," but pre-1887); the letter ends in a postscript: "All my questions will keep except the one about the fair lady" (MacColl Papers, H166; copies, Harrison Papers, boxes 8 and 22). For one version of Harrison's relationship

with MacColl, see Peacock, *Jane Ellen Harrison,* 65–71, 83–89; from MacColl's side, Borland, *D. S. MacColl,* 51–58; see also below, Chapter 8.

32. R. Browning, *The Poems,* vol. 1, ed. J. Pettigrew (Harmondsworth, 1981), 416–447.

33. The obituary appeared in *The Times,* September 21, 1943, 6; for MacColl's reply, see Strong Papers, box 27.

34. Strong Papers, box 15.

35. Mirrlees, "Further Notes and Memories of My Own," Harrison Papers, box 15. For what little is known of "Get" (Jane) Wilson, who shared a home with Harrison for many of the years between 1882 and 1898, see Peacock, *Jane Ellen Harrison,* 64–67.

36. Margaret Smith to Sellers, February 3, 1889 (Strong Papers, box 2).

37. For the moment I am treating "German archaeology" as if it were a single "school"—and indeed that is how it was often treated by the English (Harrison and Sellers included) in the late nineteenth century. We shall see later in this chapter, unsurprisingly, that it had its own tensions, disagreements, and disputes; to admire one German archaeologist was not to admire them all.

38. Harrison to Elizabeth Malleson, September 9, 1881 (copy in Harrison Papers, box 8).

39. The trip is evoked by Harrison herself in *Reminiscences,* 64–65; a narrative (largely based on information from the Mallesons) is given in Mirrlees's draft biography (Harrison Papers, box 15). Copies (made for Mirrlees) of other letters from Harrison (abroad) to Mrs. Malleson, between September and December 1881, are preserved in the Harrison Papers, box 8.

40. Harrison to Elizabeth Malleson, September 9, 1881 (copy in Harrison Papers, box 8).

41. See Beard, "Casts and Cast-Offs."

42. Autobiographical notes (Strong Papers, box 15), reprinted in Thomson, *Mrs. Arthur Strong,* 30.

43. Autobiographical notes (Strong papers, box 15), reprinted in Thomson, *Mrs. Arthur Strong,* 34–35.

44. Diary entries for 1895 (Strong Papers, box 1). The trips to Munich are described at loving length in her autobiographical notes (Strong Papers, box 15) and partly reprinted in Thomson, *Mrs.*

Arthur Strong, 26–35 (though Thomson wrongly implies that the main visit was in the 1880s).

45. *Berliner Philologische Wochenschrift* 10 (April 12, 1890): 461–471.

46. Joint communiqué: *Classical Review* 5 (1891): 284–285. Loring (who was the effective site director, under the name of Gardner) broke ranks much more comprehensively than the others, though the timing was (and remains) confused. In the main publication of the site (E. A. Gardner et al., *Excavations at Megalopolis, 1890–1891 Journal of Hellenic Studies,* (supp. 1, 1892), Gardner more or less sticks to his guns (while genuflecting to Dörpfeld); however, the chapter "The Theatre" (pp. 69–91), jointly authored by Gardner and Loring, is followed by a note to the effect that "Mr. Loring . . . since passing a proof of Chap IV . . . has changed his opinion"; this is explained by Loring in "The Theatre at Megalopolis," *Journal of Hellenic Studies* 13 (1892–93): 356–358, which reprints a letter he had previously published in *The Athenaeum.* The background to Dörpfeld's visit is not entirely clear. It seems plausible that the British excavators *invited* Dörpfeld to the site; that certainly is the impression given by Gardner in his Preface (puzzlingly dated May *1893*) to the report published in *1892*—completely disguising the horrible animosity that marked the controversy.

47. Though no one likes to admit it, the excavations at Megalopolis were frankly a disgrace. No wonder they barely find a mention in H. Waterhouse, *The British School at Athens: The First Hundred Years,* British School at Athens, supplementary vol. 19 (London, 1986), and no wonder the British have always claimed to be better at Greek *prehistoric* sites.

48. Harrison, *Reminiscences,* 65

49. *Classical Review* 4 (1890): 274–277; she is quoting A. W. Verrall, reviewing Haigh, in *Classical Review* 4 (1890): 225. Her reference to Dörpfeld's "suggestive" work is a delicate understatement, but unmistakable in its allegiance. Her *Mythology and Monuments of Ancient Athens* (with M. de G. Verrall) also follows Dörpfeld's line on the theater (pp. 271–295).

50. *Classical Review* 5 (1891): 239–240.

51. Jebb to Sellers, June 26, 1891 (Strong Papers, box 2).

52. Sellers to George Macmillan, July 19, 1891 (Macmillan Archive,

14/215). Sellers was, in fact, the first ever female student of the British School at Athens.

53. Campbell to Sellers, June 20, 1891 (Strong Papers, box 2; partly quoted (and misquoted) in Thomson, *Mrs. Arthur Strong*, 25); the "joint letter" of Dörpfeld and Gardner is presumably the communiqué in the *Classical Review* (above, n. 46).

54. Sellers to Waldstein, July 13, 1891, Waldstein Papers.

55. It is worth spelling this out, and reflecting on how differently this story would run if I had come across (as was nearly the case) only the letters to Macmillan and Jebb, or only the "reluctant victim" letter to Waldstein. So, too, on a larger scale (and this is one of the main morals of this book) with our image of Jane Harrison: inevitably diffused and multiply diffracted through different contexts, observers, and addressees.

56. For a brief history of intellectual tourism to Bassae, see M. Beard and J. Henderson, *A Very Short Introduction to Classics* (Oxford, 1995), 21–32.

57. MacColl to Mrs. J. S. M. MacColl, May 25, 1888 (MacColl Papers, M256; copy in Harrison Papers, box 22, wrongly entitled "*Diary* of a Greek Journey"). He appears to have no inkling that the muleteer might not have been telling the whole truth. "We told the man to make for Bassae & towards 8 or half past we reached a little village in the hills called Dhromovoi. Here our guide thought he had us & led us to a cabin where he said we could sleep. We should sleep I said at Bassae. The village was round us, exclaiming, screaming. We could not sleep there—could not get there—it was dark, it was cold, it was wet. 'The English, it was explained, do not fear the cold. The κύρια [*sic*; MacColl's grip on the principles of Greek accentuation is forgivably shaky] does not fear the cold. You are a man, why should you fear it?' Then the muleteer had to confess he did not know the way." Other letters to Mrs. MacColl and to his sisters Lizzie and Letitia describing this trip are preserved in MacColl Papers, M252–255, E59 (copies, Harrison Papers, box 22). See also Harrison, *Reminiscences*, 66–69; Borland, *D. S. MacColl*, 52–58.

58. So much is clearly implied in her own notes on the chronology of their letters during the 1890s: e.g., "Letters written between Jan 1894—after my attempt to settle in Paris—and Jan 95, when I

determined to leave England altogether and to settle in Germany. In 1894 occurred our delightful meeting in Dresden" (Strong Papers, box 2).

59. Hope Mirrlees's words, from her draft biography (Harrison Papers, box 15).

60. MacColl to Sellers, 1889 (Strong Papers, box 13).

61. Lizzie MacColl to Sellers, May 4, 1890 (Strong Papers, box 2); Harrison had recommended Miss Godkin's to MacColl in 1887 as a convenient place to stay ("Friday" [1887], MacColl Papers, H159; copies in Harrison Papers, boxes 8 and 22).

62. MacColl Papers, E59 (copy, Harrison Papers, box 22).

63. Harrison to Elizabeth Malleson, June 6, 1888 (copy in Harrison Papers, box 8).

64. Their itinerary can be reconstructed from MacColl's letters home (above, n. 57); for "the return to civilisation," see MacColl to Mrs. J. S. M. MacColl, May 21, 1888 (MacColl Papers, M255). If they had any sense, the party would have taken with them J. E. Sandys's helpful guide, *An Easter Vacation in Greece* (London, 1887); Sandys had made his Greek odyssey exactly a year before Harrison and party, and had published his diary, combined with useful pieces of practical information, such as steamer and train timetables. (The copy of Sandys that I have been using was originally owned by Sir James Frazer. Typically, he bought it [August 13, 1890] just after he had *returned* from Greece, on a trip that was preliminary to his great edition of Pausanias.) For Pausanian tourism, more generally, see Beard, "Pausanias in Petticoats."

65. MacColl to Mrs. J. S. M. MacColl, April 12, 1888 (MacColl Papers, M253; copy in Harrison Papers, box 22); Harrison to Mrs. E. Malleson, June 6, 1888 (copy in Harrison Papers, box 8).

66. *Archäologischer Anzeiger* (1889): 63.

67. See, for example, C. A. Abbott to Sellers, January 15, 1888; A. Lucas to Sellers, January 27, 1888; J. P. Postgate to Sellers, March 3, 1888; George Lewis to Sellers, April 1, 1888 (Strong Papers, box 2).

68. Diary (Strong Papers, box 26). On Sellers and Vernon Lee, see below, Chapter 6.

69. O. Hikelas to Sellers, August 2, 1888 (Strong Papers, box 2).

70. See, for example, D. Traill, *Schliemann of Troy: Treasure and Deceit*

(London, 1995), plate 24, not to mention a bizarre picture among Strong's papers in Rome of "Dörpfeld and his groom," in Greek national dress—in which he is, in fact, quite closely reminiscent of the portly man in the background with his drooping mustache.

71. For brief biographical sketches, see R. Lullies and W. Schiering, eds., *Archäologenbildnisse: Porträts und Kurzbiographien von Klassischen Archäologen deutscher Sprache* (Mainz, 1988), 110–113; and A. E. Furtwängler (a relation), in Briggs and Calder eds., *Classical Scholarship,* 84–92. The general context is discussed in S. L. Marchand, *Down from Olympus: Archaeology and Philhellenism in Germany, 1750–1970* (Princeton, 1996), 116–151; she nastily (and slightly unfairly, on Winckelmann no less than on Furtwängler) encapsulates the achievements of Furtwängler's *Meisterwerke* on pp. 144–145.

72. The meeting between Harrison and Furtwängler, at the German Institute in Athens, is described by Jessie Crum (Stewart), who obviously saw the joke: "D[örpfeld] introduced him to J. 'You know Miss H. I think you met in Berlin' *v. smilingly*" (my emphasis; quoted in Stray, "Digs and Degrees," 126–127. Note also Harrison's review of *Meisterwerke* in *Classical Review* 9 (1895): 85–92 and Furtwängler's reply, 269–276.

73. Jex-Blake to Sellers, November 8, 1885 (Strong Papers, box 2).

74. This briefly summarizes one influential version of the history of female same-sex relations: see, for example, L. Faderman, *Surpassing the Love of Men,* and Smith-Rosenberg, "The Female World of Love and Ritual" (also incorporated in Smith-Rosenberg's *Disorderly Conduct,* 53–76). Both works clearly delineate a historical development—from "romantic" or "sentimental friendships" between women in the late nineteenth century to specifically "lesbian" (and, in conventional terms, "abnormal" or "inverted") sexual relationships in the early twentieth century.

75. Many of these doubts (which I share) are raised by Vicinus, "'They Wonder to Which Sex I Belong,'" and Moore, "'Something More Tender Still Than Friendship.'"

76. For Harrison, anachronistically conscripted as a model for modern lesbian-feminism, see Passman, "Out of the Closet and into the Field" ("The real problem was that Jane Harrison wrote like a dyke and lived like a dyke, as any Lesbian could see," 181).

77. Notebook, Harrison Papers, box 15.
78. "Further Notes and Recollections of My Own," Harrison Papers, box 15.
79. Notebook, Harrison Papers, box 15.
80. Throughout Mirrlees's drafts (Harrison Papers, box 15) *Schwärmerei* is used of a childish "crush" (she writes, for example, in the draft biography of the young Harrison's changing relations with her teacher Miss Beale, "Another probable cause of her dislike for Miss Beale is the sense of grievance of having been defrauded in which a young girl's schwärmerei for purely biological reasons, is apt to end"). The word (which evokes the swarming of bees) is briefly discussed by Prins, "Greek Maenads, Victorian Spinsters," 51.

6. Alpha and Omega

1. Strong Papers, box 15; a comic (anti-)image of the "New Woman" is illustrated in Marshall, *Actresses on the Victorian Stage,* 169. A poster for Sydney Grundy's play *The New Woman,* it shows her sitting on a stool, glasses on her nose, surrounded by books (*Man the Betrayer, Naked But Not Ashamed*) and sheaves of paper—and to one side a cigarette burning; the poster also appears on the front cover of J. Chothia, ed., *The New Woman and Other Emancipated Woman Plays* (Oxford, 1998). See also S. Ledger, "The New Woman and the Crisis of Victorianism," in S. Ledger and S. McCracken, eds., *Cultural Politics at the Fin de Siècle* (Cambridge, 1995), 22–44.
2. Thomson, *Mrs. Arthur Strong,* 24–25.
3. "Further Notes and Memories of My Own," Harrison Papers, box 15.
4. *Pall Mall Gazette,* November 4, 1891, 1 (see above, Chapter 5).
5. *Classical Review* 9 (1895): 85–92. Harrison's review appears, appropriately enough, directly under George Warr's memorial lines (in Greek) for Charles Newton (who had died on December 4, 1894). Furtwängler's muscular riposte followed shortly (*Classical Review* 9 [1895]: 272–276), written in perfect English—translated by Sellers, I imagine.
6. See Thomson, *Mrs. Arthur Strong,* 24–25, 43.

7. Lee's career is discussed in Gunn, *Vernon Lee;* her wartime fiction, by G. Beer, "The Dissidence of Vernon Lee: *Satan the Waster* and the Will to Believe," in S. Raitt and T. Tate, eds., *Women's Fiction and the Great War* (Oxford, 1997), 107–131. A small selection of her correspondence was edited and published by I. Cooper Willis (Lee, *Letters*) in 1937; thousands of letters to her are preserved in the archive of Somerville College, Oxford, and Colby College, Maine. "Very nasty" are the words of the critic W. C. Monkhouse, writing to Lee (quoted by Gunn, *Vernon Lee,* 102).

8. Gunn, *Vernon Lee,* 11–24 (quotes on pp. 13 and 22).

9. "I feel my summer's fate is rather in your hands, as I am decidedly too poor to afford lodgings," Lee to Sellers, March 20, no year stated (1892?) (Strong Papers, box 16).

10. Lee to Mrs. M. Paget, July 10, 1886 (*Letters,* 221).

11. Lee to Mrs. M. Paget, September 13, 1893 (*Letters,* 367). See also July 11, 1887, p. 256 (on the photograph); July 2, 1887, p. 253; July 17, 1887, p. 258 (on the Cambridge visit); on Florence, see above, Chapter 5.

12. Thomson, *Mrs. Arthur Strong,* 43.

13. All these quotations are taken from the Preface, v–viii.

14. See, for example, Ackerman, "Jane Ellen Harrison," 223–225; Peacock, *Jane Ellen Harrison,* 75. MacColl's attack is discussed above, in Chapter 5 (the lectures), and below, in Chapter 8.

15. All the information (and quotations) about the origins of the trouble is taken from a draft copy of a letter, Sellers to Lee, October 16 (1886) (Strong Papers, box 16).

16. So runs the reply, Lee to Sellers, October 20, 1886 (Strong Papers, box 16), from which all the quotations in this paragraph are taken.

17. How we interpret this dismissal depends on whether we think that the "Miss Harrison" that Lee met at dinner in early June (just a month before the dinner with Sellers) was "our" Miss Harrison or not; Lee to Mrs. M. Paget, June 6, 1886, (*Letters,* 207). Lee *was* seeing some other Harrisons at the time, and in fact Frederick Harrison had "taken her into dinner" the very night she met Sellers; Sellers to Lee, October 16 (1886) (Strong Papers, box 16).

18. Draft copy of a letter, Sellers to Lee, October 22, 1886 (Strong Papers, box 16)

19. Sellers to Lee, January 16, 1887 (Vernon Lee Papers); the letter is dated January 16, 1886, but that must be a new-year error— Sellers and Lee had not yet met in January 1886.

20. Her major contributions to aesthetics at this period were *Studies of the Eighteenth Century in Italy* (London, 1880) and *Belcaro: Being Essays on Sundry Aesthetical Questions* (London, 1881). See also Gunn, *Vernon Lee,* 79–82.

21. The third side of this triangle—the relations between Harrison and Lee—is much less clearly documented; the tone of Lee's first letter to Sellers ("I had not seen her or heard of her for four years," October 20, 1886, Strong Papers, box 16) suggests that they may never have been on particularly cordial terms.

22. See above, Chapter 5.

23. MacColl to Sellers, December 20, 1890 (Strong Papers, box 13), recording his rather weak excuses for spoiling her book; June 19, 1891, on Dörpfeld—though he does go on (his recollection of the boredom fading over time) to recognize Dörpfeld's "cheerful energy and conviction."

24. Strong Papers, box 13.

25. Strong Papers, box 13 (Christmas Day, note; MacColl was not a man to let anything rest). Sellers obviously replied instantly—for on December 27 he writes to say how relieved he is that the misunderstanding has been cleared up (Strong Papers, box 13). This broken confidence *could,* of course, be the first rumbling of trouble with Miss Harrison.

26. January 18, 1891 (Strong Papers, box 13).

7. Ancient Art and Ritual

1. *Myths of the Odyssey in Art and Literature,* vii.

2. In *Juvenal's Mayor,* Henderson bravely explores the "anecdotage" of teaching and lecturing in late nineteenth-century Cambridge, trying to reach "the personal politics of the *performative* within the semiotics of scholarship" by a different route (p. 61; my emphasis).

3. Buxton to Sellers, March 2, 1892? (Strong Papers, box 2). If the date is correct, this was a judgment that shortly followed the "terrific bust-up."

4. *Introductory Studies in Greek Art,* vi.

5. Though now rather down at heel, the building has survived bombs and road schemes—its grand classical portico still reminding visitors of the social pretensions of those who once occupied the relatively modest flats within.

6. *Pall Mall Gazette,* November 4, 1891, 1.

7. Though he does retaliate, and in the end it is hard to tell who gets the better of this encounter. Later on in the interview the ladies ask him to admire a battered bit of sculpture. "Isn't it beautiful?" they prompt. "'Very,' I replied emphatically, and thought of the beauty of ugliness."

8. Mostly collected in Harrison Papers, boxes 9 and 18.

9. Quoted from Oxford University Extension Lectures, syllabus for a course of six lectures on "The Mythology of the Parthenon Marbles" (n.d.). Most of the course syllabuses ("Homeric Greece and the Myths of the Homeric Cycle," with Walter Leaf; "Athens: Its Mythology and Art") lay down exactly the same principles in very similar slogans.

10. Quoted from advertisement prospectus, with prices, University Extension Society, Chelsea Centre, Lent Term, 1890.

11. "These are freely lent up to the time of the return of the papers. If students desire to keep them they can be retained at the price marked on the back. Great care is requested in the use of the photographs" (correspondence course prospectus, Harrison Papers, box 9); sometimes reminders were necessary ("Could you kindly send back those of the photographs that you do not keep"; Harrison to Miss Marshall, dated by postmark, July? 3, 1889, Harrison Papers, box 9).

12. Harrison Papers, box 25.

13. From a Chalcidian hydria (550–530 B.C.E.) by the so-called Inscription Painter, now in Munich, *Corpus Vasorum Antiquorum* München 6, 24–26, pl. 281; illustrated and discussed in P. E. Arias and M. Hirmer, *A History of Greek Vase Painting,* trans. and revised B. B. Shefton (London, 1962), 310–311, pl. 25.

14. The restoration of the various archaic poros pediments from the Acropolis is a long-running game, with shifting fashions. In this case, current orthodoxy keeps the two monsters in the corners but inserts two vast fighting lions in the center; the fragments of the

two male fighters in Harrison's photograph (Herakles and Zeus) have now been assigned to a quite different pediment.

15. "Archaeology in Greece," *Journal of Hellenic Studies* 9 (1888): 118–133 (see 120–123).

16. E. Gardner, "Archaeology in Greece 1888–89," ibid. 10 (1889): 254–280 (see 262–263); A. Brückner, "Porosskulpturen auf der Akropolis," *Athenische Mittheilungen* 14 (1889): 67–87.

17. A solution desperate enough to accommodate the fact that our Bluebeard differs in two crucial respects from the monster on the vase: he has no wings and three heads.

18. Taken from E. Gerhard, *Auserlesene griechische Vasenbilder: Hauptsachlich etruskischen Fundorts* (Berlin 1840–1847), pl. 237.

19. Most of the photographs are labeled, like this one, "Miss Marshall" (and the letters and notes of comment from Harrison are also almost all addressed to her—presumably passed on, as a collection, directly or indirectly to the archive; apart from the example described here, they are now in box 21). But a similar exercise for "Miss Lathbury" also survives, and the prospectuses refer to this form of teaching almost as Harrison's trademark. We can be pretty certain that Sellers, formally or informally, went through the same course.

20. Dated by postmark, February 8, 1889 (Harrison Papers, box 9).

21. Harrison to Marshall, December 31, 1888 (Harrison Papers, box 9), congratulating her on good work.

22. *Themis,* 158–211; for a recent discussion, see N. Marinatos, *Minoan Religion: Ritual, Image and Symbol* (Columbia, S.C., 1993), 31–36.

23. *Times Literary Supplement,* March 21, 1912, 115, D. G. Hogarth (Keeper in the Ashmolean Museum, Oxford) writing anonymously, as was then the *TLS* rule.

8. Hellas at Cambridge

1. Published in 1959. The long, difficult, and contested genesis of this biography will be discussed in Chapter 9.

2. P. iii (her emphasis).

3. For a start, claims about the *priority* of ritual over myth always beg the question: In what sense "prior"? Chronologically or logically

prior? These and other issues of the myth/ritual debate are discussed by Versnel, "What's Sauce for the Goose Is Sauce for the
Gander."

4. P. 26, n. 1.

5. He was a leading figure in the League of Nations, a vociferous
   supporter of the rights to "conscientious objection" during the
   Great War, an advocate of multilateral disarmament after it.

6. Murray's career is reviewed by Fowler, "Gilbert Murray," and discussed by P. E. Easterling, "Gilbert Murray's Reading of Euripides," *Colby Quarterly* 33, no. 2 (1997): 113–127. For a more general treatment, see West, *Gilbert Murray: A Life;* Wilson, *Gilbert
   Murray O.M.*

7. For a brief account of Cornford's career, see Kellogg Wood, "F. M.
   Cornford." Johnson's *University Politics: F. M. Cornford's Cambridge
   and His Advice to the Young Academic Politician* is an engaging account of his political and intellectual context, written from the
   political center of 1990s Cambridge; it includes a text of the
   Microcosmographia (originally published Cambridge, 1908). The
   significance of Cornford's *Thucydides Mythistoricus* (London, 1907)
   is outlined by V. J. Hunter, *Thucydides, the Artful Reporter* (To-
   ronto, 1973), 6–7; and that of his *Origin of Attic Comedy* by
   Versnel, "What's Sauce for the Goose Is Sauce for the Gander," 35.

8. *Zeus,* 3 vols. in 5 (Cambridge, 1914–1940).

9. I discuss Frazer as a classicist in "Frazer, Leach and Virgil: The
   Popularity and Unpopularity of the *Golden Bough.*" The history of
   the *Golden Bough* itself, from 1890 to 1915, is tracked by Fraser,
   The Making of The Golden Bough. *Pausanias* (Cambridge, 1898)
   weighed in at six volumes.

10. See Ackerman, *J. G. Frazer,* 183–184. There is no reason to sup-
    pose that Harrison was particularly close to the workaholic Frazer,
    although they met in Rome in 1901, as she wrote to Mary Murray
    (February 1901, letter reprinted in Stewart, *Jane Ellen Harrison,*
    36–37): "Mrs. Frazer (your double!) has been sitting on my bed
    for two hours, telling me 'who not to know,' ie who has not paid
    Mr. Frazer 'proper attention'! This is the price I pay for a few shy
    radiant moments under the Golden Bough."

11. Murray, *Four Stages of Greek Religion,* 6.

12. Cook, *Zeus* 1: xiv–xv.

13. Cornford, *Origin of Attic Comedy,* viii.

14. *Cambridge Review,* January 30, 1943, 164–165. It is instructive to compare with this Murray's obituary of Cornford. Murray always writes Harrison *up,* but here (predictably) he is slightly more guarded than in his Harrison lecture: "Jane Harrison was a teacher who combined certain minor defects, due in part to a lack of early training in the drudgery of exact scholarship and in part to a natural impulsiveness, with a width of learning, a force of historical imagination, and an infectious interest in her subject which amounted to genius . . . In Cornford's work this seed ripened into critical maturity" (*Proceedings of the British Academy* 29 (1943): 421–432).

15. Ackerman offers a helpful account of Frazer's debates (with R. R. Marett) on the explanatory force of ritual in the understanding of religion and culture; *J. G. Frazer,* 224–235.

16. Murray, *Four Stages of Greek Religion,* 7.

17. P. 1; note, too, the ironic "I was always a ritualist at heart (that form of Churchmanship still holds me by sentiment), but there was too much Protestant blood in my veins for it to take real possession; so I lapsed into Broad Churchism, and finally, as I thought, into complete Agnosticism" (*Alpha and Omega,* 184). So far as I can tell (unless *I* have misconstrued), Renate Schlesier utterly misconstrues this passage, taking ritualist (with a small *r,* in Harrison's sense) as if it were Ritualist (with a capital); see Schlesier, "Prolegomena to Jane Harrison's Interpretation of Ancient Greek Religion," 188.

18. Some of the complex processes of (selective) rereading that underlie the invention of the Ritualists can be traced in the writing of S. E. Hyman and others. In the conclusion of *The Tangled Bank: Darwin, Marx, Frazer and Freud as Imaginative Writers,* Hyman writes (p. 439), "In the work of Murray and the *Cambridge ritualists*—Harrison, Francis Cornford, and A. B. Cook—the influence of Frazer permanently transformed and revitalized the field of classics" (my emphasis). Paradoxically, however, in the main body of his text he never refers to them as a group—and the fact (as Richard Gordon points out to me) that here the term is inserted casually, without quotation marks, suggests that he was not in-

tending to coin a title for the group as a whole (but rather to find a convenient rhetoric for identifying Frazer's legacy). In a later article, "The Ritual View of Myth and the Mythic," in Vickery, ed., *Myth and Literature,* Hyman makes no reference to a Cambridge "group," although he does see the publication of *Themis* as a crucial moment when "a 'Cambridge' or 'ritual' approach became generally available" (p. 50). The editorial introduction, however, by J. B. Vickery, does refer (p. 47) to the "work of the so-called Cambridge group"; and again in *The Literary Impact of the Golden Bough* Vickery writes of "what came to be called the Cambridge School of Anthropology" (p. 89), and he summarizes the Cambridge contribution as "research in Greek myth and ritual." Also in Vickery's *Myth and Literature,* an article by C. Moorman, "Myth and Medieval Literature," refers to a pupil of Gilbert Murray as "a thorough-going ritualist, a disciple of the Cambridge school, represented chiefly by Frazer, Miss Harrison, Cornford, Murray and Miss Weston" (p. 174). But if all the elements for the Cambridge Ritualists are by this point in place, a glance at the notes that follow suggests that the (in many ways pioneering) work of Robert Ackerman has been supremely influential in "naturalizing" the term.

For different slants on the terms "Cambridge School" or "Cambridge Group" (sometimes with the carefully inserted "so-called") see, for example, G. S. Kirk, *Myth: Its Meaning and Function in Ancient and Modern Cultures* (Cambridge and Berkeley, 1970), 4; Fowler, "Gilbert Murray," 326; F. Graf, *Greek Mythology: An Introduction* (Baltimore and London, 1993), 40–42. Needless to say, they didn't refer to themselves in those terms either. The fluidity of the "Group" has recently been emphasized by A. Robinson, who shares my impatience with the idea of a distinct movement, though for rather different reasons: "A New Light Our Elders Had Not Seen: Deconstructing the 'Cambridge Ritualists,'" *Echos du Monde Classique* n.s. 17 (1998): 471–487.

19. Edited by W. M. Calder.
20. S. Arlen.
21. R. Ackerman, *Greek, Roman and Byzantine Studies* 12 (1971): 113–136.
22. R. Ackerman.

23. Ackerman, "The Cambridge Group," quotes on 1 and 2; similarly Ackerman, *J. G. Frazer,* 3: "He was not part of the group, but rather their intellectual parent"; Ackerman, *The Myth and Ritual School,* 89: "Although there were only 4 Ritualists, the classicists and ancient historians and historians of religion of Cambridge and Oxford constituted an indispensable auxiliary."

24. Arlen, *The Cambridge Ritualists,* 2–3.

25. For a recent attempt to construct a movement out of the untidy and improvised reality of academic life, see A. J. Boyle in a special issue of *Ramus* (vol. 20, 1991) entitled "The New Cambridge Latinist"; Boyle constructs a programmatic "movement" in Latin studies out of what is (at the same time) a motley assortment of Latinists, Hellenists, and art historians, many of whom have not spoken to each other for years. The point is that Boyle is not *wrong,* but he's not straightforwardly right, either—for he willfully occludes the disagreements, uncertainties, and animosities that divide these individuals as much as any common project unites them. Likewise the character, even existence, of the "Paris School" (of Vernant et al.) seems much more elusive when you're actually in Paris than it does in the pages of modern Anglo-American commentators.

26. Murray to Jessie Stewart, April 23, 1952 (Harrison Papers, box 11)

27. Murray to Jessie Stewart, October 26, 1953 (Harrison Papers, box 17).

28. Gilbert Murray is strangely marginal as an *intellectual* presence in Dodds's own memoirs, *Missing Persons,* but crucially it was his lectures on the *Bacchae* that convinced Dodds that "the study of Greek literature *could* after all be worth the expenditure of one's only lifetime" (p. 29).

29. Stewart, *Jane Ellen Harrison,* 83–88; quote on p. 83. She claims that Harrison's aim was that her group should (collaboratively) rewrite the whole history of Greek religion, including both philosophy and the attitudes of literary authors. The philosophy she earmarked for Cornford, "the delicate literary task she assigned to GM" (p. 84).

30. J. A. K. Thomson to Stewart, November 8, 1955 (Harrison Papers, box 11). On this occasion Murray had conveniently agreed

with the idea that Stewart's book was "unpublishable"—not, needless to say, what he had been writing to her. Thomson reassures Stewart with the comforting thought that the old man no longer had a mind of his own.

31. Franklin's story is told by Jenifer Glynn, "Rosalind Franklin, 1920–1958," in Shils and Blacker, eds., *Cambridge Women: Twelve Portraits*, 267–282. The fact that Harrison has not been written out in this way must be connected, I guess, with the "feminizing" of Ritualism as an intellectual approach, the sense that it is founded on a female agenda (via the aesthetics of art criticism—strikingly associated with Harrison rather than the men).

32. Farnell, *An Oxonian Looks Back*, 281.

33. "Jane Harrison," p. 32. Could that ever have been written of a male scholar?

34. Ackerman, "The Cambridge Group," 2; in similar vein, "Gilbert Murray was (and is) clearly the best known . . . nevertheless I maintain that Jane Harrison was the center of the group" (Ackerman, *The Myth and Ritual School*, 8). We shall see in the next chapter how this gendering underlies the story of her "passions" for younger male scholars, her series of (in the words of Lloyd-Jones, "Jane Harrison," p. 34) *amitiés amoureuses.*

35. Arlen, *The Cambridge Ritualists*, 2.

36. Schlesier, "Jane Ellen Harrison," 134.

37. See, for example, Lloyd-Jones, "Jane Harrison," 36–37 (though—very carefully—Lloyd-Jones does not use the word *Ritualist*); Schlesier, "Prolegomena to Jane Harrison's Interpretation of Ancient Greek Religion," 189–196 ("I. On the Genesis of Jane Harrison's Ritualism").

38. This paragraph essentially summarizes the views of Ackerman in "Jane Ellen Harrison," (quotes on pp. 223–225); see also Ackerman, *The Myth and Ritual School*, 74. Most writers on Harrison take a broadly similar (if not so extreme or mystical) view; a notable exception is Schlesier, "Prolegomena to Jane Harrison's Interpretation of Ancient Greek Religion," who argues that Harrison developed "a coherent model of the history of ancient Greek religion, the fundamental conceptions of which remain consistent; only the nuances and emphases vary" (p. 195). In an outline of his relations with Harrison, written by MacColl for Mirrlees (Har-

rison Papers, box 15), he notes only that he encouraged her to-ward folklore by "introducing her to Mannhardt's *Wald und Feld Kulte*" (which is, of course, a very long way from Harrison's later work).

39. See, for example, Ackerman, "Jane Ellen Harrison," 225.

40. Harrison, "Hellas at Cambridge," a review of the brand-new Museum of Classical Archaeology in Cambridge and its inaugural speeches and celebration. ("It was necessary, of course, on the opening day to pay some courteous compliment to the 'squalid savage' with whom Hellas is thus perforce unmetely mated"). On this occasion, and the necessary but awkward juxtaposition of Greek and Roman sculpture with prehistoric and ethnographic material, see my "Casts and Cast-Offs."

41. Pp. xii–xiii.

42. P. ix; she continues: "Frequently we have plain evidence that it is not the artist who is borrowing from Homer, but that both Homer and the artist drew their inspiration from one common source, local and national tradition." For the modernity of this view, cf. A. M. Snodgrass, "Poet and Painter in Eighth-Century Greece," *Proceedings of the Cambridge Philological Society* n.s. 27 (1979): 118–130, and *Homer and the Artists: Text and Picture in Early Greek Art* (Cambridge, 1998).

43. P. 122. Such prequels of her later position are occasionally pinpointed by Ackerman. See, for example, *The Myth and Ritual School,* 74: "But in that [early] work can also be found the elements typical of the mature work of the next decades."

44. Quote on p. 7. The book was explicitly addressed "to artists and to the amateurs of fine design" (p. 5). The complexity of Hellenizing aestheticism at this date (and its compatibility with what we would define as a more "anthropological" approach) is well discussed by Prins, "Greek Maenads, Victorian Spinsters."

45. P. xxi; this was something of a topos among anthropological theorists at the time (according to newspaper reports in the 1930s, J. G. Frazer was "fond of saying he has never seen a savage in his life"; see Beard, "Frazer, Leach and Virgil," 216).

46. L. R. Farnell, for one, did not take it *à la lettre,* referring in his review of *Themis* (*Hibbert Journal* 11 [1912–1913]: 453–458) to

"her sympathetic delight in savages, which she in vain disclaims in her preface" (p. 458).

47. Pp. v–vii.

48. *Edinburgh Review* 185 (1897): 441–464, reviewing Percy Gardner's *Sculptured Tombs of Hellas* plus thirteen other books on Greek art and religion (quotes on pp. 442 and 464); briefly discussed by Stray in his review of Peacock's *Jane Ellen Harrison, Liverpool Classical Monthly* 16 (1991): 110.

49. *Epilegomena*, 26, n. 1.

50. E. E. Evans-Pritchard, *Theories of Primitive Religion* (Oxford, 1965), 72–73; there is a similar emphasis in Di Donato, *Per una antropologia storica*, 255–263 ("Jane Ellen Harrison e i Durkheimiens"). Lloyd-Jones, "Jane Harrison," also places considerable emphasis on her "in several ways unfortunate . . . dependence" on Durkheim (p. 55).

51. I recognize, of course, that in formal terms Harrison (as a woman) was not a member of the University and so, strictly speaking, had no Faculty. In some respects this had serious practical (as well as symbolic) consequences (she could not, for example, borrow books from the University Library), but it would be naive to represent her position as one of simple exclusion. Paradoxically the University of Cambridge was much more accepting of women lecturers than women students. Harrison was an active member of the Cambridge Philological Society (the Faculty club) and gave lectures in university lecture rooms (the first woman to do so, in fact). I am meaning "Faculty" in this combined intellectual, social, and institutional sense.

52. There is (obsessive) discussion of the background to this reform, as well as of the content of the early archaeology papers, in my essay "The Invention (and Re-invention) of 'Group D.'" The particular characteristics of this section of the Tripos that I describe here were retained until a further reform in 1918 that effectively removed the study of religion from archaeology.

53. It leads out his *Essays on Art and Archaeology* (London, 1880), 1–38; quote on p. 2.

54. P. 35. "I am a human being, I count all human affairs as my business" (Terence, *Self-Tormenter,* 77)—the comic busybody's slogan,

in Newton's essay conscripted (as it almost always is) into a proverb of humanistic idealism.

9. *Pandora's Box*

1. Hope Mirrlees to Jessie Stewart, August 23, 1946; Agnes Horsfield to Stewart, March 24, 1943; Mirrlees to Stewart, July 18, 1954 (Harrison Papers, box 14).
2. Hope Mirrlees to Jessie Stewart, June 26, 1959 (Harrison Papers, box 14).
3. Lorimer was later classical tutor at Somerville College, Oxford; author of *Homer and the Monuments* (London, 1950), dedicated to Gilbert and Mary Murray.
4. The best account of Stewart's career is Stray, "Digs and Degrees," which includes extensive quotation from Crum's diary (now lodged in the Cambridge University Archives, University Library).
5. Harrison to Edith Crum, Jessie's sister, n.d. (Harrison Papers, box 10). Peacock, *Jane Ellen Harrison,* 104–106, quotes from a variety of letters from Harrison and Stewart's later friendship.
6. This is one element in Hope Mirrlees's parody of the life of a don's wife (along with "practising glees in the Choral Society"), in *The Counterplot,* 17.
7. See Henderson, *Juvenal's Mayor,* 63 and 129; Stewart edited Mayor's *Twelve Cambridge Sermons* (Cambridge, 1911), prefacing it with a long biographical memoir.
8. Henig, "Queen of Lud, 10, presumably drawn from an interview Henig conducted with Mirrlees. My information on Mirrlees's pre-Newnham career is taken from Henig (with Mirrlees herself as the ultimate source); apart from this, the fullest account of Mirrlees's life (with Harrison, at least) is in Peacock, *Jane Ellen Harrison,* esp. 99–102, 109–115.
9. Harrison to Mirrlees, April 2, 1912 (Harrison Papers, box 9).
10. Harrison to Mirrlees, dated by postmark, July 3, 1910 (Harrison Papers, box 9). Peacock (*Jane Ellen Harrison,* 111–112) doesn't recognize the classic style of the Newnham don in this letter, claiming: "Hope proved her fidelity early on when she broke off her engagement to a young man in 1910 . . . She was 'truly glad'

Hope planned to return to Newnham, as well she might be: unlike the other members of Jane's circles, Hope had consciously rejected marriage and returned to the fold of the college community."

11. Harrison to Mirrlees, n.d. (Harrison Papers, box 9).

12. Harrison to Mirrlees, n.d. (Harrison Papers, box 9); many other similar letters are quoted by Peacock, *Jane Ellen Harrison,* 111–115. One of their most extraordinary communications is a "memorial rhyme" on the use of the dative case in Latin; though very similar to such rhymes collected in Kennedy's *Revised Latin Primer* (and familiar to my senior colleagues), I have so far found it in no edition of Kennedy—nor in any other similar source. It was presumably copied out (or conceivably invented) for Mirrlees by Harrison: "A dative put remember pray / After enjoy, spare, obey, / Persuade, believe, command; to these / Add pardon, succour & displease. / With *vacare* to have leisure / And *placere* to give pleasure / And *nubere* of the female said / The English of it is 'to wed'" (n.d., box 9). Inscribed as a gift ("H.H.M. / d.d. / J.H.") and sent on its own in an envelope to Miss Mirrlees, it is hard not to detect a romantic tone masquerading as an aide-mémoire to some pretty basic Latin grammar.

13. The (linguistic) world of early women's colleges, as well as the closeness of the relations within them, is well captured by Vicinus, *Independent Women,* 142–145.

14. Henig, "Queen of Lud," 10. Mary Berenson to Strong, March 19, 1913 (Strong Papers, box 15): "Karin and her friend Hope Mirrlees will arrive in Rome tomorrow, to stay 2 weeks . . . They know you are *very* busy & don't want to add to your burdens. But sometime, when it is convenient, they would like to come to the School."

15. The message around the edge of the postcard reads: "I was living peacefully not munie-d with any pièces till I tried cabling to you. The official βάτραχος has a consuming passion for this photograph. In fact as the converted Bourget *used* to say 'il se grise de mes bottines' small wonder—see left foot!" To decode: a letter sent to Murray the same day (Harrison Papers, box 6) tells the story of her dealings with French bureaucracy when she tried to send him a telegram and they demanded she be *"munie d'une pièce*

de justification" (in possession of a permit); βάτραχος is an Anglo-Greek pun: "frog" in Greek, the English slang for Frenchman; the "official frog" is probably the man she refers to as her "usher" in other letters to Murray (see June 30, Harrison Papers, box 6); the "converted Bourget" probably refers to the novelist and critic Paul Bourget, who dramatically gave up his radical past in 1889 (on the publication of his *Le disciple*) and became the voice of conservative morality; *"il se grise de mes bottines"* (he's carried away by my boots) may be a wry joke on the rather staid foootwear peeping out from under her skirt.

16. Harrison and Mirrlees, trans., *Life of the Arch-Priest Avvakum*—another Hogarth Press production (there was greater literary and historical interest to this than my simple summary implies); Harrison and Mirrlees, trans., *The Book of the Bear: Being twenty-one tales newly translated from the Russian.*

17. Translation: "If, o heart, you become cleansed of the dust of the body, / You, a pure spirit, will ascend to the firmaments above. / Your seat is the Throne; may you be ashamed / That you should come and be resident in the realm of dust."

18. Woolf to Margaret Llewelyn Davies, August 17, 1919, *Letters of Virginia Woolf,* ed. N. Nicolson and J. Trautmann (London, 1975–1980), 1075 (2: 384–385); to Lady Cecil, September 1, 1925, *Letters,* 1574 (3: 200–201). See also *The Diary of Virginia Woolf,* ed. A. O. Bell (Harmondsworth, 1979–1985), 1: 258; 4: 140 (for her close friendship with Ottoline Morrell, whose literary executor she was).

19. Harrison's word in *Reminiscences,* 90 ("In my old age [Fate] has sent me, to comfort me, a ghostly daughter, dearer than any child after the flesh"); "the chosen companion of her latest years" (as Murray tactfully genuflected in his *Jane Ellen Harrison,* 21).

20. Henig, "Queen of Lud," 15. Henig, in "Queen of Lud," is an avowed (and not always very accurate) partisan for Mirrlees, always eager to make it seem that Mirrlees's work anticipates the great classics of modernism. Julia Briggs is currently working on *Paris* and other works of Mirrlees.

21. *Paris: A Poem* (London, 1919).

22. The lesbian life of the Left Bank is commemorated in Benstock, *Women of the Left Bank.*

23. *Themis,* 473–474. Harrison and Mirrlees must have been only too well aware of the Latin gender of this constellation: the great *female* bear.

24. Woolf to Margaret Llewelyn Davies, August 17, 1919, *Letters* 1075 (2: 384–385).

25. The historical De Scudéry (whose first name, significantly, was Madeleine) is discussed by J. De Jean, *Fictions of Sappho: 1546–1937* (Chicago and London, 1989), 96–110.

26. Woolf to Clive Bell, September 24, 1919, *Letters* 1083 (2: 391).

27. *Times Literary Supplement,* October 9, 1919, 547 (reviewed anonymously, according to the standard conventions of the time). Woolf's letter to Lady Cecil (September 1, 1925, *Letters,* 1574, 3: 200–201) tells one story of the book's history and of her review ("I was asked to review it, and of course found it an awful burden and didn't like the book as much as I should have done, and when my review came out, Hope was very much disappointed: however, we've made it up now").

28. My quotations are drawn from the explanatory advertisement next to the title page.

29. See, for example, *Poems* (Cape Town, 1962); *Moods and Tensions: poems* (privately printed, Oxford, 1976).

30. L. Gordon, *Eliot's New Life* (Oxford, 1988), 54

31. To Mary Hutchinson, February 10, 1941, *Letters* 3691 (6: 471–472).

32. This is a nice example of the unfathomability of *influence.* Of course, we know (see above, Chapter 1) that Eliot had discovered Harrison long before his friendship with Mirrlees, but it would be naive to imagine (as most accounts of Harrison's work and influence do) that she had nothing to do with his continuing enthusiam for Harrison's writing. For an account of Eliot's lodging *chez* Mirrlees, see P. Ackroyd, *T. S. Eliot* (London, 1984), 258–259.

33. *Newnham College Roll Letter* 1929, 60.

34. Mirrlees to Stewart, May 10, 1932 (Harrison Papers, box 14).

35. Mirrlees to Stewart, December 29, 1932, ibid.

36. Mirrlees to Stewart, May 22, 1933, ibid.

37. Ibid.

38. Mirrlees to Stewart, May 21, no year (Harrison Papers, box 14).

39. Mirrlees to Stewart, May 22, 1933, ibid.
40. Mirrlees to Stewart, May 3, no year, ibid.
41. Mirrlees to Stewart, March 4, 1951, ibid.
42. Mirrlees to Stewart, February 3, 1936, ibid.
43. De Bunsen to Stewart, dated by postmark, ibid.
44. Mirrlees to De Bunsen, March 26, dated 1943 in another hand, ibid.
45. Agnes Horsfield to Stewart, March 24, 1943, ibid.
46. Mirrlees to Stewart, August 26, 1943, ibid.
47. Mirrlees to Stewart, March 29, 1943, ibid.
48. Mirrlees to Stewart, August 23, 1946, ibid.
49. Mirrlees to Stewart, June 11, 1950, ibid.
50. Mirrlees to Stewart, May 19, 1946, ibid.
51. Ibid.
52. Stewart to Mirrlees (draft), May 5, 1946 (Harrison Papers, box 14).
53. Mirrlees to Stewart, June 6, 1950, ibid.
54. R. F. Willetts, *Cretan Cults and Festivals* (London, 1962); *The Law Code of Gortyn: Edited with Introduction, Translation and a Commentary* (Berlin, 1967); and so on. He was later to be Professor of Greek at the Univesity of Birmingham.
55. Mirrlees to Stewart, June 6, 1950 (Harrison Papers, box 14).
56. Mirrlees to Stewart, July 14, 1946, ibid.
57. Mirrlees to Stewart, July 9, 1953, ibid.
58. Mirrlees to Stewart, March 4, 1951, ibid.
59. John Johnson to Stewart (including Leonard Woolf's comments), May 6, 1954 (Harrison Papers, box 21).
60. Stewart to Gilbert Murray (draft), August 3, 1954 (Harrison Papers, box 16).
61. John Johnson to Stewart, March 7, 1955 (Harrison Papers, box 21); Mirrlees's refusal, Stewart to Gilbert Murray (draft), August 3, 1954 (Harrison Papers, box 16).
62. E. Tillyard to Stewart, April 1, 1954 (Harrison Papers, box 16).
63. J. A. K. Thomson to Stewart (referring to a letter from Murray to Jocelyn Toynbee), November 8, 1955 (Harrison Papers, box 11).
64. Murray to Stewart, October 15, 1955 (Harrison Papers, box 16); a subtly different line from his letter to Stewart, September 9, 1950

(Harrison Papers, box 11): "Of course the fame of any 'savant,' especially perhaps a scholar, lasts a very short time. Think of Jebb."

65. Murray to Stewart, April 23, 1952 (Harrison Papers, box 11).
66. Harrison Papers, box 14.
67. Mirrlees to Stewart, October 14, 1957, ibid.
68. Stewart to Mirrlees (draft), June 28, 1959, ibid.
69. Mirrlees to Stewart, June 26, 1959, ibid.
70. Ibid.
71. Mirrlees to Stewart, Sept 27, 1959 (Harrison Papers, box 12).
72. Notebook and draft biography (Harrison Papers, box 15).
73. This should not be read as any unwillingness on my part to "face the facts" of Harrison's lesbianism. The "evidence" concerning her relationship with Mirrlees is compatible both with passionate erotic physicality and (in our terms) rather quaint—and aggressively nonphysical—sentimentality. My objection is to those who think they *know* what went on in the bedrooms of the past (or those of today, for that matter).
74. A. Powell, *Faces in My Time: Memoirs* (London, 1980), 3: 181–182.
75. G. Stein, *The Autobiography of Alice B. Toklas* (London, 1933), 158–159. It is part of a wry description of Stein and Toklas lunching at Newnham: "Miss Jane Harrison . . . was much interested in meeting Gertrude Stein. We sat up on the dais with the faculty and it was very awe inspiring. The conversation was not however particularly amusing. Miss Harrison and Gertrude Stein did not particularly interest each other."
76. Woolf to Jacques Raverat, February 5, 1925, *Letters,* 1534 (3: 164).
77. Woolf to Molly MacCarthy, April 22, 1923, *Letters,* 1381 (3: 30); the published edition (which appeared while Mirrlees was still alive) omitted the words "who have a Sapphic flat somewhere"; I reproduce them here courtesy of the Lilly Library, Indiana University, Bloomington.
78. This is hinted, at least, in the closing paragraphs of Harrison's *Reminiscences,* 90–91.
79. Mirrlees, draft biography (Harrison Papers, box 15); it is a passion to which Mirrlees's manuscript repeatedly returns: "Her Newnham love-affair was not a tragedy of unrequited passion. The par-

ticular plot of the drama I do not feel at liberty to divulge"; "a man of singular beauty and fascination"; "Her last year at Newnham was one of intense misery . . . Her double dream—the marriage of two scholars—had vanished in smoke."

80. When MacColl married in 1897, it was, according to Mirrlees, "a great blow," draft biography (Harrison Papers, box 15).

81. Mirrlees, draft biography (Harrison Papers, box 15).

82. Stewart, *Jane Ellen Harrison,* 101–113; above, n. 69.

83. Mirrlees, Notebook (Harrison Papers, box 15).

84. At the time of the break with Cornford, Harrison had just had an operation on her feet (here painted as a close encounter with Death); needless to say, the relationship of Mirrlees's quotations to the *ipsissima verba* of Harrison is unclear but presumably more remote than she presents. For the context of these events, see also Peacock, *Jane Ellen Harrison,* 151–178. Frances Darwin's account is reprinted in Stewart, *Jane Ellen Harrison,* 106–109.

85. Pencil note, apparently copied from "letter from Hope Mirrlees April 28, 1946," Harrison Papers, box 14.

86. Peacock, *Jane Ellen Harrison,* 165, 111; although she discusses Mirrlees's investment in Harrison's biography, Peacock *repeatedly* fails to recognize the influence (wishful thinking? invention?) of Mirrlees in the many "quotations" she draws from Mirrlees's Notebook. How, for example, should we evaluate *Mirrlees's* claim that *Harrison* said that she regarded "a phallus the most degraded of all objects"? (Peacock, *Jane Ellen Harrison,* 206: "This startling statement reveals not only that Harrison feared male sexuality but also that she emphatically rejected all masculine power and authority as symbolized by the phallus.")

87. For a crudely explicit version of Harrison's distinctive female contribution to the group, see J(acquetta) Hawkes, *New Statesman,* June 20, 1959, 870–871: "What was most splendid about the collaboration was that Jane Harrison participated essentially as a woman. Her greatness lay in creative imagination of a deeply intuitive feminine kind."

88. Ackerman, "Jane Ellen Harrison," 210–211; similarly Lloyd-Jones in "Jane Harrison": "Jane Harrison was prone to fall in love, and her love-affairs were closely connected with her work"—

though she was, apparently, "old-fashioned enough to connect sexual relations with marriage" (p. 60).

89. Anyone who doubts the folly of this procedure should try it on their own life.

10. *Epilegomena*

1. The closest contact I have tracked down is at one remove, via Mirrlees (who, as we saw in Chapter 9, almost certainly met Mrs. Strong at the British School when she visited Rome with Karin Costelloe).

2. Harrison Papers, box 20.

3. Harrison to Gilbert Murray, November 8, 1903 (Harrison Papers, box 1): "If giving up drink is like the wrench from a lover—who all the time you half despise—giving up smoke is like parting from the best friend who always comforts and never torments."

4. Mirrlees, Notebook (Harrison Papers, box 15); it is not clear from the notes whether this is a remark of V. de Bunsen (above, Chapter 9) or an editorial comment by Mirrlees herself (which would make quite a difference to how we read it). De Bunsen was certainly capable of an ironically waspish view of her old teacher: "She could not help dominating any situation," she wrote in her obituary notice, *Newnham College Roll Letter* 1929, 68.

5. She was buried in Rome on September 18, 1943, with a "little ceremony" in the Chiesa Nuova to follow in 1946 (Thomson, *Mrs. Arthur Strong*, 123); in England there was a low-key requiem mass in a chapel of Westminster Cathedral (attended by the MacColls, among others), reported in the *Times* October 1, 1943, 7.

Major Archival Sources

This book draws particularly heavily on two Cambridge archives: the Strong Papers, Girton College, and the Harrison Papers, Newnham College. Documents are cited, wherever possible, by box number within each collection. The draft biography of Jane Harrison, and the accompanying notebooks, compiled by Hope Mirrlees, have presented particular problems of referencing. Mirrlees did not use consistent pagination, and she often produced new drafts of essentially the same material in similar, but not identical, wording. In the face of these difficulties, when quoting from Mirrlees I have usually cited only one of her versions, and I have not attempted to provide exact page references within her manuscript (on the grounds that it would be more misleading than helpful). Those who wish to check this out will have the fun of exploring this extraordinary material for themselves.

Material from these archives is reproduced by permission of the Mistress and Fellows, Girton College, Cambridge; and the Principal and Fellows, Newnham College, Cambridge.

I have also made considerable use of the following archives:

Strong Collection, British School at Rome (BSR)

Vernon Lee Papers, Special Collections, Miller Library, Colby College, Waterville, Maine

MacColl Papers, Glasgow University Library, Department of Special Collections

Macmillan Archive, University of Reading

Todhunter Papers, University of Reading

Waldstein Papers, Historical Archives of the International Olympic Committee, Olympic Museum, Lausanne

I gratefully acknowledge permission granted by each of these archives to reproduce material in the collections.

I wish to thank the following for their permission to cite from unpublished material: Valerie Eliot (Hope Mirrlees's letters and papers); Robert Elton and Andrée MacColl (D. S. MacColl's letters and papers), Claire Pace (Jessie Stewart's letters and papers).

Bibliography

Ackerman, R. "The Cambridge Group: Origins and Composition," in Calder, ed., *The Cambridge Ritualists Reconsidered*, 1–19

———. *J. G. Frazer: His Life and Work* (Cambridge, 1987)

———. "Jane Ellen Harrison: The Early Work," *Greek, Roman and Byzantine Studies* 13 (1972): 209–230

———. *The Myth and Ritual School: J. G. Frazer and the Cambridge Ritualists* (London and New York, 1991)

Arlen, S. *The Cambridge Ritualists: An Annotated Bibliography* (Metuchen, N.J. and London, 1990)

Beard, M. "Casts and Cast-Offs: The Origins of the Museum of Classical Archaeology," *Proceedings of the Cambridge Philological Society* n.s. 39 (1993): 1–29

———. "Frazer, Leach and Virgil: The Popularity and Unpopularity of the *Golden Bough*," *Comparative Studies in Society and History* 34 (1992): 203–224

———. "The Invention (and Re-invention) of 'Group D': An Archaeology of the Classical Tripos, 1879–1984," in Stray, ed., *Classics in 19th and 20th Century Cambridge*, 95–134

———. "'Pausanias in Petticoats' or *The Blue Jane*," in S. Alcock and J. Elsner, eds., *Pausanias: Travel and Imagination in Roman Greece* (forthcoming)

Benstock, S. *Women of the Left Bank: Paris, 1900–1940* (London, 1987)

Borland, M. *D. S. MacColl: Painter, Poet and Critic* (Harpenden, 1995)

Breay, C. "Women and the Classical Tripos 1869–1914," in Stray, ed., *Classics in 19th and 20th Century Cambridge,* 49–70

Briggs, W. W., and W. M. Calder, eds., *Classical Scholarship: A Biographical Encyclopedia* (New York, 1990)

Burkert, W. *Homo Necans: The Anthropology of Ancient Greek Sacrificial Ritual and Myth,* trans. P. Bing (Berkeley, 1983)

Calder, W. M., ed., *The Cambridge Ritualists Reconsidered,* Illinois Classical Studies, supplement 2 (Atlanta, 1991)

———. "Jane Harrison's Failed Candidacies for the Yates Professorship (1888, 1896): What Did Her Colleagues Think of Her?" in Calder, ed., *The Cambridge Ritualists Reconsidered,* 37–59

Carpentier, M. C. *Ritual, Myth, and the Modernist Text: The Influence of Jane Ellen Harrison on Joyce, Eliot, and Woolf* (Amsterdam, 1998)

Cook, A. B. *Zeus* (Cambridge, 1914–1940)

Cook, B. F. "Sir Charles Newton KCB (1816–1894)," in I. Jenkins and G. B. Waywell, eds., *Sculptors and Sculpture of Caria and the Dodecanese* (London, 1997), 10–29

Cornford, F. M. *The Origin of Attic Comedy* (London, 1914)

Di Donato, R. *Per una antropologia storica del mondo antico,* Il pensiero storico 81 (Florence, 1990)

Dodds, E. R. *Missing Persons: An Autobiography* (Oxford, 1977)

Easterling, P. E. "The Early Years of the Cambridge Greek Play," in Stray, ed., *Classics in 19th and 20th Century Cambridge,* 27–46

Faderman, L. *Surpassing the Love of Men: Romantic Friendship and Love between Women from the Renaissance to the Present* (New York, 1981).

Farnell, L. R. *An Oxonian Looks Back* (London, 1934)

Fowler, R. L. "Gilbert Murray," in Briggs and Calder, eds., *Classical Scholarship,* 321–334

Fraser, R. *The Making of* The Golden Bough: *The Origins and Growth of an Argument* (London, 1990)

Furtwängler, A. *Masterpieces of Greek Sculpture,* ed. E. Sellers (London, 1895)

"Greek Plays at the Universities," *Woman's World* 1 (1888): 121–128 (written by "a graduate of Girton")

Gregory, E. *H. D. and Hellenism: Classic Lines* (Cambridge, 1997)

Gunn, P. *Vernon Lee: Violet Paget, 1856–1935* (London, 1964)

Hall, E., and F. Macintosh. *Greek Tragedy and the British Stage 1660–1914* (Oxford, forthcoming)

Harrison, J. E. *Alpha and Omega* (London, 1915)

———. *Ancient Art and Ritual* (London, 1913)

———. *Epilegomena to the Study of Greek Religion* (Cambridge, 1921)

———. "Hellas at Cambridge," *Magazine of Art* 7 (1884): 510–515

———. "Homo Sum: Being a Letter to an Anti-Suffragist from an Anthropologist," in *Alpha and Omega*, 80–115 (originally published separately, Oxford, 1909?)

———. *Introductory Studies in Greek Art* (London, 1885)

———. *Myths of the Odyssey in Art and Literature* (London, 1882)

———. "Pandora's Box," *Journal of Hellenic Studies* 20 (1900): 99–114.

———. *Prolegomena to the Study of Greek Religion* (Cambridge, 1903)

———. *Reminiscences of a Student's Life* (London, 1925); repr. in *Arion* 4 (1965): 312–346

———. *Themis: A Study in the Social Origins of Greek Religion* (Cambridge, 1912)

———. *Unanimism: A Study in Conversion and Some Contemporary French Poets* (Cambridge, 1913; repr. in *Alpha and Omega*)

———, and H. Mirrlees, trans. *The Book of the Bear: Being Twenty-one Tales Newly Translated from the Russian* (London, 1926)

———, and H. Mirrlees, trans. *Life of the Arch-Priest Avvakum, by Himself,* (London, 1924)

———, and M. de G. Verrall. *Mythology and Monuments of Ancient Athens* (London, 1890)

Henderson, J. "Farnell's Cults: The Making and Breaking of Pausanias in Victorian Anthropology," in S. Alcock and J. Elsner, eds., *Pausanias: Travel amd Imagination in Roman Greece* (forthcoming)

———. *Juvenal's Mayor: The Professor Who Lived on 2d a day,* Cambridge Philological Society, supplement 20 (Cambridge, 1998)

Henig, S. "Queen of Lud: Hope Mirrlees," *Virginia Woolf Quarterly* 1 (1972): 8–23

Hyman, S. E. *The Tangled Bank: Darwin, Marx, Frazer and Freud as Imaginative Writers* (New York, 1962)

Jenkins, I. *Archaeologists and Aesthetes: In the Sculpture Galleries of the British Museum 1800–1939* (London, 1992)

Jex-Blake, K., and E. Sellers, eds. *The Elder Pliny's Chapters on the History of Art* (London, 1896)

Johnson, G. *University Politics: F. M. Cornford's Cambridge and His Advice to the Young Academic Politician* (Cambridge, 1994)

Kellogg Wood, D. "F. M. Cornford," in Briggs and Calder, eds., *Classical Scholarship*

Lee, V. *Letters,* ed. I. Cooper Willis (fifty copies privately printed, London, 1937)

Lloyd-Jones, H. "Jane Harrison 1850–1928," in Shils and Blacker, eds., *Cambridge Women: Twelve Portraits,* 29–72

Lullies, R., and W. Schiering, eds., *Archäologenbildnisse: Porträts und Kurzbiographien von Klassischen Archäologen deutscher Sprache* (Mainz, 1988)

MacColl, D. S., and J. E. Harrison, *Greek Vase Painting* (London, 1894)

Macintosh, F. "Greek Tragedy in Performance: Nineteenth- and Twentieth-Century Productions," in P. E. Easterling, ed., *The Cambridge Companion to Greek Tragedy* (Cambridge, 1997), 284–323

Malleson, E. *Autobiographical Notes and Letters,* with a memoir by Hope Malleson (privately printed, Guildford, 1926)

Marchand, S. L. *Down from Olympus: Archaeology and Philhellenism in Germany, 1750–1970* (Princeton, 1996)

Marshall, G. *Actresses on the Victorian Stage: Feminine Performance and the Galatea Myth* (Cambridge, 1998)

McWilliams Tullberg, R. *Women at Cambridge,* 2nd ed. (Cambridge, 1998)

Mirrlees, H. *The Counterplot* (London, 1923)

———. *A Fly in Amber: Being an Extravagant Biography of the Romantic Antiquary Sir Robert Bruce Cotton* (London, 1962)

———. *Lud-in-the-Mist* (London, 1926)

———. *Madeleine: One of Love's Jansenists* (London, 1919)

———. *Paris: A Poem* (London, 1919)

Moore, L. "'Something More Tender Still Than Friendship': Romantic Friendship in Early Nineteenth-Century England," *Feminist Studies* 18 (1992): 499–520

Murray, G. *Four Stages of Greek Religion* (New York, 1912)

———. *Jane Ellen Harrison: An Address* (Cambridge, 1928)

Newton, C. T. "On the Study of Archaeology," in C. T. Newton, ed., *Essays on Art and Archaeology* (London, 1880), 1–38

Paley (Marshall), M. *What I Remember* (Cambridge, 1947)

Passman, T. "Out of the Closet and into the Field: Matriculture, the Lesbian Perspective and Feminist Classics," in N. S. Rabinowitz and A. Richlin, eds., *Feminist Theory and the Classics* (New York and London, 1993), 181–208

Peacock, S. J. *Jane Ellen Harrison: The Mask and the Self* (New Haven, 1988)

Prins, Y. "Greek Maenads, Victorian Spinsters," in R. Dellamora, ed., *Victorian Sexual Dissidence* (Chicago, 1999), 43–81

Schlesier, R. "Jane Ellen Harrison," in Briggs and Calder, eds., *Classical Scholarship*, 127–141

———. *Kulte, Mythen und Gelehrte: Anthropologie der Antike seit 1800* (Frankfurt, 1994)

———. "Prolegomena to Jane Harrison's Interpretation of Ancient Greek Religion," in Calder, ed., *The Cambridge Ritualists Reconsidered*

Schuchhardt, C. *Schliemann's Excavations: An Archaeological Study,* trans. E. Sellers (London, 1891)

Shils, E., and C. Blacker, eds. Cambridge Women: Twelve Portraits (Cambridge, 1996)

Smith-Rosenberg, C. *Disorderly Conduct: Visions of Gender in Victorian America* (Oxford, 1986)

———. "The Female World of Love and Ritual: Relations between Women in Nineteenth-Century America," *Signs* 1 (1975): 1–29

Stewart, J. *Jane Ellen Harrison: A Portrait from Letters* (London, 1959)

Stray, C. *Classics Transformed: Schools, Universities, and Society in England 1830–1960* (Oxford, 1998)

———. "Digs and Degrees: Jessie Crum's Tour of Greece, Easter 1901," *Classics Ireland* 2 (1995): 121–131

Stray, C., ed., *Classics in 19th and 20th Century Cambridge: Curriculum, Culture and Community* (Proceedings of the Cambridge Philological Society, supplement 24 (Cambridge, 1999)

Strong, E. (Mrs. Arthur). *Apotheosis and After Life: Three Lectures on Certain Phases of Art and Religion in the Roman Empire* (London, 1915)

———. *Roman Sculpture from Augustus to Constantine* (London, 1907)

Thomson, G. S. *Mrs. Arthur Strong: A Memoir* (London, 1949)

Traill, H. D. "South Kensington Hellenism: A Dialogue," *Fortnightly*

Review 34 (1883): 111–119; repr. in H. D. Traill, *The New Lucian: Being a Series of Dialogues of the Dead* (London, 1884), 59–84)

Versnel, H. S. "What's Sauce for the Goose Is Sauce for the Gander: Myth and Ritual, Old and New," in L. Edmunds, ed., *Approaches to Greek Myth* (Baltimore and London, 1990), 25–95

Vicinus, M. *Independent Women: Work and Community for Single Women, 1850–1920* (London, 1985)

———. "'They Wonder to Which Sex I Belong': The Historical Roots of the Modern Lesbian Identity," *Feminist Studies* 18 (1992): 467–497

Vickery, J. B. *The Literary Impact of the Golden Bough* (Princeton, 1973)

Vickery J. B., ed. *Myth and Literature: Contemporary Theory and Practice* (Lincoln, Nebr., 1966)

Warr, G. C., and W. Crane. *Echoes of Hellas* (London, 1887)

West, F. *Gilbert Murray: A Life* (London, Canberra, and New York, 1984)

Wilson, D. *Gilbert Murray O.M.* (Oxford, 1987)

Wiseman, T. P. *A Short History of the British School at Rome* (London, 1990)

Woolf, V. *A Room of One's Own* (1928; Harmondsworth, 1945)

Index

REVEALING ANTIQUITY

G. W. Bowersock, General Editor